VEDANTA SUVARNA MALA

MUSINGS IN VEDANTA

Dr. Debasis Bhattacharyya

INDIA • SINGAPORE • MALAYSIA

ISBN 979-8-89067-725-9

CONTENTS

PRAYER TO SELF

[A translation of the devotional song by Swami Purnatmanand Maharaj of RK Mission order.]

***

The rise of thirst, that erases thou thoughts;

Let that not arise in this.

The love that maketh this forget thee;

Let that not enamour this.

The desire that causes to loose thou;

Let that not arise in this.

The lamp of knowledge that casts a shadow on thee;

Let such lamp remain unkindeled.

The sorrow & pain that makes this remember thee;

Let that sorrow remain ever present in this.

The intoxicant that takes this away from thee;

Let that intoxication remain unborn.

The waves of joy that takes thou away from this;

Let that ocean of joy remain ever dry for this.

In melody & words, where thou is not;

Let that remain unheard of.

The flood of tears that flows unto thou;

Let that flood remain everflowing.

Hari ॐ

"ॐ सहनाववतु

सह नौ भुनक्तु

सह वीर्यं करवाव है

तेजस्वि नावधीतमस्तु मा विद्विषाव है

ॐ शान्तिः शान्तिः शान्तिः»

PREPHASE

This compilation is a contemplation on various topics on Vedanta; as deciphered by this this mind.

It is based on various texts on Vedanta and also from the understanding of various discourses by masters & teachers of Vedanta.

The writings are only a reflection of the mirror of this mind, that has tried to reflect the pure Vedantic light of knowledge from the revered masters. Any deviation or error, is of this mind alone. That shall feel blessed to be corrected.

In the tradition of Guru parampara, I offer my salutations & am indebted to the lineage of Advaita masters of past, Particularly Adi guru Shankaracharya, Swami Ramakrishna Paramhansa, Ramana Maharishi, Swami Satchidanandendra Saraswati, Swami Vivekananda & Swami Chinmayanand ji.

Of the contemporary masters; my reverence to Jagat Guru Sankaracharya Nischalanand Saraswati ji, Swami Prabuddhanand ji, Swami Atmapriyanand ji, Swami Sarvapriyanand ji, Swami Tejomayanand ji, Swami Swaroopanand ji, Swami Paramarthanand ji, Ira Schreptin ji & Sri Sri Ravishankar ji..

I also express my gratitude to all members of the (FB) contemplation group "Sankara Advaita Vedanta"; in persual of this path of enquiry.

The entire proceeds shall be as a Guru dakshina offering to "Chinmay mission".

My spiritual Guru, in this seeking.

Hari ॐ

WHAT IS VEDANTA?

Vedanta is one of the world's most ancient spiritual philosophies and one of its broadest, based on the Vedas, the sacred scriptures of India. It is the philosophical foundation of Hinduism; but while Hinduism includes aspects of Indian culture, Vedanta is universal in its application and is equally relevant to all countries, all cultures, and all religious backgrounds.

Vedanta affirms:

The oneness of existence,

The divinity of the soul, and

The harmony of all.

A closer look at the word "Vedanta" is revealing: "Vedanta" is a combination of two words: "Veda" which means "knowledge" and "anta" which means "the end of" or "the goal of." In this context the goal of knowledge isn't intellectual—the limited knowledge we acquire by reading books. "Knowledge" here means the knowledge of God as well as the knowledge of our own divine nature. Vedanta, then, is the search for Self-knowledge as well as the search for God.

What is God? According to Vedanta, God is infinite existence, infinite consciousness, and infinite bliss. The term for this impersonal, transcendent reality is Brahman, the divine ground of being. Yet Vedanta also maintains that God can be personal (immanent) as well, assuming human form in every age. Most importantly, God dwells within our own hearts as the divine Self or Atman. The Atman is never born nor will it ever die. Neither stained by our failings nor affected by the fluctuations of the body or mind, the Atman is not subject to our grief or despair or disease or ignorance. Pure, perfect, free from limitations, the Atman, Vedanta declares, is one with Brahman. The greatest temple of God is the essence of one's being.

Vedanta asserts that the goal of life is to realize and to manifest our own divinity. This divinity is our real nature, and the realization of it is our birthright. We are moving towards this goal as we grow with knowledge and life experiences. It is inevitable that we will eventually, either in this or in future lives, discover that the greatest truth of our existence is our own divine nature.

Thousands of years ago the Rig Veda declared: "Truth is one, sages call it by various names."

According to the Vedanta teachings there are four paths we can follow to achieve the goal of understanding our divine nature. These paths are known as the Four Yogas. We can choose a path based on our personality or inclination, or follow the practices of the paths in any combination.

Bhakti is the base & Gyan is the ultimate means to Self-knowledge. While Karma yoga is for mind purification & Raj yoga for mind control; as means for gyan yogyata.

Bhakti Yoga

Bhakti Yoga is the path of love and devotion. The devotee approaches God through a loving relationship. This path emphasizes practices such as prayer, chanting, and meditation on God as a loving presence in our lives.

Jnana Yoga

Jnana Yoga is the path of knowledge. In this path the seeker uses reason and discernment to discover the divine nature within by casting off all that is false, or unreal. This practice shows us that the Supreme Reality resides within.

Karma Yoga

Karma Yoga is the path of selfless work. Those who follow this path do work as an offering to God and expect nothing personal in return. Karma Yoga teaches us to practice detachment and equanimity in our work, and to understand that the results of any actions are beyond our control.

Raja Yoga

Raja Yoga is the path of meditation. Meditation is an important practice in all of the paths as it allows us to experience higher states of consciousness where we achieve a deeper understanding of our divine nature. Sri Ramakrishna, Swami Vivekananda Swami Chinmayanand ji & others, emphasized the use of a mantra based meditation technique and symbolic images of the divine.

Hari ॐ

1

THE DOCTRINE OF VEDANTA

THE TENATS OF VEDANTA

Vedas are the knowledge that is not available by inference, experience or other regular means. Thus "apaurushyea"- not of human intellect. It is accepted as an independent pramana by astikas.

Vedas are divided into poorvamimansa (karmakanda) & uttarmimansa (gyankanda).

KARMAKANDA

In poorvamimansa or karmakanda, karma is sadhana & karmaphala is sadhya. It is based on the purusharthas, viz. Dharma, Artha & Kama.

THE SADHANA/KARMA is of 3 types- physical, mental & verbal.

The sadhana has 3 imperfections or Dosha traya-

1. Sorrow, is the ultimate outcome, since all acquisitions are finite & ends. The sorrow at every end is proportional to the joy at its acquiring.

2. Atriptata- the end of one karma gives rise to another in a geometric progression of increasing desire, a perpetual unquenchable thirst.

3. Dependence on external objects of desire.

The SADHYA/KARMAPHALA is of 3 types- physical, mental & intellectual.

It is also laced with tri dosha-

The mental agitations of planning before gain.

The trepidation of hoarding & holding onto, on gain.

The anger & violence on obstruction & sorrow at loss.

POORVAMIMANSA is for most people as, to the majority-

a) These defects (doshas), are unknown.

b) One does not mind, even on knowledge of these defects, as one is happy of this world of finite desire persuals, to be done again & again..... they have no need of VEDANTA (Uttarmimansa/Gyankanda).

VEDANTA

Is for the needy. Whose need is to get rid of the imperfections (doshas).

And for the same, they are ready to relinquish the transient & finite worldly objective joys; in persual of the infinite eternal subjective bliss.

This state, sans the imperfections is Brahman/Atman; & That Thou Art, is the Vedantic declaration, about one's real nature.

Whereas worldly experience showing oneself to be finite, is a jeeva in sorrow.

Yet abundant & innumerable are the examples, where experience is a mithya. Such as- the blue ness of sky, flatness of earth, the motion of sun, the water of mirage, of the stars that all we see- some may have perished billions of years ago, the color- sound- taste perceptions of different jeevas(species) are different, all in relativity & none in absolute truth.

Vedanta is not a new acquisition, it just a revelation of one's already existing nature.

The confusion of "Who am I?"

The finite jeeva or the infinite Atman/Brahman?

Thus when a confusion arises, it has its answer in enquiry. Vedanta vichara.

THE FUNDAMENTAL TENATS OF VEDANTA

Is the synopsis of Adhyasa bhasya of Brahma Sutra -

1.   Moksha from ignorance is the goal.

2.   Gyan is the only means for mokshya.

3.   Vedanta vichara alone gives this gyan.

*METHODS OF VEDANTIC ENQUIRY

Two types of enquiry-

A)   ANAVYA VYATIREKA/DRYG DRYSA VIVEKA- Indicates discrimination between Self(Atman) & nonself (Anatman). What I am not; is indicated. It simplifies the multitudes of jagat into duality of Atman & anatman.

B)   ADHYAROPA APAVADA- Indicates the relation of Atman & anatman, by indication of ephemerality of anatman & eternity of atman. Thus proving that Atman alone is the absolute truth. The reduction of duality into nondual advaita.

ANAVYA VYATIREKA of three types-

a)   Karya karana method- pots & clay or ornaments & gold. Pots & ornaments are karya, & are effects with transient existence. While clay & gold are the karana (cause). There is no karya (pot & ornaments), without the karana (clay or gold). Not a used method for final intuition.

b)   Vyapta Vyapaka - where is smoke, there is fire. Smoke is not a cause of fire, yet the experience of Smoke, induces knowledge of fire. Not a used method for final intuition.

c)   Anavritra Vyavritta sambandha- The used method for intuitive indication.

In the simultaneously experienced multitudes, that which comes & goes is incidental transient- Vyavritta. That which is always, is the essential nature- anavrittam. As seen in Avasthaya traya vichara (waking- dream- deep sleep).

WAKING- experience of I am(self) (constancy) + gross body + mind(transient & changing).

DREAM- experience of I Am (Self) (constant)+ Mind (transient)= Anavya. While gross body experience is absent= Vyavritti.

DEEP SLEEP- experience of continuity as self (anavya); while absence of body mind experience (Vyavritta).

Thus gross (body) & subtle (mind); comes & goes- incidental/Vyavritta- not one's nature= non self=anatman.

The self as anavya is Atman, ones real nature.

The Causal body is the seed form of gross & subtle body, thus not different from it as non self/anatman or vyavritta.

The three states or three bodies are are not the self, they being anatman; Whereas I am the Atman. Yet there is no Advaita Siddhi, since there is duality of Atman & Anatman.

This is an experience of ASANGATVA, What not am I.

Entering of Adhyaropa apavada Naya.

ADHYAROPA APAVADA

[THE TYPES OF EXISTENCE =

Real/SAT= that which is ever existing across all time frames=Atman/Brahman. The eternal.

Unreal/Asat= that which is not there in any experience, horns of a hare.

Illusory/Mithya= that which Appears in experience of space-time -causation; but is with an origin & end, hence transient & ephemeral.]

1. ADHYAROPA is intentional superimposition of reality on an appearing effect as jagat/body/mind/intellect etc.

2. To determine the cause (Atman/Brahman) which lends existence to the effect (Jagat & Jeeva).

3. TO establish the non existence of effect without the cause- denial of independent existence of effect (jagat/jeeva).- MITHYATVA. This is apavada.

4. Intuitive realisation of the cause Brahman alone as the only truth (existence)- EKATVA- ADVAITA.

Ayam Atman Brahman.

I am the cause- in form of total consciousness (Hiramyagarbha), which experiences the dream of jagat. I alone lend existence to all the contents of that dream of jagat. Jagat is the dream of total consciousness.

Like the individual consciousness of mind of jeeva in dream (taijasa), that creates the contents of individual dream.

Thus when the limited jeeva realises its essential nature as that of tri dosha Rahita limitless essence, the upadesha vakya "TAT Twam Asi"; becomes the intuitive "Aham brahmasmi"... Moksha.

The gyan of vedanta vichara or GYAN is a philosophy only, unless it be integrated as a way of living, as GYAN YOGA. For this to happen, there is the need of preparatory sadhanas to make the mind intellect receptive for integration of such knowledge. These are the ways of=

* CHITTASUDDHI or Sadhanas of GYAN YOGYATA.

Two ways for this-

1) KARMA YOGA. 2) ASTANGA YOGA

KARMA YOGA= KARMA + YOGA.

***

ON KARMA

Karma can mean 1) Action 2) Karmaphala (as sanchita- prarabdha) 3) sometimes object of action - as in Iswara gyan.

In karmayoga-

*Karma is only about actions in proper form.

*YOGA is the attitude of action.

KARMA is of 3 TYPES-

A) ADHAMA KARMA- the lowest karmas in the Tamasic predominance, that harms others & also oneself. Those that are prohibited by shastra, as it takes one away from mokshya. The attitude (yoga), towards such karma should be of dislike & avoidance. It is to be given up.

B) MADHYAMA/KAMYA KARMA- Neither enjoined or prohibited in shastra. It gives primarily material benefits & less chitta suddhi, depending on the attitude of doing.

Can not be instantly given up by samsari, thus; to grow out of it gradually.

The attitude of kamya karma is to be of Iswara Arpana, instrumentship or ambassadorship of lord in doership & Fala Prasad buddhi in enjoyership. The realisation of any outcome as that, as was bound to happen. The feeling of injustice to any outcome, is the result of ignorance of past karmas & a rejection of the law of Karma.

C) UTTAMA KARMA- Enjoined in scriptures. These are nihita or compulsory karmas that gives maximum chittasuddhi & sometimes less material benifits. It's non doing takes one away from mokshya. It is of the nature of 5 yagyas, as oblations to-. 1. DEV yagya- worship related. 2. PITRY yagyas- parents, forefathers, all departed, gurus- second parent. 3. BRAHMA or Rishi yagyas- sages & shastras. 4. BHUTA yagya- all living & nonliving. 5. MANUSYA yagya, for the good of all humanity.

All these are of equal importance & should be done together & not at the expense of another.

The attitude towards These karmas should not be of burden & compulsion, but of love & understanding, for one's own good.

ASTANGA YOGA OR SAMADHI

The body is the chariot, the senses are the horses, the mind is the rein, the intellect is the charioteer, that will enable the spiritual journey.... Katha upanishad.

For the journey to be smooth & successful, there are 5 prerequisites-

1. The chariot (body) should be healthy.

2. The senses should be healthy for sravana

3. The reins (mind) should be healthy for sense control & mañana.

4. Intellectual health for discrimination, mind control & niddhidhyasana.

5. The harmony of body- mind- intellect, to function in unison.

The body should not be ignored in unkept neglect, nor should it be ultimate end of purpose. It should be a healthy means for vedanta vichara, on this spiritual path.

Astanga yoga is a means towards integration of a healthy body mind intellect, as a means of Gyan yogyata.

It is not a gyan sadhana as it not any of the six pramanas (prataksha, anumana, Upasana(comparison), arthapatti- postulation, anupalabdhi, sabda).

It is not a mokshya sadhana as it does not remove ignorance.

The Astanga yoga of Patanjali is accepted in vedanta as gyan yogyata, but not its philosophy, which accepts multiple Atmans.

It's 8 steps are-

1. YAMA- (5 prohibition)- Ahimsa, Satya, Aparigraha- no hoarding, Asteya- no covetousness, Brahmacharya- passion control.

2. NIYAMA- (5 injunctions)-Saucha- purity, Santosa- satisfaction, Tapas - wilful denial- sense control, Swadhyay- study of vedanta, Iswara pranidhana- surrender to Supreme.

    The Yama & Niama pertains to moral health.

3. ASANA- integrates health & develops dhyana, is for the health of annamaya body.

4. PRANAYAMA- improves health of pranamaya, and being middle of annamaya & manomaya; helps in their integration. Of the 5 pranas, 4 are involuntary, while only breath is both voluntary & involuntary, thus its voluntary control gives control over all pranas. All mantra incantation are also pranayama. When done as dedication to Iswara, gives chittasuddhi. Kundalini association to pranayama, pertains to anatman, hence not vedanta.

5. PRATYAHARA-withdraewl of sensory desires.

6. DHARANA- mind fixed on a choosen Chakra, superimposed by ista Devata or Iswara.

7. DHYANA-retaining the fixity of Dharana, on the Iswara.

8. SAMADHI- uninterrupted dhyana. In yoga, on Chakra & in vedanta, on Iswara or Brahman.

Astanga yoga gives focused intellect.

Shastras give sharp intellect.

*GYAN YOGA

Bondage is in ignorance. Gyan is the only means to liberation. Vedanta vichara is alone that gives that gyan.

Sadhana of gyan yoga is by SRAVANA -MANANA & NIDDHIDHYASANA.

SRAVANA from guru or shastra, removes the abhavana of gyan.

MANANA removes intellectual doubts & removes asambhavana. Till oneself (not others) is convinced.

NIDDHIDHYASANA removes emotional doubts in form of contrary thoughts (viparita bhavana). Most of the qualities of Jeevan Mukta is pertaining to the removal of emotional doubts.

Jevanmukta is one established in vedanta vichara, without intellectual or emotional doubts.

*BHAKTI (As LOVE) & ITS YOGA (As UPASANA)

BHAKTI AS LOVE & devotion for the divine is a must in any religious or spiritual path. Depending on its intensity & purity, it is of three types-

A) ADHAMA BHAKTI- It is either for removal of sorrow (ARTA) or for worldly gains (ARTHARTA). The gain of worldly & the removal of sorrow is the end. God is the means. The end is greater in love than the means, thus this is a false devotion, of least intensity & purity. Yet better than nastika. This is the commonest form of Bhakti.

B) MADHYAMA BHAKTI- When worldly gains are found perishable (viveka); there arises the quest for eternal (Jigyasu Bhakti). In such a state, the finite worldly objects become unimportant & renouncable (vairagya) & there develops intense yearning for the Supreme (mumukshutwa). When the worldly desires can be forsaken for God; then God is the end & the worldly, is the means. Thus a bhakti of higher intensity & purity. Yet, there is duality in that too- me & God; and God is yearned for MY sake... "Atmaneyeshu kamayae atma Priya bhavati."

C) UTTAMA BHAKTI- When the means & end has merged in oneness - all is in God & God is in all. There is none other than God, this is unconditional Bhakti- nondual advaita. The highest & purest - "Aham brahmasmi." & "Isavasyam idam sarvam."

The state of a Gyani. This is not selfishness, as to reach this state; there is already the realisation of Brahman as my self & as the Self in all.

BHAKTI AS YOGA

Any Upasana, be it religious practice or sadhana, when done in an attitude of devotion- is Bhakti yoga. Also of 3 types.

A) KARMA BHAKTI- Action done as yagya or oblation or as agentship of God & results accepted as prasadam, is Karma yoga or karma Bhakti. The lower Bhakti yoga.

B) DHYANA sadhana done with an attitude of devotion to saguna or nirguna Brahman, is Dhyana Bhakti- the madhyama Bhakti yoga.

C) GYAN BHAKTI- as Sravana- Manana- Nidhidhyasana of vedanta vichara, with love & Shraddha, for the lineage of Gurus, Rishis, Shastras & Atmagyan; Gyan Bhakti, the uttama Bhakti yoga.

All spiritual practice can be a form of Bhakti in vedanta vichara.

* MEDITATION

is an adjuvant to Gyan yoga. It is helpful in preparation or assimilation of gyan; not in gaining gyan. Another method of Gyan yogyata.

It is for preparation of mind, to accept the gyan by sravana mañana; by making it relaxed, concentrated focused, expanded or virtuous. When done before gyan.

a) Relaxation meditation -imaginations of relaxing nature, thought of guru, Devata or that which relaxes the mind.

b) Focused meditation- as Manasa Puja, mantra or nama japa.

c) Expansion meditation- contemplative unison with the concept of Virat purusha or Hiramyagarbha.

d) Virtue meditation- on that virtue which is is deemed deficient in oneself.

It is for assimilation of gyan by niddhidhyasana, a constant contemplation of vedanta vichara. Sometimes repeated sravana, writing & satsanga in vedanta vichara is also niddhidhyasana, that helps in assimilation of the gyan as a living realisation.

Hari Om.

2

WHO AM I?

The observer (asmat) & observed (yusmat) are not the same.

The observer is one, the observed are many.

The observer is unchanging relative to the changing observed.

The observer is sentient (conscious), the observed is not (gross).

I (the SELF), do observe=

IN WAKEFULNESS-

A) Multitudes of JAGAT,

B) This BODY of mine,

C) The PRANAS of this life,

D) This Mind of mine,

E) The emotions of INTELLECT & the feelings of ego in doership & enjoyership.

IN DREAM SLEEP-

Also, do I observe; all that I experience as in waking standpoint.

IN DEEP SLEEP-

I am the observer of the BLISS OF OBJECTLESSNESS.

Thus I am the Subjective consciousness;

Which is-

NOT THE BODY, NOT THE PRANAS, NOT THE MIND, NOT THE INTELLECT OR EGO, NOT THE SUBTLE DREAM, NOT THE CAUSAL BLISS OF DEEP SLEEP.

"Naham deha janmamrytyu krutoh me.

Naham pranah shatipasey krutoh me.

Naham chittam shok moho krutoh me.

Naham karma bandhan moksha krutoh me"

Since I am not the body, how could there be birth & death to me?

As I am not the life forces, whence could hunger & thirst be to me?

The mind is also, not Me; then where is grief & delusion to me?

Since I am not the ego & intellect; who is in bondage or or who is it that seeks liberation?

The ADHYAROPA Teachings- (deliberate superimposition of Sakshi)=

I am the SUBJECTIVE consciousness that illumines as SAKSHI, all that appears as OBJECT (body mind prana intellect bliss & jagat).- The duality of WITNESSING subject & the WITNESSED object; is a deliberate distraction of mithya duality, created on the absolute truth of nonduality.

So as to wean one away from the grave ignorant notion of- I as the Body mind intellect & the world as real.

Into the relatively lesser ignorance of the Self(I) as Sakshi, & the rest as an observed dream.

The APAVADA teachings of desuperimposition =

After the shift in notion, of I as Sakshi; from I as body-mind- intellect- ego.

Is the lightening that strikes to destroy the illusion of Sakshi-

"Na nirodho na chotpartin na ca sadhaka.

Na mumukshurna vay muktah ityesha paramartha."

There is no dissolution, no birth, none in bondage, None aspiring for wisdom, no seeker of liberation & none liberated.

This is the absolute truth.

"Brahma satwa jagat mithya;

Jeevo brahmaiva naparah."

All the world is an appearance only, in the truth of Brahman. &

"TAT TWAM ASI"

"AHAM BRAHMASMI."

I AM THAT NON DUAL POORNA ETERNAL TRUTH THAT ALONE IS. THE REST IS AN ILLUSION IN ME.

Hari ॐ

3

EKAM ADWITIAM BRAHMAN

HOW IS THIS POSSIBLE, WHEN THERE IS THE EXPERIENCE OF JAGAT OF MULTITUDES.

"nahi bhanad- rte sattvam narte bhanam chito citah,

Chit sambandho pi nadhyasad rte tenaham advayah."

Experience is the only factor, that substantiates the existence of;

gross objects & subtle thoughts & emotions. The world or any object, can not be said to exist without experience.

For Experience,(that is needed to substantiate any existence); a conscious principle is imperative.

The totality of existence is composed of Asmat (Self) & Usmat (objective gross & subtle). The components of Usmat (world & thoughts - emotions) are not self revealing, hence inert non conscious. Thus the conscious principle has to be the Asmat (Self), that illumines all and beyond (infinite) & is also Self revealing (there is no need of proof, for the experience of - I am ness.).

In the act of knowing, there is an interaction/contact or association; between the subjective Self & the objective inert gross (objects) or subtle (thoughts).

But such an association though it appears; is not possible in reality as =

1. Opposite is their nature, which can't coexist, as Darkness-Light; Knowledge- Ignorance; Silence - Sound.

2. Facts of different realms of reality can not really interact. Conscious pertains to Absolute reality, while world is transactional. The water of waking world by bedside does not quench a dream thirst.

   Nor does the the water of mirage, wet a grain of sand.

3. That without a form or attribute (consciousness) is without a change, hence without a beginning or end -Eternal.

   In the objective world of thoughts & objects, change is the only constancy; these everything is with a beginning & end with change in the middle, eg. Ephemeral.

   The Eternal can have no real interaction or transaction in & as the Ephemeral.

4. "nasto vidyate bhavo, nabhavo vidyate satah".- The unreal has no being & the real has no non being. (BG. 2-16).

That which is absent before birth & after death, has no true existence in the middle.

This is the sin qua non of the objective world.

While the subjective Self/Atman/Brahman/Consciousness; is beyond time - space, everlasting as the answer to the questions of - what BEFORE time? & what BEYOND space?

The consciousness, which is beyond time space; can have no relationship to elements of causality which are in space time dimensions.

Thus the relation of Asmat/Self/Atman/Brahman; With the Usmat (gross world & subtle thoughts & causality);

IS AN UNREAL RELATION.

An APPEARANCE ONLY (of world & thoughts), AS A SUPERIMPOSITION; (on the substratum of Self/Brahman).

Like the Rope on Snake.

Or Mirage water on desert sand.

Where the substratum rope (Brahman), is not the cause of appearance snake (jagat).

Nor is the a appearing (snake/jagat); a part of the substratum (Brahman).

The Self/Brahman, is the Ekam Adwitiam substratum on which Space Time causality is an appearance of superimposition, due to ignorance of-

1. Ignorance of reality of Self/Brahman, as truth.- Abhavana & Asambhavana.

2. Wrong knowing of the world as truth & the body mind as the Self -Viparita bhavana

4

BIOLOGY & GOD REALIZATION

In our body we have billions of cell. Each has a life's purpose(karma). Let me tell you the story of a single RBC. Supose in its world of RBC's it has a name alpha. Alpha thinks, in its miniscule awareness that it has a life of 120 days and its karma is to carry O2 from lung to tissue and CO2 from tissue to lungs. After 120 days all is finished for it. But in reality it is transformed into iron and protein an is used up as a part of different tissues(liver andmuscles) So it is the death of RBC and birth of muscle and liver. There is death of only the name and form(nama/roopa) whereas the existence in a different form is always there. TheRBC with its miniscule consciousness does not realize itself to be a part of the bigger body-you. It considers itself complete and a separate entity which is false. Similarly we ourselves are a part of the greater truth-the eternal existence consciousness of which we are unaware of due to the veiling and projecting power of Maya. We are actually a part of that eternal totality which we call God.

All in me, Me in all, that is what Krishna said to Arjun (This is actually the philosophy of VisistAdwaita of SwamiRamanujacharya and also Adwaita of Swami Sankaracharyaa's; as this mind feels.)

HariOm.

5

LAW OF KARMA..

IS IT ONLY FATE?

Karma is only in realms of pratibhasika (dream) or vyavarika (waking), so long as there is doership & enjoyership.

Karma is the basis or substratum of future embodiment, to start with.

But it is bondage, only with karta bhokta bodha, when there is mind intellect... the double edged sord.

Doings of lower life forms, without enjoyership doership, there is no agama karmaphala, it is only exhaustion of sanchita karma. A progress in the evolutionary path of consciousness.

With advent of mind intellect of human birth; there is doership enjoyership with free will.

The karmic substratum at birth (body mind), is like a material to work upon with free will.... mud, marbel, gold or stone or cow dung.... But is not the final end. With free will and present karma, a Michaelangelo will make a master piece of stone, more precious than gold. While in hand of Iconoclast, a priceless creation will become rubble. Thus very evident like said in Vedanta, that karma though gives the substratum to start the transaction, is modifiable by free will and color of mind (varna), at the time of transaction.

Atman is in the realm of paramarthika, non transactional. Neither a witness nor a dispenser of justice, but the unbiased consciousness which envigors both the enjoined & nissiddha karma, like the light of sun which equally lights up the the karmas of Shankara & a Killer.

The result of karma may or may not be instant. It is a complex interplay of fructifying past sanchitas & the mental element. Thus is explained different outcomes for same effort by different people at different time frames.

The atman is a pure non doer, like light. It is the reflecting or refracting media of mind, colored by gunas due to fructifying karmas of past & free will, that is the doer & enjoyer. This mind intellect since is the one with karta bhokta bodha (subtle), based in ignorance(causal); is the one that has to dream the dream of life, in transmigration.... to dream a better dream in free will (atmagyan).

The gross body, is just an instrument without karta bhokta bodha, like the weapon of a killer, thus spared the outcome of karma phala, in transmigration... so left behind to the panchabhutas.

Thus in the law of karma, the entire gamut of future outcome of work & embodiment, is for the doer enjoyer mind intellect (subtle), (causally) ignorant as the superimposed self or false Ego. Such a mithya Ego alone is responsible for ones karma phalas, no Iswara or Atman, is responsible for it.

Yes, Manonasha, dissolves the objective mind intellect, in subjective pure consciousness, by Atma gyan, to transcend vyavarika into paramarthika.

Karma, since it pertains to Maya, is not False(in vyavaharika), nor true (in paramarthika).

It is neither True nor False, it is Mithya.

Hari Om.

(as this mind feels).

Why and what is Karma?

Karma is action(Rajas). The body mind complex is the outcome of sanchita and prarabdha karma. The prarabdha karma is infallible and, is the so called lifespan of a jeeva; till it ends. In this background new karmas are done (agama karma). All this is in the play of Maya. All karmas be it good or bad has its equal reaction.. and thus continues the apparent game of birth and death (samsara).

Tamas(gross ignorance) can be obliviated by Rajas(karma), only by incorporating the element of Sattwa in karma. Karma persay is unattached. Only the fruits of karma gives sorrow and joy. So to kill Tamas, there is the need of karma sans the fruits of karma which can be dedicated to the supreme/ Universal totality. Then it is niskama karma. In nishkama karma there is the benefit of DESIRELESSNESS, which is the basic need of spiritual life/ self realization (from the individual self to the universal self/Brahman.) This State Of Desirelessness and universal yagna is Sattwa, which obliterates Rajas (karma). The body mind becomes a seeker of what is the only truth in this mirage of transition. Naturally next to follow is Gyana. For this to happen there is the need of a tranquil mind directed in the inner universe of infinite (possible by meditation/Raj yoga) and a belief in the truth of prasthana traya (this belief is Bhakti).

When The Universal truth of Asangatwa, Ekatwa and Mithwatwa dawns, all the Maya powers= Tamo, Rajo and Satwa gunas, vanish and you are that. Tat Twam Asi.

There is no more Karma, Bhakti, or Ignorance or Gyana.

Hari ॐ

6

MAYA & THE UNREAL WORLD

World is perceived by the five senses and that is an apparent truth, for every jiva.

If one is blind from birth then the world is composite of sound, taste, smell and touch; to that bodymind.

If one is born blind and deaf then to such a bodymind the world is of taste, touch and smell...

and similarly if one is born without the five senses, then to such an existence the world does not exist at all.

Let Us Take The Five Senses Individually.

VISION: The electromagnetic spectrum is vast; extending from cosmic, gamma, ultraviolet, visual spectrum, infrared, microwaves and radio waves. The human eye perceives only apart of it; the visual spectrum. And that we feel as, the complete & real; where as the greater total truth is much more. Coming to color, we see the seven colors and its various combinations; that is the world of vision for humans. A lion or tiger sees only black and white and grey; that world is also true for them. Cats and nocturnal animals perceive vision even in infrared spectrum; that world is true for them. Aquatic animals see world in a media with different refractive index, where others will have blurred vision. Is this true or that is true?..... Astavakra.

World of SOUND:

The world of sound is nonexistent in space. Even on Earth, humans hear from 20 to 20000 decibels. To the rest we are deaf. The world of sound is much more vast for a dolphin, bat, rhino and elephant. It is a relative awareness that we consider as real whereas it is a relative truth or vyavarika.

The world of TOUCH:

Touch that we feel as contact is in reality an illusion. When two objects are in contact there is a micro nanometer space between them. A real contact will be an overlap of electron orbits and forming a compound. But in spite of the non real contact we perceive it as real. A relative functional reality.

Similarly the world of Taste and Smell is different for different jivas and each considers its relative reality as the truth that ever was and is.... This is the scientific MAYA with its avarana of the real and prakshepa of the unreal. How the unreal becomes real.

In all animate and inanimate objects the only one truth in common is.. SAT(Existence). The rest in the process of evolution has been a gradual increase in consciousness. Evolution is not evolution of body (otherwise dinosaurs would be the top product), it is actually the evolution of consciousness, finally as the human brain/mind.

Right here in this world there are other realms of senses, which does not exist for us since we are not endowed with such perception. The world of geomagnetism so real for birds, the world of electromagnetism so real for whales and sharks; does not exist for us.

In the cosmic order of things as propounded in relativity, it is the bending of space that there is.

In the Quantum Order Of Microcosm; uncertainty and dual nature of existence predominates.

Science has only now started its search on the Unifying principle which has long ago been propounded as the existence/consciousness in VEDANTA.

Science Considers Energy (existence in vedanta) to be indestructible... same.

In a black hole where when all energy/existence goes into, there might be a passage (wormhole) ending on the other end into a white hole through which new universes may emanate with different dimensions of existence. Similar to the metaphorical stories in puranas.

Even in present life, perceptions of sense may change. Sound can be seen. Colors can be touched. Sweetness can be heard, motion can be perceived as flight; when the mind brain under influence of drugs likeLSD.

Adwaita is science told in allegorical stories. The great Unified theory of everything, yet to be found in science. It is the Brahman (existence/consciousness) of Vedanta).

Jagat Mithya.. Brahma sattwi.

World Plurality is unreal, only existence/consciousness is the SAT.

Hari ॐ

7

MANDUKYA UPANISHAD AND NIRVANA

Manndukya the shortest of all upanishad is most profound (as said by Rama to Hanuman). It is actually a map guiding a seeker home (to that what you are).

Life being a game (leela) of finding:Who am I?

The rules of the game is Maya and Yoga. In this game you have many many lives to reach the endpoint (which everyone shall ere long. -B. G).

The eternal homogeneous Brahman(singularity/existence.....) started the game by obscuring itself in ignorance (avarana) and then bending space into forms (prakshepa) of jiva and jagat. It (existence and maya) is beginningless and unidirectional (time).

When a weary traveller transmigrating on the path of evolution of consciousness, searching for happiness (name/fame/wealth/knowledge...); realises that all is impermanent (happiness). The jeeva transforms from samsaric, to a seeker. Finding the unifing principle of quantum/newtonian and cosmic reality (spiritual), which is infinite, eternal, nondual, omnipresent, existence and consciousness...(God/Brahman.. in Aitet. Upanishad).

When Brahman appears as, gross individual name and form, it is viswa nara, which when becomes a seeker does action for the benefit of all rather than the individual self(karma yoga). In the process the individual gross body(viswa nara) becomes the cosmic gross body (Virat).

Raj yoga follows in form of meditation and chitta vritti nirodha and one becomes dream like in the mental world (not the body), that is Taijasa. When meditation turns into samadhi, one becomes the cosmic dream state(subtle body) which is Hiranyagarbha. Then the sun shines in all its glory and darkness is gone (gyana yoga takes away ignorance). The state of Pragya (you are not the body not the mind.. causal state) The beginningless Maya since it acts the bodymind complex, fails to exert its power now.

Continually being in this state one becomes: Ayam atman Brahman, that what you are. The homecoming.

HariOm.

A SEEKERS DILEMA= WHY THIS CREATION?

If I am that eternal nondual Brahman Full Of Bliss (ayamatmanBrahman) why was this jagat and jeeva, created in this game of birth and death?

Answer=

1. In bhakti yoga it is God's Leela.

2. In Adwaita:You were never created/born. You're always Brahmam, rest is mithya, due toMaya/ignorance, this mithya appears to be real as it is experienced.

3. Reply by Tapovanswami to Chinmayanandji.

"Chinmaya get me some water to drink". Chinmayaji went and got a lota(vessel) full of water from the Ganges and gave it to the swami. Tapovan swami was furious. Why did you disobey me? I asked you to bring water and what is this? Chinmayaji said Gurudev this is a lota full of water. Tapovanswami said, why the lota, I asked for only water.

Chinmaya ji understood. You need a nama roopa & mind (vessel/lota) to experience the bliss. Nondual bliss is beyond experience. That's the need of the mithya called jiva and jagat.

HariOm.

9

PURPOSE OF GYAN YOGA

for atma gyan.

Has two Purpose=

1. There arises true knowledge of the impermanence of sense objects to which MIND attaches.

2. It becomes known by the MIND that the only true knower (atmana/ Brahman) is the only permanance to which the mind should attach and also the fact that it (knower/atmana/brahman) can not be known by the MIND, (then it will not be absolute knower and will be a known object).

Thus the MIND knows that what it knows is false/impermanent) and that, it ought to know is beyond its realms. Knowing Its (MIND'S) futility it dissolves its egoism, into that what it is... existence, consciousness only. That Is Bliss.. absolute. The dissolution of MIND... JIVANMUKTI...

HARI OM.

BHAGWAT GITA SAR

For the jeeva in ignorance (Maya), there is Sakama karma(with desire of karma phala) which are bound by the various combinations of Gunas (Tamo/Rajo/Sattwa), to be done in the vedic tradition of dharma- artha- kama (in that order).

For the seeker of liberation, there is karma without desire of karmaphala (Niskamakarmas). This is the stage of renunciation of desire and not renunciation of karma; which at this stage is Tamasic.

Later with knowledge when one, no more identifies with the body and mind (I am not the body, not the mind, rather i am the witness consciousness of all at first of jagat & later the witness or substratum of all the appearing illusions), at this stage of enlightment (Brahma Jnana); there is total renunciation of both Karma and its Phala. The eternal witness, consciousness - bliss.

Bhagwat Gita is not to goad a body mind into incessant karma. Rather it uses karma as a stepping stone to reach the stage beyond it... Liberation.

HARI OM.

Avidvadvisayam karmavidvadvisaya ca sarvakarmasannya sapurvika jananistha... BG. 18. 66

11

THE MOVIE OF LIFE

Directed By:Maya

Produced by:Free will of the mind.

Screen:Brahman.

Projector:mind.

Audience:jiva and jagat.

This is a 4 D movie with feelings of time and space. The mind projects this movie in three parts namely -waking, dreaming and deep sleep(states).

In the waking part there is a physical and mental element. In the dreaming part there is onlya mental element and in deep sleep there is the experience of absence of physical and mental elements.

One can enjoy the movie while it lasts and go for another movie if one is a movie buff (in the cycle of transmigration). One may laugh in a comedy, cry in a tragic, feel the adventure in awar, love in a romance or suspense in a mystery. All these are after all experiences of the mind which enjoys them. Thus continues the movie of transmigration which ensnares the jiva and jagat in this cosmic mirage.

Why is there so much sorrow, war, strife, joy, yearning for peace in the world? This is because the mind in duality searches for answers in duality and the producer called free will asks the director Maya to produce such a film to cater to the needs of the audience (jeeva andjagat).

The movie of waking part vanishes with the onset of dream state. The movie of dream vanishes with deep sleep onset and the movie of deep sleep vanishes with the onset of the waking state. None of the party remains throughout (truth), so all this is mithya.

When the audience is a Vedantin seeker, then the focus remains on the screen only; the movie of life is enjoyed without attachment to the projected images which are known to be transient and illusory. The only constant, being the screen (Brahman) on which stories of love-hate, violence- peace, joy-sorrow etc. are projected, which are like the snake on the rope. Thus to the vedantin audience there is no snake due to the true knowledge of rope (gyan yoga); and to the substratum (rope/screen) there never ever was a snake/movie.

Only the substratum is the truth(Brahman) rest all is mithya, viewed as a mirage by the projection of mind, courtsey : Maya.

When a movie ends one may see another movie depending on latent desires in a different hall (transmigration), or one may not go to a movie again if one has focussed on the screen only, feeling it to be an illusory interplay of emotions and sequences; on the only truth of substratum (screen/Brahman).

The producer, director produces movies depending on the demand of audience(jeeva and jagat). When the free will of the jeeva and jagat becomes Vedantin then the need of the movie will vanish. All will merge back into the substratum (Brahman) which it always was.

There is also, the need for such a film critique like Shankara to make the audience understand the true essence of the movie of life.

Hari Om. Sankara namaha.

12

SPIRITUAL PURPOSE OF STORIES

In Puranas

Every story is a mythology at face value and easily discarded. But actually the stories are allegorical means of meditation to a deeper spiritual meaning. Letus today meditate on the story of Samudra manthan and Neelkantha.

Once the Devas and Asuras (your own mental and thought states) decided to churn the Ocean (the Mind-an ocean of thoughts.)

The Mandara mountain (intellect) was the churning staff. The rope for churning was Vasuki the serpent (OurEgo). So when the mind in maya is churned by the ego in the light of intellect. There comes out many gifts (Samsaric fortitude, visions, tranquility, intuitions, yogic powers.. etc.) If you still continue the churning there will be the ultimate benefit of Amritya/ Immortality (Brahmagyana/. TatTwamAsi). But before the final benefit, the serpent (Ego) will spew its final Venom which is capable of destroying all (spiritualpractices). This venom is the latent desires and vasanas collected over many life times. These latent pravittis are not to be given a place in the mind (intellect/Head) or the heart (emotion) and thus to be untouched by both in a place in between (neck). That is possible only when nUma (prakriti) places her hand of grace, on the neck of Shiva (purusa), who then goes into Turiya.)

(From punya Gurudev, Swami Chinmayanand ji's teachings.)

Hari ॐ

13

EFFORT & GRACE

FOR THE SEEKER OF SELF.

No amount of effort in form of Sadhana, Dhyana, Satsanga or Sravana, Manana or Niddhidhyasana can lead to Self realization (Brahma gyana). All these efforts are bound by space, time and cause- effect relations of the mind and intellect and body. Whereas Brahman is beyond these, completely unbound by body- mind- intellect. Should one stop these practices? It is said if one leaves the samsara to be a recluse one has lost the way. Similarly if one leaves spirituality and immerses into samsara, that too has lost the way. What is the need of such efforts? Since seeking does not lead to Brahma Gyan. What's Its use? It develops discrimination of sat and asat.

Gyan yoga as atmagyana has two purpose =

1. There arises true knowledge of the impermanence of sense objects to which MIND attaches. It becomes known by the MIND that the only true knower (atmana/brahman) is the only permanance to which the mind should attach and also the fact that it (knower/atmana/ brahman) cannot be known by the MIND, (then it will not be the absolute knower and will be a known object).

Thus the MIND knows that what it knows is false/impermanent) and that it ought to know is beyond its realms. Knowing its (MIND'S) futility it dissolves into that what it is (beyond namarupa into.. existence, consciousness, bliss.. absolute.) The dissolution of MIND..

A state of complete helplessness and abject surrender; one becomes a true disciple as Arjuna had surrendered to Kfishna after all his doubts; finally saying "my lord guide me" then dwelled the Grace of the lord/Atnan and one is enlightened.

In Isa upanishad one prays to the Sun (as the lord) to reveal itself to the ignorant failing which no amount of effort will result in Brahmagyan. It is for Brahman the absolute, beyond attributes to reveal itself by GRACE to the chosen. And chosen is the one who has choosen the Self above all the worldly. Because Brahman is not a purchasable entity which can be purchased by the currency of dhyana, dharana, nididhyasana, satsang or gyana. Till then waiting for GRACE; continuing in the path to mind dissolution... A state of deep sleep in wakefulness.

"Sahana vabhatu, Sahanav bhunaktu, Saha viryam karva wahey, Tejaswina adhitamastu, mavidh viwahsawhey."

Hari ॐ.

14

MANAGING RELATIONS

Divinise your worldly relations and

Humanize your Godly relations.

The first is a fusion of Karma and Gyana yoga. The second is fusion of Bhakti and Gyan yoga.

The result is a state of unattached bliss, akin to Samadhi (Rajyoga).

In divinising the world one sees the supreme Brahman as the substratum of all nama roopa in the form of a stone, tree, animal or human. After all Ishwara is a Sattwic maya (nama roopa) of Brahman. In this state of mind there is a realization of & about; "sarvaidam Brahman & about;.. All is in me.(Gyan yoga). Then any work in samsara becomes a worship as it is done in a spirit of niskama karma =Karma Yoga. Every work can be done as a worship the supreme God/Brahman, if one is in duality. And when gradually duality is absolved there remains no one to worship, no worshiper and no act of worship. Endgame.. Jivanmukti.

In humanising the godly and supreme relations the supreme lord can be loved as a child (balgopal); as a friend - sakha (Arjuna-Krishna); as beloved (Mira-Giridhar); mother(kali) or father or son(Jesus). Such a love is intense Bhakti (yoga). Progressing ultimately into the truth & quot; you are me; I am you.. TatTwamAsi. The finality of Gyan Yoga.

Thus after divinising the jagat and humanizing the divine, one lives in a trance of the unity every one and everything... Ekatwam... living in Adwaitic unity (Samadhi), which is Rajyoga. The need of predominance of a particular yoga depends on the intellect, that particular mind body complex is; that's how one is led into the one in the many -the ultimate truth:

Life as an Adwaitin; a fusion of Yogas. Hari ॐ.

15

THE SINGULARITY TO MULTITUDES

How the singular (Brahman), became many(Jagat.)

The nondual singularity is the only true bliss, consciousness and existence; without changes either in space, time or object. The rest (Jagat) is all changing in space, time and as objects; hence is not eternal/absolute. It is Mithya: neither truth nor untruth. It is not truth since it is changing, thus not eternal. It is not untruth because it is vyavaharik (apparent) reality.

The nirguna non dual Brahman appears to play (leela) with the power of Maya/ignorance; which is Avarana (veiling) and Prakshepa(projection) because of ignorance. First the Avarana power deludes itself from, knowing its true self of who am I; then the projecting power manifests itself first as its image in mirror which looks and moves like real but is only virtual; this is probably Ishwara (nirguna Brahman+nama roopa); then when the universal mirror of mind-intellect breaks into multitude of smaller finite mirrors of mind intellect; there arises multiple images of the one and only absolute reality (Brahman); into multiple virtual images(Jagat and jeeva). Like the single sun casting and appearing as multiple smallerimages in multiple water bodies; all of which are mithya except the one self luminous one. The ignorance/maya is inexplainable as it is beginningless like Brahman, but is different from Brahman by its finite end; while Brahman is both beginningless and endless. The human mind is perplexed by its inability to fathom the nature of Maya/ignorance; because in ignorance one can't find details of ignorance as if searching darkness with darkness. Contrarily with the advent of Gyana; ignorance vanishes instantaneously. Just As One Is Unable To See Or Understand Darkness (ignorance) in a blazing light (gyana). Thus Maya the creator of the illusory Jagat and Jeeva remains unknown. The only facts being known of it is =1.

That it is the power of the saguna Brahman and it needs Brahman (existence/ consciousness) as its substratum to manifest its veiling and projecting power into an illusory world, while itself (sagunaBrahman) remaining unaffected like the poison of snake which does not affect it.

2. Though beginningless it is finite with an end.

Like if one does not know Hebrew and is asked "since when do you not know Hebrew?... it is unanswerable. beginningless. But when one learns Hebrew there is an answer to the same question. And Ignorance Is finished. You Know what you are.

* Nirguna Brahman+cosmicMaya=Ishwara.

* Brahman+individual maya=Pragyana.

* Ishwara(Brahman+maya)+cosmic mind=Hiranyagarbha.

* Brahman+maya+cosmic mind+cosmic body=Virat.

* Brahman+maya+individual mind =Taijasa.

* Brahman+maya+individual mind+individual body=Viswanara.

From the above it is seen that Brahman with different additions of body, mind and intellect takes various nama roopas of Iswara, Pragyana, Hiranyagarbha, Taijasa, Virat and Viswanara.. this is the illusory Jagat, all of which is transitory (mithya); so if there's the realisation that one is not the body, not the mind or not the intellect then what remains is the only Adwaitic mahavakya "AhamBrahmasmi".. That What One is.. Tat twam asi.

Hari ॐ

16

THE END GAME OF SAMSARA

Adwaita as a path to escape Transmigration (death to death journey.)

Why is there Birth?

The gross body passes into the pancha bhuta (five elements) at death. The Subtle and causal body searches a womb according to its sanchita KARMA and takes birth as a new gross body with the seed of causal body.

Why the KARMA?

Karma is due to desires. Desires are always in duality, when one perceives a difference between oneself and anything to be desired (which is not considered, as one self). One does not desire a hand so long, one has hands; but there is desire of hand if one does not have it. Desire is always for something which one feels that one does not have. Then there is karma to acquire it and its subsequent karma phala leading to the continuation of Transmigrating experiences over and over and over again.

In Gyani with Brahma dristi, there is complete oneness with everything (non duality). There is nothing other than me The Self, in every thing. The Shiva is me, the food is me, the music is me, the fragrance is me, the sensuality is me, the universe is me; all of the essence of Self. So what else is there to desire.. I am fullness itself. A state of complete satiety. A state of desirelessness. This is the result of knowing and living Adwaita. Since there is no desire, there is no sanchita karma; thus there is no birth and hence no death.

Escape From Transmigration...

Since all this happens in the illusory projection of Avidya/Maya; this is actually a mithya which appears real like a magic/mirage. But when there is an explanation of the magic/mirage; the apparent reality vanishes though the magic/miragestill continue to happen and the bodymind complex continues till prarabdha is exhausted...

Hari ॐ

17

TRANSCENDING MAYA/AVIDYA

The jagat is created in illusion by the veiling and projecting power of Maya. Then the jeevas and jagat are bound in an endless game of death to death by the three Gunas(Tàmo, Rajas and Sattva).

The Tamo guna is signified by lust, gluttony, inactivity and somnoloscence. These are the easiest to give up by a seeker as these are mainly pertaining to the gross body(annamaya kosha). With a little effort of activity and action, these vices of Tamo guna can be oblivated. Since action signifies Karma which is Rajoguna; thus Tamas can be erased by Rajas.

The characteristics of Rajo guna are activity, restlessness, anger, conquest, action etc. all of which needs the gross body(annamaya kosha) and the life forces (pranamaya kosha) to perform them. These vices can also be given up with a little effort of love, compassion, truth and benevolence; which are the qualities of Sattva guna.

The qualities of Sattwa guna mainly pertain to the mind and intellect(manomaya and vigyanmaya kosha). Thus it is seen that Sattwa guna can erase Rajo guna. In other words as the journey from annamayya to pranamaya to manomaya leads to the vijnanamaya kosha; there is evolution from Tamas toRajas and then to Sattwa.

This Sattwa is also a guna which binds to the illusion Maya and probably the strongest binder which is the final barrier before one becomes Gunatita (beyond the guns of Maya). The deeds in Sattva guna as helpfulness, benevolence, charity etc. lulls the intellect into complacency called punya with the promise of punya phala. But like adharma(papa); punya(dharma) is also a cause unto the endless journey from death to death.

This sattva guna of mind intellect can only be overcome by gyana of the higher intellect (dhi); and thus one becomes "na punyam na papam.. na saukhyam na dukham,... (only the unattached witness of all).. Shivo Hum.. Shivo Hum... The One realized beyond the Gunas.

Hari ॐ.

18

DILEMA IN ADWAITA

If atman is same in all, why did the realization of Krishna, Rama, Shankara, Ramanmaharishi, Ramakrishna.. et. al did not liberate all?

A:The atman common to all (the realized masters, the jeevas of jagat) is the one and only Brahman which is ever free (beyond bondage and liberation). It is the body mind complex of nama rupa which has veiled the true self (atman/brahman) and projected the I; as the bodymind complex, which is in bondage; due to ignorance or false notion of the real me, like a mirage.

The body mind complex of the realized masters realized the GYANA of I as the atman and not the body, not the mind. Thus those body minds realized the true nature of Jagat to be mithya like a mirage. Once the physics (gyan) of mirage is known, there is no reality in it.. only an illusion (maya); yet the mirage does not vanish.. it remains (like Jagat).

But it is to those, body minds not knowing physics (in avidya), when water is pursued after, in a mirage (Samsara).

There is thus no bondage or liberation in the substratum (atman/Brahman), it is only in the body mind complex.

The body mind complex of liberated masters realised and lived this Gyan and so those nama roopa were liberated.

We the nama roopas of Jagat do not realise and live as such; thus our body minds are in bondage of samsara (Maya). The atman in us was, is and will be ever free. So there is no bondage to it. Thus what is liberation to be achieved other than this Gyan and of course living it.

Hari ॐ.

19

THE NEAREST POINTER OF BRAHMAN

"Satyam gyanam anantam Brahman".. Taitr. up. This is probably the nearest description of the indescribable Brahman.

Brahman means Vast, not as an adjective to anything (vast ocean etc). It's just Vast.. anything.

Anantam is infinite. Infinite in space, time and object. Infinite in space means Omnipresence (it's everywhere).

Infinite in time means Eternal. It Was, is and will be. Without a beginning and end. Birthless Deathless.

Infinite in object means it is in everything. In any object one has an experience of existence, name and form (Sat/Nama/Roopa). The Sat/existence aspect is constant, while the Nama Roopa keeps changing. That which is constant unchanging is the only truth while those which are changing are relative/mithya, in Adwaita. Due to ignorance (Maya) the mind is focussed on the interesting and changing nama roopa and thus the continuation of Jagatic experience of origin to cessation. Death To death... transmigratory mithya (illusion).

Gyanam is knowledge. It is associated with aspects of knower, knowing and the knowable. The knower and knowable is in form of nama roopa while the act of knowing is karma (kartabodha); all this is in duality. Only knowledge just it.. is consciousness only which illumines the triad of knower, knowing and knowable. It is beyond duality. Nondual.

Satyam (Sat) is existence. Existence can be intrinsic (its own nature) Or borrowed (extrinsic). All that one experiences has borrowed existence. Our body borrows existence from cells. The cells from molecules. Themolecules from atoms, the atoms from subatomic particles, which then borrows from quarks, and quarks from strings and waves. Thus biology borrowed existence from Chemistry, which from particle physics. Now economics states that all cannot be borrowers without a lender. The only lender which lends existence is Brahman in Adwaita. The only truth. The rest is relative reality which changes and is mithya (Maya). Thus Brahma sattwa Jagat mithya, Jeeva Bramhaivo naparah.

Since Brahman is consciousness only and also unknowable. When associated with ignorance (Maya), it maintains its intrinsic property of consciousness. But what is there to be conscious about? except itself, which is also unknowable? So it projects (by the projecting power of Maya) while veiling its true self, the mithya/mirage called Jagat which binds the body mind into the gunas to continue the endless transmigratory game of death to death. Knowledge of Brahman (Gyana yoga/Brahma gyana) alone removes this ignorance. And when the body mind lives in this reality of gyana; is what is probably the

answer to Who am I?

Aham Brahmasmi (inspiration); Sarva idam Brahman (expiration)

Hari ॐ.

20

CONTRADICTION OF KARMA & GYANA

Is there no karma for a Gyani?

How does the body mind of a gyani continue in prarabdha. The body mind has to respire, take food, move and also most of those body minds had the karma of preaching knowledge as guru to enlighten the ignorant body minds. So it seems that no karma for a Gyani is a misconception.

The karma of an ignorant body mind is bound by karma phala of body mind. There lies the problem from which originates doership. Doership leads to enjoyment and suffering Depending on karma for that particular body mind. If one body mind suffers gangrene of hand then one readily agrees for amputation to save oneself. The hand then ceases to be thought of, as a part of the body mind. When one has terminal cancer, then there is the feeling of loosing onself; as thebody mind is considered as the self.

The story of a Gyani. When Ramakrishna had throat cancer, he was in great pain and was unable to swallow food. His disciple asked "Swami why don't you ask mother Kali to let you off this suffering so that you can have food" Ramakrishna said "I did ask her and she replied that why is the Adwaitin worried about one mouth not being able to eat. You who are all, is eating through the innumerable other mouths. So There is no hunger for the real you.

The karma of a Gyani is very much there but there is no association with the karma phala pertaining to one or few bodyminds. It is probably associated to the cosmic whole (infinite). And what is infinite other than Brahman. Thus infinite divided by infinite remains infinite.

"Poornamidaha poornamidam poornat poornamudacchate....:

The karma of Gyani is by the Brahman, for the Brahman in Brahman sans the body mind and this is probably the misnomer karma, perceived by the ignorant bodyminds who witness a Gyani in so called Karma.

SriKrishna in BG: Be just my instrument and do" that what is ordained; without the ego of doership. The scalpel of a surgeon has no karma phala as it has no ego of doership, but the surgeon is affected by the outcome of operation as there is doership of body mind ego, if only this ego is erased; then it is the so called karma of a Gyani. That one perceives to be doing has already happened. Only the time frame is relative. Adwaita is probably time travel into future where one is a witness only of all karmas ofbodyminds..

The Karma of an ignorant is real; as (perceived) water; in mirage is real to an ignorant; which one body mind runs after.

The karma of a Gyani is like the water in mirage wich still appears but is known as mithya and one does not run after it.

Hari ॐ.

21

SAILING THE SEA OF GRIEF

How To overcome grief of loosing a loved one, in Adwaita.

There is extreme sorrow in loosing a loved one for any body mind. The pangs of sorrow remain so long as one is living, though Maya as time masks it (it is still present). The only way to get over this sorrow is to stop living; not by taking ones so called body mind life. But By enquiry and realization.

The greatest sorrow is present in the waking and also in dream state. Yet in deep sleep the sorrow completely vanishes. The waking state is synonymous to the body mind perception of me as I in gross state. Similarly in dream state the I is perceived as body mind in subtle state. While in deep sleep the I is perceived just as it is without body mind and senses... and there is no greif.

In waking state the ego wakes up as body mind and there is grief. In dreaming state the ego wakes up as the subtle body mind and there is grief. In deep sleep there is no body mind ego either in gross or subtle state and thus I AM ABOVE SORROW.

So the only way to get over such sorrow is to stop living as a body mind complex and start to live as actually what you are= The eternal, nondual ATMAN/BRAHMAN.

The Atman in Adwaita is the:

"Satyam jnanam anantam brahman"

It means Vast, Infinite in time- space- object, the only non dual existence and consciousness. This Is who I AM and ALL THAT THERE IS.

Thus since all is me and all is eternal. Who was it that died, who was it that perceived it and who was it that was born?... I am, I was and I will be. Only a part of me as a different nama roopa transmigrated in its body mind state but it' s existence and consciousness exists and is eternal. The death of body mind is there but there is no death to me, which is all (aham brahmasmi-sarvam idam brahman).

The birth/death; joy/sorrow and all the dualities were the projections of mirage (mithya) in the substratum(desert Brahman), by Maya; which though exists but is non existent toMe/I, which is not the body, mind or intellect but the screen(Brahman/atman) on which the movie named life is being projected and, I am all, the eternal witness(without joy or sorrow) as an Adwaitin.

Hari ॐ.

22

THE MIND. (AS PERCEIVED BY THIS MIND)

The mind is a conglomerate of thoughts; either in form of memories from past or apprehensions or desires in future.

Though the present is the only state of certainty, yet the mind hardly rests on the present and vacillates between past and future, which are its only activity so long as it is in ignorance/Maya. If Mind can be focussed just on the present by oblivating the past and future. This in a way, is killing the activities of mind. The benefits out of such a state are many. By obviating the past, memoirs of joy and sorrow; vanishes the vicissitudes of mind resulting in sthitaprajna. By negating the future, desires; it's subsequent sakama karma vanishes. Meditation is a way of achieving such a state of present tense by abolishing the past and future vacillations of mind. To be just at Present Moment.

Amongst the waves of thoughts and doubts which makes the mind; there is always the background thought of "I Am"; without which there is no meaning or existence of any thought or anything at all.

So finding out who am I? Is the true essence of self realisation. This substratum is the infinite ocean of pure consciousness in which arises the waves of thoughts in form of mind; only to merge back into it (consciousness).

Is there a free will of mind? So long as there is Ego of body mind complex, there is duality. To overcome the Ego of body- mind/duality; one needs effort by the mind. This is the free will of mind which exists in the Ego and the Ego in it's turn is actually a mithya. So when ego is shed; there is no free will. All is just pure (conscious mindlessness): nonduality -ADWAITA.

Hari ॐ.

23

THE PERMANENT (SAT) & IMPERMANENT (ASAT)

The perspective of the JEEVA;

Though in life, there is death of a moment with birth of another moment at all times; yet there is a sense of continuity like that in a movie where the individual pictures are telescoped so rapidly, as to give a feeling of uniform continuity.

Looking back in life, every moment is death of the past and birth of a future moment as the present. There has been death of the infant and birth of the child, the death of the child and birth of the youth, death of youth and birth of adult, death of the adult and birth of the aged. Then there is death of the body and most mind of this body and a birth anew, after search of another womb depending on the residual seed of ignorance in form of sanchita karmas (punarapi jananam punarapi maranam, punarapi janani jathare sayanam). This is a state of continuous change. The photos in the album of a Jeeva as a child, youth, adult, aged; are absolutely different from one another in all gross aspects, yet one says that all

this as me, without the feeling of change. There is thus something which is permanent and without a change in every body mind which witnesses these changes without being affected by these changes. This is the Atman; so named in the shrutis.

BRAHMAN is "satyam gyanam anantam" eg. Existence, Consciousness, Bliss, Infinite.

The Scientific perspective:

From Birth To Death Is A Process Of Continuous Change.

Change is there in Space and Time. In general relativity there is no separate space and time, rather there is a space time continuum. The changes (birth-death) is there only in space time.

Any thing that changes; according to the laws of entropy and enthalpy; is bound to go from organized to disorganized.

In other words, from birth to death.

That Which is changeless thus has to be beyond space and time since everything in spacetime is changeable.

It is also known that the entirety beyond space and time is infinity. Thus Except infinity everything's changing (from birth to death).

Summary:

In me there is an unchanging element which witnesses over the changing gross & subtle elements of body mind. Since that unchanging is infinity; and in me there is something unchanging; thus it has to be INFINITY and nothing else.

Mathematically infinity can never be two as one will limit the other infinity and make it finite.

Since BRAHMAN is infinite as per shruti (Aitt. up.).

In me; the I (atman), the unchangeable is the infinite witness.

Since there cannot exist two infinities.

The I (atman) and Brahman are bound to be the same infinite.

Thus"aham brahmasmi"

Hari ॐ.

TatSat.

24

WHAT HAPPENS WITH ENLIGHTENMENT

There is no change in the physical world. It being so called mithya, does not vanish. The viewpoint of the one enlightened; only changes.

This changed viewpoint is probably Brahmadristi. Assuming from vedanta, this Brahmadristi is Atmagyan/Brahma gyan either as "neti-neti" (not this, not this); as in Brihadaranyaka, Chandyo. up or mandukya up.

Or as yati-yati(this also, this also); as in isha, katha, prasna up. Ultimately both achieves the same.

The neti neti path negates all as illusion, accepting only the unexplainable existence, consciousness, bliss (BRAHMAN) as the only truth and avyavarika reality; the rest being a vyavarik sat or mithya. To stay in such a state is like being in deep sleep while being in full consciousness along with destruction of the seed of ignorance, from which there is no coming back. Turiya. Such a living is possible only by a

body mind in vidwat sanyasa of complete relinquition.

Jivanmukti.

Living a life in samsara, such a state is difficult to achieve. The Tamasic and Rajasic elements of life (gluttony, violence, anger, material and physical desires) can be relinquished with effort. But how to overcome the Sattwic elements like compassion, benevolence, helpfulness? How can one negate these?The yati-yati (this also, this also) path is the answer to this dilema of a body mind in samsara.

The initial verses of Isha Up. states that; "all that there was, is or will be is clothed in isa/iswara/Brahman." So every thing and every body is Brahman in essence with appearance of, different nama roopa and every karma is for Brahman, by Brahman, in Brahman. The yati- yati Brahmadristi. There is no doership (thus no karma phala & hence no transmigration) in such a state, though work and life goes on till prarabdha. And then Videhamukti at prarabdhas end.

The perspective view point of life (mind) is only changed with gyan; while the body states remain the same, till it is shed.

For a female body mind, a certain male as lover, is an object of desire; a similar male body mind as son is an object of love and protection, another as a father is an object of respect and a different love, as a brother. A different love and devotion, as a male body of deity (iswara Krishna/Shiva), a different love with complete faith and surrender. The single element Love manifests as a spectrum of multiple feelings in the ocean of consciousness only by taking different nama roopa (Maya).

When this multiplicity of nama roopa is erased by the gyan of unity(all in me/Brahman and nothing else.. neti neti-OR- me/Brahman in all.. yati-yati); the conflicting waves of emotions vanish in the sea of sthitaprajna/consciousness.

Nothing more to be achieved as there is no more an achiever. The end of dualities. Ekam eva Adwaitam. Tat Sat.

Hari ॐ.

25

LIVING IN ADWAITA

Shankara:"brahma sattwa jagat mithya, jivo brahmaiva naparah"

Brahman is the only truth and the world is mithya (vyavarika) and you are Brahman.

"Aham brahmasmi" &"sarva idam Brahman".

You are Brahman and all that there was, is and will be is Brahman.

One who says that one knows it; or one who says that it(Brahman) does not exist... actually does not know it. While one who knows that it (Brahman) is, but does not know it; probably is in the path to be that, which is unknowable.

Swami Vivekananda:

one who has renounced the world to live in the cave has missed the way. One who plunges in the routine samsaric life has also missed the way.

So how to live the paradox of the truth called Adwaita?

A story from the himalayan masters:

A gold smith with a store of ornaments in his safe asked his daughter to bring some gold to work upon. The daughter came back to inform that there is no gold in the safe. The goldsmith asked her what was there in the safe. She replied there were necklace, tiara, bracelets, bangles etc. but no gold. He said daughter all this is gold in different name and form, any of these will do to work upon.

So if one throws away the world (ornaments) as in reclusive sanyasa and searches for the gold (Brahman), one does not find it.

Similarly if one takes them as bangles, rings etc. as the only truth(jagat nama roopa) and searches for gold(Brahman) else where; one has lost the way.

The only way out, is to look at every thing as it's essence of (existence-consciousness-bliss) and to renounce the nama-roopa (theMaya elements). This is true Sanyasa.

Living life in such a way considering everything as Brahman in essence. Then work is Brahman, forBrahman, by Brahman.

This can be done in bhakti as" you are my lord, i am your instrument and all results of work; good or bad is your blessings to me. Complete surrender.

This can be done as a gyani as, Brahman is the essence of me and all the work is the play of Brahman towards the realization of itself (Brahman). Finding who am I. Just like the waves, the sunami, the ripples and bubbles finds; what the ocean is.

Of the five elements of a being: existence, consciousness, bliss, nama & roopa. The first three are beginningless and endless, so called Brahman.

The later two are beginningless but with an end (Maya/Ignorance).

The ignorance elements are eliminated by the light knowledge as darkness vanishes witha bright light.

Since Maya functions only through its elements of ignorance as nama roopa, thus so long as there is the ego element of nama roopa in mind there is transmigration of body mind complex, from death to death. Once with knowledge when there is sanyasa of name and form (nama roops); Maya has no hold on the existence, consciousness and bliss(Brahman)... "ayam atman brahman."

Lead this body mind from the maya of jagat to the truth of Brahman.

Lead this body mind from ignorance to knowledge.

Transcend this body mind from the chains of death to death transmigration, unto immortality.

"Asato ma sad gamayah, tamaso ma jyotir gamaya. Mrityur ma amritam gamaya.

Om Shanti, Om Shanti, Shanti Om."

To achieve this state there is the need of rigorous practice of sama, dama, titiksha, uparati etc.

And in every action to discriminate and choose the good (eternal) over the preferable (transient). There lies the importance of saying No to desires= not for me.

To look upon every thing and every action and result as the self in essence. (don't look upon anything as other than God in essence.) Then when all is in me, what is there to desire (nishkama karma).. and when all is me -what is there to renounce?.. sthitaprajna.

And finally to wait for the grace of Brahman to reveal itself, that forgotten one what one is.

Hari ॐ.

26

TEACHINGS OF NATURE

The subtle teachers that guides the mind to the only truth is the real way to see. But ignorance veils the reality.

1. The male elephant is trapped by the lure of a female TOUCH.

2. The moth plunges to death in fire, on SIGHT.

3. The fish is lured to death on the hook by food and TASTE.

4. The bee is trapped in a closing flower at dusk, drawn to it by its SMELL.

5. The deer is trapped by drums and bells causing a SOUND.

The organs of sense and the senses (touch, taste, sight, smell, & hearing) are verily aits of alure, in to bondage. The five gates of bondage.

Human body mind is enslaved in all five sensory prisons.

Knowing this remain ever free. Let the senses be your slave by constant discrimination of neti neti or acceptance of the essence as yati yati; rather than the other way round.

The mind which on enquiry of these lf becomes nonexistent, is the master of all five enslaving senses. A nonexistent virtual master.

Thus self enquiry is the only weapon to kill the mind and thus the enslaving senses.

The death of the body is not the death of mind. The Causal vasanas transmigrates into another body.

The death of the mind; though the body may live on in prarabdha is Jivanmukti. Then when the body falls it is Vidheyamukti. No birth, no death.. that thou art.

Hari ॐ.

27

THE PLAY OF LIFE. (SAMSARA)

The Rule of the play: when "mine" becomes the "me".

The eternal non dual consciousness; that what is there as all, being projected by the ahamkara of mind (primordial ignorance) or the Pseudo I maker, unto the body mind; makes what is mine as me. The body mind which is not me but my possession; becomes me. Thus when the infinite is falsely limited by the body mind; the unfathomable real infinite is sensed as discrete finite duality/multiplicity. Then the infinite/eternal/immortal/unchanging or SAT becomes falsely: finite/temporal/mortal/changeable or ASAT.

From immortal existence, consciousness (Brahman); to the mortal birth to death experience of the illusory body mind in jiva jagat consciousness.

Adwaitic spiritual gyan is all directed to remove this primal ignorance of eternal existence-consciousness-bliss, being superimposed into a state of finite existence, body mind consciousness and duality of transient joy and sorrow. I can observe and experience the changes and impermanence of both the body and the mind. That what is observable and changing and impermanent is an object (body- mind); while that what is giving the first person experience is the Seer or Observer (Atman/Brahman).

"Tat Twam Asi."

"Ayam Atman Brahman".

The illumined knows oneself to be the swayam prakasha Atman and views the seen world as the play of Maya or Consciousness in adhyasa (superimposition).

The jeevas take this play seriously by considering the mine (body mind) as me. Thus suffering with the mind and dying with the body.

For the seekers it is a practice to see the happenings of the world including the happenings of one's body mind as a play or leela. Striving to live as a Sakshi/witness consciousness. Till the practice becomes a living reality. Even before complete realization, this practice gives a blurred sense of something timeless and limitless about our being; and that too is a joy unparalled.

UntilGrace..

When the "mine" is renounced and only"I" remains.

Regaining the Self, that what was lost in illusion, but that I, always was and is.

Hari ॐ.

28

LEARNINGS FROM THE; STATES OF BEING

Life is an oscillation between waking, dreaming &deep sleep states. These three states convey the depths of Vedanta Like a guru. One Has Only to enquire.

The waking, dream and deep sleep states are constantly changing. To observe a change there has to be an observer which is unchanging or relatively unchanging. Since that what is unchanging is eternal. This is an enquiry of what is eternal.

The waking state seems different from dream and deep sleep because of the concept of continuity. The continuity is temporal (in time) and is expressed as physical (body)& mental(mind) elements. So when waking is regained from sleep it falls back into the physical and mental elements which has changed very little in that time, and is perceived as continuity. This continuity will vanish in case of time travel or in the RipVanWinkle sleep. This wakeful world vanishes completely in dreams and in deep sleep, thus it is not permanent. It is a world of external mental projection as viewed by the brain and mind with which one experiences birth- death, elation- sorrow and all the dualities in both body and mind. This waking world is also relative. The world as seen by other animals is not what we see or hear or smell or taste or feel. Thus what I experience is doubtable. But the I that experience it is undoubtable.

The dream is a world in ones mind. The body plays no part in it. All the objects in dream are real so long as the dream lasts. There are experiences of elation, pain, sorrow in dreams. This state is also not permanent as it dissolves in deep sleep or into waking state. The dreams are realised to be false on waking, but the I that dreamt can not be doubted. Since dream is only metal with no physical element. There is no falling back into physical continuity on the end of a dream.

In deep sleep there is no perception of the body and mind (Ego) but on waking one says "I slept like a log, I did not experience any pain, pleasure, elation or sorrow. But the I the experiencer of this nothingness remained. This I experiencer remained only with a veil of ignorance of the real I. There was no mental projection of objects (ekatvam.). Since there is no mental or physical element in deep sleep there is no remembrance or physical continuity after it passes off. But since there is a veil of ignorance of the real I. One wakes up into the projected I as body mind complex of this world. Thus deep sleep is not no experience, but experience of partial veiling and complete absence of projection. We experience ignorance (Maya= veiling & absence of projection).

In waking and dream the mind in Maya is with complete veiling of the atman/I and complete projectionas the world of waker or dreamer.

There is no cognition without consciousness but consciousness exists even without cognition (as seen in deep sleep).

Deep sleep is thus nearer to removal of the veil and projector of Ignorance (Maya).

But practically the waking state is important as the mind has free will, absent in dream or deep sleep state. With free will the mind only is the only weapon to eliminate its own veiling and projecting power without which there will be no spiritual progress. Thus one becomes Manonasa by stilling the mind completely (a door to realization: YogaVasistha).

Thus the desirable is to use the free will of mind by preparing it with sravana, manana and niddhidhyasana; to enter into a deep sleep state in complete wakefulness. Since the ego (body-mind) does not exist; there is no elation, no sorrow, no birth, no death.

And also since there is no veiling, there is no falling back into the dreams of waking or sleeping world. One is just the witness consciousness, un attached;

viewing the goings on in the movie called life, immersed in the joy of self (knowing who am I).

The sakshi (witness) consciousness is also an act of mentation & is only a means to grasp the pure consciousness. Then when "tat twam asi" is understood as "aham brahmasmi", then the unexplainable state beyond words and thoughts beckon.

The only waveless ocean of consciousness- existence- bliss, alone. Neither I nor You, No God-no jeeva, no death- no birth, no bondage- no liberation. One has tranced the three gunas of duality.

Hari ॐ.

29

THE TAT & TWAM RELIGIONS

Religions are basically of Tat (That) & Twam (Self) types; in its method of explaining, the essence of the supreme divine.

The Tat(That) philosophy explains the supreme as the God in heaven, something separate from you (duality); who is to be worshiped (as deeds), loved (as emotion), feared (for adharma) & as an expected provider demanded from(for dharma). There remains the mind elements in form of desire, joy, fear & love for a name or form or both. Where ever there is mind there remains a modulator for it. In such a scenario of duality where one considers oneself as finite, there is ignorance and fear leading to submission. This is used by the dealers of religion in various faiths to keep the jeevas in bondage of religion and its subsequent biased views and fanaticism. I am Hindu, I am Christian, I am Muslim, Jew, Buddhist and so on. But the common factor in all this dualistic statements "I AM this, that and so on" is I AM."

But this is not explored into. This- Tat philosophy however has a greater control on the ignorant minds (which are many). The EGO sense is promoted in form of "my religion is superior" & this leads to conflicts in Tamas and Rajas. Moreover the Tat philosophy is something of postmortem type, you will see God after death in heaven, not now.

The TWAM philosophy explains the supreme as the self, not something different from your own essentiality. The most beloved of every being is the self, the most unfeared is the self, the most unknown yet the constant presence is the self. The Twam philosophy is only the exploration into the inner essence of every being" Who amI?". This gives a complete independence to mind resulting in freedom from religious and franatical bondage. Is not freedom (liberation) the desire of all? This is Vedanta;

The magna carta of liberation of all beings.

THE SCIENTIFIC mind: is a quest for exploration. The exploration in the outer world is the physical sciences. The exploration into the inner world is sprituality. Man's basic nature is the search for unity. To beunited as a family, society, nation, world & so, on. Even in physical science there is the exploration into the theory of everything (StevenHawkins); which will explain relativity, quantum, newtonian, gravity, all in one. Thus, the basic ques of science is very Upanishadic. Kena up.-" Knowing which one knows all that there is to know". The ancient Rishis of Vedanta had sought and found the answers that (TAT), eternal existence/& consciousness/& bliss as ones basic nature (TWAM); and knowing it, all is known. There remains no duality, no separation, no conflict, no fear. The World is the heaven that one seeks; The supreme is the essence of, all that one senses & also one's self. There is the peace and bliss of oneness, of deep sleep in wakeful activities. Heaven and the Supreme is achievable right here & right now. Not post mortem.

Vedanta is the religion of science and future minds. It withstands the debate of science and explains much more than science. But is this also not a thought in duality? Vedanta as a superior philosophyor religion. No.

Vedanta is bold enough to state that all is mithya, even the Vedas & Yagnas. OnlyYou - The SELF, are the truth and you are all. TAT TWAM ASI & SARVA IDAM BRAHMAN.

All these teachings are a deliberate superimposition of a lesser untruth, on the Truth of the unknown Self (adhyaropa), till the wrong knowing are shed. Then the teachings are also discarded (apavada).

Then one realises AHAM BRAHMASMI.

Hari ॐ.

30

NIRVAN SHATAKAM [VIEWED DIFFERENTLY]

I am the mind, I am the intellect and the Ego. I am also the faculty of recollection. All, as its essence.

I am the substratum of senses (hearing, sight, taste, smell and touch). I Am The five elements of space, air, fire, water, and earth.

I am the eternal consciousness and bliss. I am the five vital airs in form of Pranas.

I am the gross bodies, as the seven fold materials that make it. I am the five sheaths that makes this existence.

I am the substratum of the karmendriyas in form of speech, hands, legs, genitals and organs of excretion.

I am the consciuosness bliss, in which all is. I am the gross in wapking,

I am the subtle in dreaming. I am the causal in deep sleep.

I am also the substratum of the waking, dreaming, deep sleep and beyond. I am the imagination that plays in itself.

I am the mind with its hatred and love, greed and detachment, pride and humility, knowledge and ignorance, dharma and adharma. Yet I have the free Will to choose and play with the dualities or to be the witness of it all.

I am the substratum consciousness of this body mind appearing in me.

The good and bad karmas, the pilgrimage, the sadhanas, the Vedas and, chantings all arise transiently in me, only to merge back into me.

I am the food, I am the eater and also the act of eating as body (gross) and the subtle (mind). Iam the doer of gross as Viswa and Virat.

I am the doer of the subtle as Taijasa and Hiranyagarbha. I am the enjoyer of Pragyana and Iswara.

I am also the unaffected essence of gross, subtle, causal and that beyond these.

I am the death and the birth, as a body and mind. I am also the immortal existence, consciousness beyond the body and mind.

I am the father and the mother, I am the guru and the disciple. I am the friend and the foe. I am the known and unknown universe.

I am all this in my Maya.

I am the only I, without my Maya (body-mind).

I am the changing and changeless, with and without form. I am the one, two and.. infinite. The only I.

I appear to be limited in gross, subtle and causal appearance. I am also the limitless essence of all.

All is in me, and I am in all.

Sarveyidam Brahman.

Shivo hum Shivo hum.

Hari ॐ.

31

THE INFINITE BLISS

Infinite bliss is the experience of absolute freedom. When one thinks of absolute freedom as a thought of mind; it usually encompasses freedom of the sense organs & the organs of action. A little more thought into this; one realises their changing & finite nature. A finite & changing object is never absolute. The only absolute is infinite (that beyond time, space & causation). This infinite is eternal (beyond time); omnipresent (beyond space);& omnipotent (beyond causation). Infinite is always one (ekam eva adwaitham) as a second, will limit the other & thus make it finite.

It is non dual. Infinite Is The Only Absolute.

To comprehend infinite by finite means (the senses) is mathematically impossible & it gives rise to error. The error called ignorance Of Absolute consciousness.

Since absolute is Infinite. So absolute freedom is in finite freedom. As infinite cannot be comprehended by finite senses &mind it gives rise to an error called Maya or ignorance. Thus infinite can not be known. The one which can never be known is never an object & is the only subject. The only knower. Knowing the knower as self in one & all, makes one know that; by knowing which all is known. One becomes the knower.

Though it is impossible to comprehend or describe the infinite; it is possible to be the infinite, by that all encompassing knowledge. This is freedom from the error of comprehension called jagat/Maya. This is infinite freedom or absolute freedom; the realization "brahma sattwa jagat mithya" &" sarvey idam brahman."

Hari ॐ.

32

WHY WAS THE UNIVERSE CREATED & BY WHOM?

Initially it was only the pure consciousness & nothing else. It is the only knower. The knower has an intrinsic property to know. Since there was nothing else, except itself; there was nothing to know but itself. The game of knowing WHAT AM I?; started with a big bang of projections in itself (the pure consciousness).

The five elements are there; as objects of cognition. They are a projection of the pure consciousness existence only. The pure consciousness is that without object. So there is no experience. The five elements are the precursors to five senses. It is through senses only that the mind experiences. What is the universe, to a person born with neuronal impairment of sight, hearing, taste, smell & touch? The universe does not exist to such a person but the feeling of I am is there.

The experience of Jagat is not bad for all. Most body minds enjoy it in the different gunas, though with with occasional sorrow. Most body mind desires to come back again in this movie as an actor to play their role again to fulfill unfulfilled desires. Till the time one bodymind desires to quit playing. Even this game of how to quit; is enjoyment, otherwise there will be no adwaitins. So the search for enjoyment to some is end game while to the rest it is the game itself.

A lump of clay serves no purpose like Brahman which is avyavarika (useless). To serve a purpose it needs a formt hus this projection is for the experience of finding : what am I?

If one throws away all the pots, vases & utensils and searches for clay thinking them to be an illusion. Clay will never be found. The clay/Brahman is in all this we call jagat and jeeva. In the quest in Adwaita, the vision only changes like X ray vision to penetrate beyond the nama roopa & remain stabilized in the existence consciousness which is same in all. This is sthitaprajna.

There never was a creation. Only projection in pure consciousness.

The eternal consciousness is infinite. When infinite is explained by finite means there is a mathematical error. So when finite minds and senses tries to find the infinite; there is an error which our rishis called Maya.

A movie has a story only when light falls in patterns of nama roopa. A haphazard interplay of lights wil lnever give a story to experience. Thus it is Brahman appearing to experience itself as a movie. A movie appears real but is only an illusory projection.

With adwaita the universe does not vanish. But the limited viewpoint of limited body mind, changes to the infinite perception of the infinite... very similar to the probable theory of everything. Knowing that; by which all is known.

Hari ॐ.

33

ADWAITA IS ESCAPISM

Doubt arises in mind when people say that practicing Adwaita is escapism. There need not be any doubt about it. Because it really is.

A glass is half empty or half full. Both are true. Only. the viewpoint is different.

For a jeeva in samsara; there are the parents, wife, children, friends, enemies, society, nation, world & one's own body & mind. Towards these there are desires to be fulfilled; for which one has work (karma- good & bad). Each karma has its karma phala which one has to endure in this or other lives by transmigration. Thus goes on the play of life cycle through eons. The samsaric jeeva is in ignorance. The ignorance which veils the basic query of WHO AM I?; with a subsequent projection of I as the body & mind. This creates a separate limited individuality of body mind which is distinct & separate from others. Then there arises subject object relationship. This relationship is the seed of emotions (love/hate; desire/rejection;) The world of duality and multiplicity. Emotions give birth to thoughts & a conglomerate of thoughts is the so called mind. The mind becomes the ruler of the body with differentiation of swagata, swajati & vijati veda. In such a state there is attachment (sangatwa); a perception of truth in the mento- physical world (projected sattwa) & the samsara continues in its quest of impermanence. When such a body mind comes across an advaitin who is non attached (asangatwa); lives but knows this to be an illusion (mithyatva) & does not perceive duality (ekatva); it thinks it as escapism from samsaric duties. A glass half empty.

To a seeker or knower of self. There is only self & nothing else. There is only the subject & no object. Who is the teacher? Who is taught? Who is father & who is mother? Who is a beloved & who loves? Who is an enemy & who hates?What is work & for whom it is done?Who is in bondage & who is liberated? What are the Vedas & who does it preach?The answer to all this who; is the bodymind; which is impermanent. The only permanence is the absolute consciousness (the nondual subject without object/chit); which always exists (eternal sat). Finding this eternity; that all is self; there is no fear, no hate, no love, no death, no joy, no sorrow. Transcendence of duality. An escape from a finite being into all prevailing infinity. An escape to the realms of immortality from the mortal body mind, me. The greatest escapism. A glass half full for the seeker, till it overflows limitlessly fora jivanmukta.

TatSat..

Hari ॐ.

34

DREAM IS UNREAL
HOW CAN WAKING BE UNREAL LIKE A DREAM?

The world of dreams does not come back when one wakes up, but the world of waking comes back when one wakes up from sleep.

Dream state is real so long it lasts. It appears false only when analysed from waking viewpoint.

No state is continuous as they are interspaced by the other.

Waking state is not continuous as it is interspaced by dream & deep sleep for the subject. Waking state appears real because of the appearance of continuity in the objects which seems to remain as it is when one regains a waking state from a sleep. This continuity is however relative and not absolute as it happens in time space. Timespace is not separate but a continum. The continuity of objective world after dream appears samec because of relative small time frame. There is entropy & enthalpy going on continnually. Take the example of RipVanWinkle sleep or time travel or an amnesic state of waking for few years. Then the objective world will have changed so much when the waking state is regained and will appear not as continuous.

The dream world appears unreal from the waking perspective not while in dream.

Similarly the waking world appears unreal from Turyia perspective and not whileawake. This is a waking bias. The objects of dream does not come back when one is awake. The objects of waking world does not come back to one who wakes up to realization (Turyia); all becomes the eternal I from the noumenal you and that.

Very Similar.

This is true, or that is true?

Janaka; neither this (waking), is true nor that (dream) is true. OnlyYou that remained continuous in all the three state as consciousness is true.

Tat Twam Asi Shwetketu.

Hari ॐ.

35

LIVING NONDUALITY

FEEL only Tat (that divine) in everything.

SEE only Tat in everything.

SMELL only Tat in every thing.

HEAR only Tat in everything.

TASTE only Tat in everything.

THINK only Tat in everything.

As an adhyaropa of, divine on the worldly.

This releases one from the bondage of the worldly tamas & rajas;

into the divine bondage of sattwa.

Finally to be initiated into the apavada truth, that; all senses & thoughts are observed, hence not the Self/Atman.

The Self being the pure subjective consciousness.

Which is the eye of eye; ear of ear; mind of mind ….

The indescribable & intuitive nature of being -The Self of one & all.

"Tat Twam Asi";

becomes a living reality right hear & now.

Hari Om.

(is this jivanmukti/manonasha?)

LIVING IN ADWAITA

Shankara:"brahma sattwi jagat mithya, jivo brahmaivo naparah"

Brahman is the only truth and the world is mithya/vyavarika sattwa and you are Brahman.

"Aham brahmasmi" & "sarva idam brahman"

You are Brahman and all that there was, is and will be is Brahman.

One who says that one knows it or one who says that it (Brahman) does not exist... actually does not know it. While one who knows that it (Brahman) is, but does not know it; probably is in the path to be that which is unknowable.

Vivekananda:one who has renounced the world to live in the cave has missed the way. One who plunges in the routine samsaric life has also missed the way.

So how to live the paradox of the truth called Adwaita?

A story from the himalayan masters:

A gold smith with a store of ornaments in his safe asked his daughter to bring some gold to work upon. The daughter came back to inform that there is no gold in the safe. The goldsmith asked her what was there in the safe. She replied there were necklace, tiara, bracelets, bangles etc. but no gold. He said daughter all this is gold in different name and form, any of these will do to work upon.

So if one throws away the world (ornaments) as in reclusive sanyasa and searches for the gold (Brahman), one does not find it. Similarly if one takes them as bangles, rings etc. as the only truth (jagat nama roopa) and searches for gold (Brahmana) else where; one has lost the way.

The only way out is to look at everything as its essence (existence-consciousness- bliss) and to renounce the nama-roopa(the Maya elements). This is true Sanyasa.

Living life in such a way considering everything as Brahman. Then work is Brahman for Brahman by Brahman.

This can be done in bhakti as" you are my lord, i am your instrument and all results of work good or bad is your blessings to me. Complete surrender.

This can be done as a gyani as, Brahman is the essence of me and all the work is the play of Brahman towards the realisation of itself(Brahman). Finding who am I. Just like the waves, the sunami, the ripples and bubbles finds what the ocean is.

Of the five elements of a being: existence, consciousness, bliss, nama& roopa. The first three are beginningless and endless, so called Brahman.

The later two are beginningless but with an end(Maya/Ignorance).

The ignorance elements are eliminated by the light of knowledge as darkness vanishes with a bright light.

Since Maya functions only through its elements of ignorance as nama roopa, thus so long as there is the element of nama roopa in mind there is transmigration of the body mind complex from death to death. Once with knowledge when there is sanyasa of name and form(nama roops); Maya has no hold on the existence, consciousness and bliss(Brahman)... ayam ataman brahman.

Lead this body mind from the maya of jagat to the truth of Brahman.

Lead this body mind from ignorance to knowledge.

Transcend this body mind from the chains of death to death unto immortality.

Asato ma sat gamayah, tamaso ma jyotir gamaya. Mrityur ma amritam gamaya. Om shanti shanti Om.

To achieve this state there is the need of rigorous practice of sama, dama, titiksha, uparati etc.

And in every action to discriminate and choose the good (eternal) over the preferable(transient). There lies the importance of saying No to desires, not for me.

To look upon every thing and every action and result as the self(dont look upon anything as other than God) then when all is me what is there to desire(niskama karma).. and when all is me what is there to renounce?.. sthitapragya.

And finally to wait for the grace of Brahman to reveal itself, that forgotten one what one is.

HariOm.

36

ROPE SNAKE STORY

Three persons saw a shining elongated object lying on the path while walking in dusk(dimlight). The object was a shiny rope.

One said it is a silver chain; he wanted to get it.

The second person said it to be a snake and jumped back in fear.

The third person with a torch explored & found it to be a shiny rope and was thus neither desirous or fearful of it.

This is one of the greatest story of experience in Vedanta. This Story Is a Guru in itself.

1. There is always a causality for any effect. There will never be experience of illusion of desire (chain); fear (snake) or truth (rope), without the existing substratum (rope). Is there a substratum for all that there is?

2. To the rope (truth), there never was the snake or the chain. The substratum may appear as the transactional or illusory adhyasa but to it the illusion is never there.

3. To see the snake, chain or rope. There has to be an impression of such objects in the mind. There can never be an experience of what the mind does not know. Mind is the creator of illusion (rope& snake); it is also the revellor of truth (rope). If the mind rules on the jeeva there is illusion. When The jeeva rules on mind by intellect the illusions start to clear.

4. There has to be something in common between the truth (rope) & the illusion (snake or chain). The rope cannot be mistaken as

an elephant. Here the slender undulating existence is the common factor. Similarly there has to be something common between the eternal truth (Brahman) and the observed truth (jagat). The swaroopa of everything is the common essence.

5. There is the illusion of snake, chain or rope in partial light; never in complete darkness or bright light. Similarly there is no illusion in a gyani or in one with no gyan. Illusion is there only in avidya where there is partial gyan; the gyan of the" I exist" is there but what am I, is not.

6. With enquiry into "what is it" The snake (fear) & chain (desire) vanishes and the reality of rope (existence) remains. With Vedantic enquiry the desire & joy of birth and also the fear of death vanishes as adhyasa (superimposition) on the eternal existence consciousness.

7. The superimposition of rope and snake appears only in waking (bodymind) & dreaming (mind) states. There is no adhyasa in deep sleep when there is no body or mind; but I am.

Desire & fear is only in the body & mind (which; one is not).

1. The mind as knower knows by the act of knowing the rope as snake, chain or rope. But to the consciousness which is knowledge itself there never is any illusion.

2. The illusion and truth both occurs only in consciousness(subject). Illusion is only in object (matter & mind). Thus there is no hard problem of consciousness. Consciousness is fundamental (eternal). It is only the hard problem of matter. The more one delves into matter, from the gross to atomic to subatomic & quarks & strings & waves; matter is found to vanish into duality and then into uncertainty. The hard problem of matter (jagat mithya/vyavarika or prativasika). What appears is not what it is.

3. What is; Is- but is not as it appears.

    Brahman is of the nature (essence) of jagat & jeeva. Jagat & jeeva are not of the nature of Brahman.

4. In a blinding light there is no rope, snake or chain. There is only light. Probably this is like Brahmagyan where there is only the light or self... no snake(fear); no chain (desire) & no rope (duality).......

Hari ॐ.

37

VEDANTA AT THE GOLD SHOP

The Gold is the basis (substratum); from which was made the Ring & later melt to create an Ear- ring. The Ring & Earrings are the, name & forms of Gold.

The Gold is the same substratum & of same value to a goldsmith (seer of substratum/advaitin), in all the ornaments of name & forms. It is not another - thus nondual.

The different ornaments, hold different values to the wearing enjoyer (samsari), and has likes & dislikes depending on the desire, needs & mindset. The dualities of emotions that come with a view of duality (the view as ornaments).

The golden Laxmi has special value & reverence to the owner (the seer of name & forms), far more than the golden Owl (Laxmi's vahana). However to the goldsmith (seer of substratum = advaitin), the Laxmi & Owl has same value.

The different ornaments (name & forms), came into being (creation), due to desire. The existence of substratum (gold), preceded the desires (creation). Before creation; Substratum alone was.

The goldsmith (Guru) asked the apprentice (seeker), to bring some Gold from the vault. The apprentice saw the vault contents & came back empty handed (unrealized) & said there were bangles, rings, Earrings, necklace etc.; but no Gold. The Guru goldsmith, said that all those are Gold only in reality. The name & forms are just appearances only for transactions. That declaration of the Guru to the seeker, opened the vedantic vision of Gold (the vision beyond nama roopa), for the seeker.

So if one throws away all the names & forms of jagat (ornaments) & then searches for the substratum (Gold), in ignorant sanyasa. The essence (Gold/ Brahman); is unknown.

As also, for the revellor who is engrossed in the enjoyership (Samsaric jeeva) of ornaments (name & forms), in ignorance of the substratum (Gold/ Brahman). The essence is unknown. Ignorance is the nemesis, of both the samsari & sanyasi in the search of the essence (Brahman) & not the state of varnashrama.

The Golden crown was melt & made into some ring, some bangles, a necklace & anklet. The same substratum of Gold is the beholder of different name & forms. The same Atman/Brahman pervades all the creation. The one in all.

Space/Time/Causality in Gold shop.

Time=

The ring (name & form) did not exist prior to gold & also did not exist at the end, so also might be with ear ring. Whereas Gold (substratum) was there at beginning - middle & at end. That which is not present in the beginning & at the end; does not really exist in the middle. The name & forms have no real existence. Only the substratum is real. Brahma sattwa, jagat mithya.

SPACE=

Is the ornament (jeeva/jagat), in Gold or outside Gold (Brahman/ Substratum)?

It is neither inside or outside, it is Gold (Brahman). Jeevo brahmaiva naparah.

Gold (Tat) are you (asi),

O ! ornament (Twam).

Tat Twam Asi.

Hari ॐ.

38

THE MISSING TENTH PERSON

Ten persons cross a river on a boat, then decide on a head count to find if any one is missing. The counter counts all others as 9, except his own self and starts to grieve about one person being missing, presumed drowned.

The story of missing tenth man, it is an act of ignorance, resulting in non cognition of self and mis apprehension of absence of the tenth man, resulting in sorrow.

In a group of ten persons, any one person will see only nine faces, except, ones own self. The seer is unseen.

The experience of other nine persons by senses of the tenth, is pratyaksha pramana.

When someone knowledgable other than the ignorant ten persons, comes to count and explains to the greving person, that he himself is the tenth person and no one is missing. This is paroksha gyan from the eleventh person/guru, to the greving tenth person/disciple, which indicates the self which is nearest, yet farthest due to ignorance. That thou art the tenth.

The instant realisation by negating ignorance, that "aham dasam asmi", is neither Pratyaksha or paroksha. It is aparoksha

jnana.

Self existence needs no pratyaksha or paroksha evidence. It is aparoksha-spontaneously ingrained. One considers oneself Mr/Ms. soanso, spontaneously out of aparokshaamubhuti of ignorance of body mind. When after sravana (from guru/shruti) the abhavana of ones divinity is known, manana (of satsang/contemplation), removes the asambhavana of ones being divine.

Then nididhyasana (constant contemplation) on that, removes viparita bhavana(contrary doubts). Then there is mithyatva of finiteness of, I am so and so and realisation of infinitude of Aham brahmasmi, the aparoksha anubhuti of gyan (self realisation).

Hari ॐ.

39

CLAY (SUBSTRATUM) & POT (CREATION) : (VEDANTIC VIEW)

1. The pot is not different from clay, as it is non existent without it.

2. The pot is not identical to clay, as there is no forms of pot, in the formless clay.

3. The pot forms as the result of an invisible force (of potter), acting on the clay.

4. The pot origins in clay, sustains in clay & is destroyed into clay.

5. The potness is an added name, form & transaction in clay due to an external force.

6. Of the cause clay, force & product pot. The force & product (pot), exists at a time. The cause (clay) remains throughout, even after destruction of effect.

7. Substantiality of panchabhuta is only in clay. The pot is noumenal only.

8. The force of creation is not visible before operation, later manifests as the product of pot.

9. Before creation of pot, the capability of giving rise to pot was inherent in the clay.

10. The force of creation is different from the cause (clay) & effect (pot).

11. Knowledge of clay does not destroy the pot in transactional usage. But it destroys the ignorance of the idea of pot as an independent reality, into an idea of borrowed reality.

12. With knowledge of clay, the knowledge of substratum is established & potness as appearance only is accepted.

13. From pots, on destruction, clay is recoverable (also gold from ornaments); instances of vivarta.

14. By knowing substratum clay, all pots in its essence is known. Knowing that, by knowing which, all is known.

15. Throwing away all pots & searching for clay is possible but difficult. Clay is easy to search in pots with discriminative viewpoint.

16. The clay of creation (substratum); is one Brahman. The creation are pots of infinite names, forms & transactions. The force of creation is Maya. The potter iscIswara (saguna Brahman).

17. From the formless cause (Brahman); appears formed effects with space time qualities, which was not present before creation, nor after destruction. That which has no existence in the beginning (creation) & nor in the end (pralay), has no real existence even in the present. All the name & forms.

18. Negation of all name & forms results in nothingness OBJECTIVELY. Yet the indescribable subject remains & "Tat Twam Asi."

Hari ॐ.

40

CONTRADICTION & THE LANGUAGE OF PARADOX

"ISAVASYA IDAMSARVAM"

&

"BRAHMA SWATHI JAGAT MITHYA"

How can these two dictums be confirmative. It appears opposing while declaring jagat mithya.

Anything that has avidya as its causality is bound to disappear with vidya. The jagat does not vanish with gyan. So how is jagat, a mithya?

The basis/essence of all there is; is Brahman. So the jagat whose essence is Brahman; is always there; either in potential form before creation or the kinetic form after creation. The creation is probably there to expend & experience the doership & enjoyership/sufferinga; of the jeevas in karma. The universe does not vanish with vidya. Thus the adhar of the universe is not avidya. The universe remains because it is the swaroopa of Brahman (by Maya); which is its adhar.

ISAVASYAM IDAM SARVAM.

Brahmavidya neither creates nor destroys. Everything & everyone, every where & at all times is only Brahman in essence. This is vidya.

The viewing of this uniform oneness as asmat usmat(duality); is trying to divide infinity into finiteness. This is an error as it remains infinite (undivisible); both mathematically & by shruti" poornamidaha poornamidam".

This is avidya; the perception of Brahman as unBrahman. Since avidya is of the jeeva & Maya is of Iswara.

The Maya of Iswara creates the universe. The Maya is eternal. The jagat it's swaroopa is also eternal ever.

The avidya of jeeva veils the uniformity of infinite Brahman in the jagat and projects finite name, forms & vyavara. This avidya is the mithya jagat; as its aadhar is avidya. With vidya this mithya vanishes. The pratyahara of asmat usmat duality & the beginning of ekam eva adwitiam Brahman. The jagat remains as it is; only perception changes in the gyani. Who becomes one with it till prarabdha is consumed. Videhyamukti.

Sri Bhagwan says in BG. With my maya I take human forms but I am all that there is, was or will be. Only the jeevas see me as human, due to avidya & find me in doership & enjoyership. Brahma swatti, jagat swatti - not as the jagat as it appears; but only as the perception of Brahman as the essence of jagat.

Hari ॐ.

41

THE VESSEL OF ATMAGYAN

The nectar of Atmagyan is contained by a vessel:

1. Made of sadhana chatushtaya.

2. Cleansed of the dirt of parigraha; into nisparigrahah (free from sense of mine).

3. Polished by nissprhah (devoid of desires of external yusmad/objects.).

4. Upturned and not inverted vessel (receptive and seeking= mumukshutva).

5. Non Leaking, so as not to revert to the emptiness of jagat & illusion.

Hari ॐ.

42

WHAT IS MOKSHA?

B. G (ch. 2-27)

"jatasya hi dhruvo mrityu dhruvam janma mratyasyaca"

Certain is the death of that which is born; certain is the birth of that which dies.

If that be the case; then there is birth of every body mind that dies, an endless transmigration......

Then, what is moksha?

There might be two logical outcomes =

An embodied birth is the result of sanchita vasanas, gunas of life which manifests so long one is in the doership of body - mind. With atmagyan when there is realization of the self, as not the body- mind; then all the karmas & gunas are burnt in the fire of gyan. There is nothing for Maya to act upon; as there has to be a body- mind to be the transactional effector. There is no more embodied birth. The mokshya. The death of body mind of such a gyani is actually not death, since the gyani is the atman which has not died (immortal); thus there is no birth since there is no death.

If death of a body, entails birth of a body literally. Then after death of a realized person who has gone beyond the dualities of desires, gunas & vasanas. There may be embodied birth; but such embodied beings are bound to be free of dualities, desires & gunas from birth... realized at birth(Sankara, Ramana, Ramakrishna..); without whom there will be no guru to show the path to the hypnotized humanity.

There may be birth or no birth in mokshya, both true.

There is the state transcending duality; embodied or disembodied as Mokshya.

Hari ॐ.

43

EXPERIMENT WITH VEDIC MATHEMATICS

*AIM:The Quotient Of Happiness.

*PRINCIPLES:

1. Anything (other than infinity) divided by infinity is zero.

2. 2. Any thing other than zero divided by zero is infinity.

FORMULAE:

Index of happiness (I)= Desires fulfilled

(d)÷ Desires desired (D).

FIRST CASE SCENARIO:

The (D); desires desired by mind (denominator), is infinite.

The (d); desires fulfilled in a lifetime is countable -miniscule (numerator).. xyz.. The Index of happiness (I) is= xyz÷infinity= 0.

SECOND CASE SCENARIO:

The numerator (d), desires fulfilled may be as many xyz till date.

The denominator (D), desires desired becomes zero by self realisation. The index of happiness = xyz...÷ zero (0)= infinity.

RESULT:

A materialistic life in perusal of desires gives ZERO (0)/No happiness. A spiritual life of no desire gives infinite bliss.

(Bhagwat Gita ch 2- verse 70-71).

Hari ॐ.

44

THE BOUNDARY BETWEEN KARMA YOGA AND NAISKAMYA SIDDHI

IS THE STATE OF YOGARUDHAH

(B. Gita, ch6-4)

"when one is not attached to sense objects or to actions and has renounced thoughts". not before is, naishkarmya siddhi.

KARMA YOGA TO NAISKARMA SIDDHI

"Yada hi nendriyarthesu na karmasv anusajjate.

Sarvasankalpa sannyasi YOGARUDHAS tadocyate."…. B. Gita. ch 6-4.

[this explains the sequence of vyavaharika karma yoga, to the paramarthika naiskarmasiddhi.]

So long as one is a seeker, even with a trace of desire. May it be the desire of liberation of atmagyan. To such a seeker the path of self perfection (chitta suddhi), lies through the highway of selfless activity (having renounced the I Ness- doership & My ness- attachment to the outcome of action). With such continued practices along with Sadhana in gyan of prasthana traya & from a guru, there comes the stage as in the sloka-

When one is not attached to sense objects or to actions, having renounced all thoughts of Sankalpa, then one has attained to yoga- Yogarudhah.

Withdrawal from activity is then to be undertaken. The meditative niddhidhyasana of self alone, in state of Naiskarmasiddhi. The renunciation of action.

Renunciation of activity before Yogarudhah, is detrimental. So is continued disturbance of mind with activities, after having reached to yoga; when quiescence is the means to attain wings in the flight of meditation, in the advaitic realms of self.

Hari ॐ.

45

TRANSACTIONS IN THE TREE OF LIFE

THE SEED: Is The ignorance of self.

THE FERTILIZER: Are the gunas of vasanas or prakriti. THE SEEDLING: germinates as the jeeva.

THE ROOT establishes as the body mind ego.

THE TRUNK of intellect develops from the root, with its sense of enjoyership (bhokta) & desires.

The trunk branches into doership, as thoughts of mind.

The mind, buds as the sense organs with dualities of attachment & rejection.

The dualities of sense organs, nourished by the thoughts of mind; attaches & transacts with the world of objects, by transaction through works(karmas); by the leaves of karmendriyas. Karmas are enjoined with Karmaphala... thus goes on transmigration. The play of Maya.

The exit path from the game of transmigration can never be achieved by working on the effect, viz. absolving oneself from karma.

The shearing of leaves of karma, results in new growth of leaves with rains of mental desires.

Physical sanyas from of external karma is never the solution. The only way is to work on the cause, or the seed of ignorance.

When the seed is roasted in the fire of knowledge (atmagyan); there is nothing but the self/all becomes the self.

The ego transforms from the immanent to transcendent. The Gunas Become Ineffective, since they need need a body mind ego to function.

In a gunatita ego, there is no enjoyership of intellect as there is no desire, since all is the self. In absence of enjoyership of intellect, the mind becomes devoid of doership & thus equanimous in thought; inspite of the body being in various karmas.

The sthitaprajna of mind, controls the sense organs & prevents attachment and detachment from objects of jagat; though the senses are functioning normally.

The absence of attachment & detachment to sense objects by sense organs, results in true absence of karma to acquire, repel, modify or purify. the state of naiskarmasiddhi; with

the absence of karmaphala. Thus released from the Maya of transmigration.

"He whose intellect is unattached everywhere, who has subdued false self, from whom desire has fled; he through renunciation, attains the supreme state of naishkarmya siddhi."B. Gita. ch. 18. v-49.

Hari ॐ.

THE EVENT HORIZON OF SELF REALISATION INTO MOKSHYA=

The steps & path of self realization is actually steps of de realization of what one perceives one to be.

Starting as the body, prana, mind, intellect & then the causal sheath; a perpetual shravana, manana & nidhidhyasana; gradually releases the self from these superimpositions.

At the penultimate point of transcendence; as the self crosses over into the realm of self knowledge from self ignorance, no luggage of language, relation, possession, shruti, smriti, guru, gyan, karma, bhakti, body, mind, sense, intellect or causal bliss is allowed. Since the preceptor of all these are, in the form of mind, senses & intellect; which remains not.

Dissolved in non duality.

Is it the shunya? neti. Is it the purna? neti. Is it not? neti.

Is it? neti.

For a self realized there is no experience or realization of it. Only one is & can be it.

Hari ॐ.

47

MUNDAKA UP. & CREATION (2. 1. 3)

"etasmajjayateprano manah sarvendriyani ca,
khamvayurjyotirapah, prithivi, visvasyadharini."

Brahman is nirakara and nirguna, the only truth. When it is associated with theunmanifested Maya, it becomes the causal- nirakara, saguna Iswara, the creator with desire of creation in the cosmic. Like a desire to make a house, as in the individual.

Then there from nirakar; saguna Iswara, arise the subtle prana or the cosmic subtle body or Hiranyagarbha, the cosmic mind of thoughts which is saguna, subtle sakara in the cosmic plane. Like the mental planning and vision of the house as in an individual plane.

The subtle cosmic totality, creates the gross totality of the creation as the gross akara, saguna -Virat purusa. Just as the physical building of house, as in the individual plane.

The manifestation of the gross also is a gradual creation from

1.   the very subtle gross (space with sense of sound), then-
2.   the less subtle gross, or Air, with added sense of touch, then-
3.   the subtle gross as fire with added sense of sight, then-
4.   the gross, water with added sense of   taste, then-
5.   the most gross, Earth, with added sense of smell.

The panchikarana of the panchabhutas, creates the gross jagat. Thus all is verily created out of the one truth, Brahman.

Hari ॐ.

THE THREE STATES OF EXPERIENCE

THE WAKING STATE

1. Maya in veiling power, veils the satchitanand swaroopa of self.

2. Maya projects the self as principally the gross body, with functional substratum of subtle and causal body, to the gross body.

3. The projection of senses to external world objects results in desires and aversion with subsequent karma of doership.

4. The karmaphala results in joy or sorrow of bhokta bodha, through physical, sensory, mental or intellectual means. The papa and punya with strong prarabdha are the bhokta bodha of waking state.

5. Waking state is the only state with doership, thus the doership of karma of liberation from bondage, to one who feels bound is possible in this state only.

DREAM STATE

1. The veiling of Maya veils the waking state and its gross body and objects to which, identification is absent. It also veils the true self (Atman).

2. The mind projects by projecting power of maya, into a subtle world of body and objects, created by the mind of jeeva (sva mayaa).

3. There is no conscious control on the initiation or type of dream, hence no doership.

4.   There is pleasure and pain depending on nature of dream, hence enjoyership is present.

5.   The papa and punya which are not so strong prarabdhas are manifested as bhokta bodha of dream state.

6.   The dream manifests out of latent imprints of gross and mental experiences of present or earlier life times, there is no element of intellect in it, nor can there be a dream of anything never experienced before in any lives.

THE DEEP SLEEP

1.   It is the rejuvenating state of tired body, mind, intellect as the sleep without dreams.

2.   There is non identification of oneself with the gross and also subtle body and also the ignorance of sat chit anand self. Veiling of maya as complete darkness of ignorance.

3.   There is no projection of maya, either in gross or subtle form.

4.   Since there is no projection of world or object, there is temporarily no desire, thus no karma or doership.

5.   As doership is absent, there is no enjoyership.

6.   Though there is no doership or enjoyership, yet it is the exhaustion of sanchita punya as prarabdha.

7.   The self and the world all merges into the causal ignorance.

8.   There is temporary absence of joy and sorrow, only there remains a temporary state of bliss arising out of non apprehension

9.   of dualities of emotion due to temporary mind dissolution.

10. Arousal from this state is dependent on fructifying prarabdha of action in waking or dream state

Hari ॐ.

49

KAIVALYA UPANISHAD.(CH1. 5-6-7)

The Six Steps For Internal Preparation Of Meditation Are=

- Firm resolve to control senses, inspite of contrary stimulus being present. By ignoring the stimuli as its witness, without delving into its lure & analysis.

- The sanyas attitude during meditation, is a state of dissociating oneself from possessions, relations, bodily constructs, of nama roopa. In to a state of oneness, in and as all. The seeker of that.

- Invoking grace of guru and Iswara, is essential as it strengthens sraddha and adds on to ones cent percent effort, which is not enough to reach that, which is beyond efforts and karmas. Effort to control the mind is like a dam on the river of thoughts, which well up on one side, unless let loose in streams of grace, it is bound to shatter the dam of resolve.

- Inward directed mind, into self-contemplation on the swaroopa lakshana of Brahman as self, like"satyam gyanam anantam brahman"or"divyo hyamurthya purusha.."As envisioned after sravana manana. This is in the transcendent space of cave of intellect.

- Meditation on saguna iswara for those who are unable to grasp the ungraspable nirguna Brahman. Meditation on Siva Shakti as representation of potential- purusha and kinetic-prakriti. The highest of all lords with three eyes, two eyes for prem -nyaya (dvaita) and third eye of gyan (advaita). The ever tranquil mahadeva, who has kept the poison of vasanas eructed by the serpent of desire, in the process of churning the sea of mind through the mandar mountain of intellect, by the daivic an asuric pravittis. Into his throat, equidistantly away from mind and heart, which makes him ever peaceful, the ever witness, beyond all ignorance.

This elevates the mind in to later nirguna nirakar contemplation.

- Meditating on Atman-in the transcendent space of heart/intellect. As the unthinkable, unmanifest, of endless forms, ever auspicious, ever peaceful, the immortal beyond beginning- middle and end, the origin of the creator, the nondual, all pervading, existence-consciousness-bliss-infinite.

Just awe !!! beyond all thoughts, emotions and words.

That thou art.

Hari ॐ.

50

THE DESIRELESS, DESIRE

The mind is the womb, where the jagat implants the seeds of objects, relation, thoughts & emotions; given importance to. A positive importance is raga & anegative one is dwesha. Both are desires, to which the mind attaches. The sense organs are the gateways of entry to the mind, with vision, hearing, taste, smell & touch, in decreasing order of importance. The capability of voluntary control over these are in the same decreasing order. The desirelessness of advaita & desires of vyavarika are two different realms & thus not explainable by same logiq.

The desires of vyavarika are governed by laws of causality & karma, where the culmination of desire is either acquisition, modification, purification of destruction. These karmas are with a predominance of either of the three gunas(tamas, rajas or sattwa). Thus desires are also of tamasic(food/lust/lethargy); rajasic (power/fame/wealth etc) & sattwic (goodness/benevolence/charity/knowledge/love etc).

The outcome of all these desires are success, culminating in greed or failure, resulting in anger. These are also transient, to be replaced by new desires; because the objects of desire are themselves finite, which can never give infinite satisfaction. So long as one is contented with finite happiness, one is a samsari in fulfilling such worldly desire. In accordance to; first -dharma, then artha and lastly kama. As envisioned in the purva mimansa of vedas. Karma yoga is important in this stage, when one is asked to work as an oblation to God, without being attached to fruits of action. This is a mind purifier.

When the question of how to get infinite happiness comes to mind, then one becomes a seeker of Advaita. For such a mind is uttar mimansa of vedas or vedanta/Upanishads.

The functioning mind is incapable; without it being attached to a desire. Then the desire for finite is transformed into a desire of infinite.

What is that; by knowing or gaining which, all is known & achieved?

Desire arises on something not considered as the self, with a view to aquire. Rarely does an embodied ego, desire a hand or breath or mind so long one has it. This is because of the notion of body mind complex as the self.

Advaita vedanta turns around this belief of ignorance & states that you are the existence-consciousness- infinite (satyam jnanam anantam brahman) that Brahman is Atman & That thou art.

You are the self, which is the self in all (Isavasyam Idam Sarvam).

This is just a realization,"Wow!!! I am & was always that, only did not know".

One is instantly transformed from the untruth to truth, from ignorance to enlightenment, from the mortal jeeva to the immortal Atman/Brahman; when one abides in such an existence of infinite consciousness. "asatoma sadgamaya, tamasoma jyotirgamaya, mrityorma amritam gamaya." Thus with such knowledge of self; when all in essence is the self.

What remains to gain or. renounce (desire)?

Is the supreme state of nondual infiniteness. Desire of infinity, merges in the desireless state of infinite self, right here & now.

Hari ॐ.

51

PRACTICAL VEDANTA

1. Do all samsaric works following; first Dharma, then artha and lastly kama.

2. All samsaric work as oblation to Iswara or Brahman. Accepting all outcomes as Iswaras prasadam.

3. To have undoubtable faith in shruti & smriti;

   after hearing & reading(sravana);

   clearing all doubts by guru/satsang/discussion (manana);

   then finally establishing oneself in such truth, so as to live that truth (nididhyasana/meditation).

4. To analyze & discriminate in every object & being; as to what is its temporary nature & what is eternal in it. Then to attach to that eternal principle in it. By contemplation of what is observable & what is the observer; till one reaches the observer which cannot be observed. The self.

5. To wean away the mind from the temporary aspect of all.

6. To detach and attach from the desires of finite to the desire of infinite Brahman

7. To continue to live in this state; till Grace of the atman relieves one from the transactional, to be one with the transcendental.

VEDANTA IN DAILY LIFE (Bhagwat Gita)

Sanyas is-

Not renunciation of Karma.

It is renunciation in Karma (of karma phala & sankalpa).

The greatest joy and output of karma is when done in the spirit of -

1. Trusteeship - "one is just an instrument in the cosmic design/hands of supreme."; thus unaffected by outcome.

2. The instrument of this body mind is shaped in the womb of past life karmas, thus none to blame.

3. Prasad buddhi- accepting the outcome of karma as prasadam of the yagya of evolution, in the path of salvation.

4. To realise mentally, that the every member of inanimate, or life form is an external manifestation (nama+roopa+vyavara =Maya); of only one supreme truth=Brahman.

Thus act according to the need of circumstance, in the limits of Dharma (Dharma, being the nature of a being); without being affected.

As in reality it is Brahman acting through Braman, by Brahman, resulting in Brahman.

Hari ॐ.

52

THE FALSEHOOD OF SAMSARIC LOVE

Spiritual yearning (mumukshutva) occurs to either-

1. One in deep sorrow resulting in vairagya (aversion to worldly desires, knowing their impermanence.). Arjuna Vishad yoga.

2. One in absolute fulfillment (Triptata), having no other desire(vairagya). Like raja Janak.

3. For those in partial sorrow or joy, there is an enticing thought, of desire to improve by karma, thus karmaphala & transmigration. The yearning of emancipation remains dormant.

Samsaric transaction is laced in falsehood, when one proclaims love for child, spouse, parents, friends, society or country. A little discrimination (viveka), bares the falsehood.

A) One says -" I love my child, my wife, my work, my parents, my country.. etc." If in all these proclamation, the MY, is substituted by OTHERS, the love lessens or vanishes. Thus the love for MY, is the utmost. Others are just a projection to hide MY and MYNESS.

B) If one's best of all desires are fulfilled, having the best of life, family, child, spouse, parents, country, work... then there remains no more desire to improve upon them, by karmas to attain better karmaphala in future life forms. Such a being naturally would seek only liberation, from this going & coming back in the play of samsara. Vairagya & Mumukshutwa is natural for such a being.

If traces of unfulfilled desires remain in any samsaric transaction or relationship, there is vasana & yearning to improve, thus rebirth; the path of karma in samsara.

Of the two initiators, eg. VISHAD OR TRIPTATA;

there is a greater (Titiksha) forebearance to dualities of emotion in those initiated by Triptata (completeness). Since such a one is so absolutely complete as the self, there is no provision to gain(desire) or loose (relinquish).

Whereas in those initiated by Vishad, a change of worldly fortunes might waver the steps on the seekers path, to the enticement of Samsara. For them is needed, constant sama, dama & niddhidhyasana (sense control, mind control & contemplation); so as not to fall from the lofty heights of sadhana, into the mundane jagat.

Hari ॐ.

53

WHO AM I?

THE IDENTITY CRISIS

IDENTITY CRISIS

Who are you jeeva?

I am Dr. Debasis Bhattacharyya.

Aham asmi D......

The Bhattacharyya, is my prarabdha, the cumulation of my sanchita karmas which fructified as the search of environment (family) of birth of present life. Depending on karmas in vyavaharika level of existence of past life. This is not a choice of this life, rather the choice of previous lives. Thus the next embodied existence, if one chooses or not; depends on karma or naishkarmya siddhi of this life. The so called free will. So long as there is karma; there will be karma phala for transmigration. This identity expresses in the waking & may or may not express as this in dream. It is completely absent in deep sleep.

The name of Debasis, is an upadhi (superimposition); given by my surrounding. A superimposition is always mithya, as the so called name could have been anything with which the ego would have been equally & happily identified itself as. Even legal affidavits can change it. Thus transient, without a real basis. It is only a superimposition for the purpose of transaction in vyavaharika. This is present in waking state, may be present or variable in dream & absent in deep sleep.

The doctor is also an upadhi of swadharma of karma, pertaining to the transaction of this body mind. Depends how one chooses the karma; in niskama or sakama of dharma or nishidha karma of dharma. Whatever that be it, is bound to generate karma phala & the resulting transmigration. This identity is only there in waking, variable in dream & absent in deep sleep.

The "I"-aham, of my identity, though less thought of(due to ignorance of veiling); is the expression of my "SELF", in the light of consciousness. This I ness is the conscious identity of self. It is present in my waking, dreaming & also in deep sleep. It has remained as it is through all my embodied states as well; though this mind does not remember it, because the body mind is new & limited in transaction and memory of the gross and subtle of this so called life. This "I", is thus the identity of eternal consciousness of the self.

The "AM"-asmi, of my identity, is the expression of existence. The existence of body- mind, that one perceives as changing from birth-growth-decay-death is actually only a change; which has to be observed by an unchanging reference frame, which is the I consciousness. The asmi - am, is matter(body-mind) as existence. Matter can neither be created or destroyed, it can only be transformed into other matter or energy. This very AM ness, as the body is transformed back into pancha bhutas on so called death, it is transformed but indestructible. The AM ness of mind existence, is transformed as residual vasanas to form a new body or merge into Brahman on liberation. Thus transformed but indestructible.

The unseen identity analysis. One loves that which gives joy. When there is no joy, there is no love. It is variable for objective desires. The love of self is the greatest love. One loves ones partner, siblings, parents, friends, job... all for the joy of the self. Since the love of self is greatest & never ending, thus the joy of the self has to be never ending bliss. The identity of bliss.

In the identity of "aham asmi such & such.."

The such & such nama -roopa, with which we strongly identify, is actually transient & impermanent. A projection of the real self on the mind as the EGO or ahamkara. This is the projection of ignorance after veiling of the real self.

The aham-" I", is the identity of unending consciousness.

The asmi- "AM", is the identity of unending existence.

The basis of all this is unending bliss; the nature of self.

Ones identity in reality is sat chit anand (existence-consciousness- bliss; which is Brahman).

The only & real (but superimposed) identity is- "aham brahmasmi".

Hari ॐ.

54

EKAM ADWITIAM BRAHMAN

HOW IS THIS POSSIBLE, WHEN THERE IS THE EXPERIENCE OF JAGAT OF MULTITUDES.

"nahi bhanad- rte sattvam narte bhanam chito citah,

Chit sambandho pi nadhyasad rte tenaham advayah."

Experience is the only factor, that substantiates the existence of;

gross objects & subtle thoughts & emotions. The world or any object, can not be said to exist without experience.

For Experience,(that is needed to substantiate any existence); a conscious principle is imperative.

The totality of existence is composed of Asmat (Self) & Usmat (objective gross & subtle). The components of Usmat (world & thoughts - emotions) are not self revealing, hence inert non conscious. Thus the conscious principle has to be the Asmat (Self), that illumines all and beyond (infinite) & is also Self revealing (there is no need of proof, for the experience of - I am ness.).

In the act of knowing, there is an interaction/contact or association; between the subjective Self & the objective inert gross (objects) or subtle (thoughts).

But such an association though it appears; is not possible in reality as =

1. Opposite is their nature, which can't coexist, as Darkness-Light; Knowledge- Ignorance; Silence - Sound.

2. Facts of different realms of reality can not really interact. Conscious pertains to Absolute reality, while world is transactional. The water of waking world by bedside does not quench a dream thirst.

    Nor does the the water of mirage, wet a grain of sand.

3. That without a form or attribute (consciousness) is without a change, hence without a beginning or end -Eternal.

    In the objective world of thoughts & objects, change is the only constancy; these everything is with a beginning & end with change in the middle, eg. Ephemeral.

    The Eternal can have no real interaction or transaction in & as the Ephemeral.

4. "nasto vidyate bhavo, nabhavo vidyate satah".- The unreal has no being & the real has no non being. (BG. 2-16).

That which is absent before birth & after death, has no true existence in the middle.

This is the sin qua non of the objective world.

While the subjective Self/Atman/Brahman/Consciousness; is beyond time - space, everlasting as the answer to the questions of - what BEFORE time? & what BEYOND space?

The consciousness, which is beyond time space; can have no relationship to elements of causality which are in space time dimensions.

Thus the relation of Asmat/Self/Atman/Brahman; With the Usmat (gross world & subtle thoughts & causality);

IS AN UNREAL RELATION.

An APPEARANCE ONLY (of world & thoughts), AS A SUPERIMPOSITION; (on the substratum of Self/Brahman).

Like the Rope on Snake.

Or Mirage water on desert sand.

Where the substratum rope (Brahman), is not the cause of appearance snake (jagat).

Nor is the a appearing (snake/jagat); a part of the substratum (Brahman).

The Self/Brahman, is the Ekam Adwitiam substratum on which Space Time causality is an appearance of superimposition, due to ignorance of-

1. Ignorance of reality of Self/Brahman, as truth.- Abhavana & Asambhavana.

2. Wrong knowing of the world as truth & the body mind as the Self -Viparita bhavana.

Hari ॐ.

55

QUEST OF ADVAITA

The enquiry is successively in 7 steps-

1. Jagat 2. Panchabhuta 3. Maya 4. Chit krida 5. Chit Vivarta 6. Chinmaya 7. Chin matra.

1) THE JAGAT=

The enchanting never ending spectrum of multitude, sernading in nama roopas of gross jeeva & jada. Addicting the ego in dualities of emotion. Leading to karmas propelled by the fuel of desires & latent vasanas. Thus goes on the cycle of karma- karmaphala, manifesting as unending transmigratory movie of bondage.

2) THE PANCHABHUTAS=

An indepth analysis of any object of the jagat, is found to be composed of the panchabhutas, in form of space(perceived as vibration, represented by hearing), Vayu(perceived as hearing & touch), Agni (as sound, touch & sight), Jal(sound, touch, sight, taste), & Earth (sound, touch, sight, taste & smell).

Pancha bhutas are the matter with associated senses, leading to mind. Thus the basis of gross & subtle.

Even scientific enquiry into nature of matter ends in Relativity (Einstein), Uncertainty (Schrodinger) or Incompleteness (Godel).

Far from absolute.

3) MAYA (NOT TRUE NOT FALSE)=

The objects of dream are a perception only, but appears as real objects, while the dream lasts. It is proved to be a perception only & not an object, from analysis in the next higher state of awareness, viz. waking.

So is an analysis of objects of waking dream, are found to be a perception only, when analysed in awareness of nonduality.

That which is a perception only & appears as an object, with no real existence, but borrowed existence; is something which is not true(like brahman/atman), neither false (like horns of rabbit); it is an erroneously(avidya) perceiving (kalpita); named mithya or Maya.

4) CHIT KRIDA=

The nondual Brahman, is without attributes & avyavarika. It alone was. Without an experience of its absoluteness (divinity). To experience something which is not real, is akin to infinite trying to perceive it as finite, a game of illusion & error- Chit krida. The game being powered by the power of Brahman, which is Maya.

5) CHIT VIVARTA=

The objects & transactions in this leela of jagat are with borrowed existence consciousness of Brahman, with no real permanent existence but ensnared in transition, change & dissolution. These are only a perception & not a thing, but appears real as a thing. An appearance only- Vivarta. The sand appearing as real water with real transactional reflections, but with no water in reality, in mirage.

6) CHINMAYA=(All pervasive)

The fan gives air, the bulb lights, the AC cools, the heater heats, the machine works, the electric chair kills. All these are different transactions, but on borrowed power of electricity; which pervades all these. There is no blame or praise for electricity, for the outcome of these. Similar is the all pervasiveness of Brahman, in all the appearances (nama roopa) & functions(vyavara). Without this all pervasiveness of Brahman, nothing functions nor appears.

7)   CHINMATRA(It only is)=

In absolute viewpoint, all that is, is Brahman (pure existence consciousness) alone, appearing only as nama roopa of jagat.

There is no real creation, nor any one in bondage, none seeking liberation.

The jagat is perception of Brahman as objects, a perception based on appearance & not absoluteness. Forgetting ones absoluteness & considering ones perceptible finiteness as real, is avidya(ignorance). This is avidya kalpita.

Only knowledge (Self knowledge/Brahma gyan); is a remedy of this avidya to dispell the effects of Maya. To realise that what one & all is.

"Aham Brahmasmi, sarvam khalu idam Brahman.

BEATING AROUND THE BUSH OF MAYA

WHY DOES MAYA CREATE DUALITY?

1.   There is no creation, it is only an appearance.

2.   The question is right, but fundamentally wrong.

Maya is avarana of the absoluteness & projection of duality in form of time, space & causation.

For such an entity there can not be a cause, since it is causation itself. Neither something beyond time, as it is eternal. Nor can there be something beyond it, as it is all pervasive space.

3.   Brahman is absolute consciousness, without attributes. However the nature of consciousness is to know. Since Brahman is one & only, there is none else to know other than itself. But it being an absolute infinite subject, to know itself; there has to be objectification of subject, finiting

the infinite, or the absolute becoming relative. The result of any of this is an error of perception, mithya (avidya kalpita).

4.   Creation of duality is because of the error of knowing.

What is the alternative? Not knowing, non creation.

That happens alternatively always.

In knowing, there is sristi & sthiti in cosmic & waking & dream in individual.

In not knowing, there is Laya in cosmic & deep sleep in individual.

The choice of the implied teaching for a mind.

5)   For one in avidya, the question persists without answer.

For a jeevanmukta, the answer is the self while the question is dissolved in mithyatva.

(Compiled from teachings of Puri Shankaracharya Nischalananda saraswati, Prabuddhanand ji & Swami Sarvapriyanand ji.)

Hari ॐ.

56

THE DELUSIONS ARE OF 5 TYPES

1. THE WORLD IS REAL.

2. I AM, THE BODY MIND INTELLECT.

3. I AM A DOER & EXPERIENCER.

4. I AM SEPARATE FROM THE SUPREME.

5. THE SUPREME PURE EXISTENCE CONSCIOUSNESS BLISS; IS NOT I; BUT GOD.

   Hari ॐ.

57

IGNORANCE-KNOWLEDGE & THE METHOD OF ADHYAROPA APAVADA

Ignorance is either not knowing or wrong knowing. As to one's true nature; both are applicable. One is a spiritual being with a worldly experience. But one does not know one's spiritual nature & wrongly knows oneself to be the limited jeeva.

This ignorance is so deep rooted by impressions of innumerable life times, that it has become a living realization of one's being as, this body mind intellect with a name & form. This needs no effort or remembrance to state oneself as a human, with a particular Name.

WHAT IS IT?

In spiritual path, first is the need of sravana, from Prarthana traya & or Guru; to remove the not knowing (abhavana) about one's eternal nature (Brahman). And also to negate the wrong knowing of oneself as that which one is not.

IS IT TRUE?

Secondly is the need of analysis about the truth of that what is heard, by discussion, deliberations & introspection. That which is Manana.

IS IT TRUE FOR ME?

Thirdly is the constant meditative contemplation of the Eternal truth in all times & transactions of waking life as Nidhidhyasana.

Till this truth becomes ingrained as ones own nature ere long. Which needs no memory or further practice for recall. Just as one previously in ignorance, responded as the Body mind name; as oneself. Then on Brahman is the only truth in one & all.

This pure being (Brahman/existence consciousness); is one's Subjective nature or Self, thus non objectifiable.

Hence beyond mind- attributes & words.

It is indescribable but intuitable.

It is a reality, as one's nature or self.

It is not a void, as that would be the erroneous saying of one; as "I do not exist".

To indicate a Subjective reality in the realm beyond words & mind. By the language of words. The method of Adhyaropa (superimposition) followed by Apavada

(de superimposition); is used in Advaita.

This is a method akin to progress from the known to unknown, like Arundhati nayay. Where a faint star is brought to cognition, by first drawing attention to any tree in that direction, then to a more brighter star & finally to the faint Arundhati. Though the last step is different in being a subjective realisation rather than an objective verification.

To indicate the attributeless Self of true knowledge (vidya) which is silence (that beyond words); by words & attributes which are avidya (attributes of ignorance).

It (Self/Brahman), is first described by a deliberately superimposed attribute of ignorance, which will negate all other ignorant attributes erroneously known as the Self; previously. This is Adhyaropa.

Then when all the ignorant attributes of body, mind, intellect, name, forms, transactions; have been shed as having been known as self, in Lieu of the the last standing superimposed ignorance that Indicates the Self/Brahman.

Then in one stroke of Neti Neti (not this, not that); the last vestige of remnant ignorant Adhyaropa (superimposition), is declared as false. To pass over the event horizon of words, into the intuitive silent singularity of Self/ Brahman. This is Apavada.

To one in the sleep of ignorance, the dream of a charging lion (adhyaropa); awakens one to the reality. The dream being known as false (apavada); fulfilling it's purpose of awakening, all the same.

Another such an Adhyaropa is the superimposition named Sakshi Chaitanya.

It is a better dream that negates the other dreams of samsara, helpful in dispassion & discrimination; to bring one to the threshold of being one with Atmagyan.

One supposes oneself as a Sakshi (witness consciousness); to be the subjective witness of the objective world, transactions, mind, intellect, body & also the ego. Thus the ignorance of oneself as the doer -enjoyer, body- mind- intellect; is transcended. Since seer (Sakshi), is not the seen (body-mind- jagat).

All ignorance of world -body-mind- intellect;

that was superimposed as self, falls away by the Adhyaropa (superimposition) of Sakshi as self. Sakshi being the last remnant vestige of ignorance. The event horizon, beyond which is the silent, attributeless realm of Advaita.

The realization of Witnessing consciousness (Sakshi), as apavada to be dropped; is the being of intuitive oneness. Whence shines forth the swayamprakasha Self -Atman -Brahman.

Hari ॐ.

58

THE TEXTS OF CREATION IN VEDANTA

The different theories are, expounded differently in different vedanta texts, about creation. Through different examples as clay- iron-gold-sparks- etc.

Only to bring down the indescribable, to the realm of descriptive discourse.

And to explain the non difference of the effect from the cause.

In no text on creation or those about effects, are any declaration on the final result of gaining such a knowledge. The absence of prayojana is a stark reminder of such a knowledge, not being anubandha chatusthaya.

Moreover there is no uniformity in the description of creation in various texts, thus indicating the irrelevance of its vakyartha lakshana. Whereas the sublime indicative pointer being more important.

The knowledge of absolute, in form of mahavakyas, that establishes the Brahman Atman eyiakam, is always with a result connected with a human end, as-

1. The knower of self, goes beyond grief.

2. Knowing that, one goes beyond death.

3. The knower of absolute reaches the Supreme.

4. Having realised that, there is no comeback.

The firm footing of prayojana, makes such teachings an essential of anubandhaya chatusthaya.

The creation texts & all such texts on effects & objects, are only an auxiliary means to establish the essence of the absolute subject (self), in all the appearing creation.

These are a descriptive superimposition of ordinary world experiences on the indescribable absolute Atman, only to be negated,

when the Absolute is intuited.

In truth, there is no differentiation in the Absolute; hence no creation at all.

Hari ॐ.

59

CREATION & VEDANTA

"There is no creation nor dissolution; none in bondage, nor a seeker of liberation." This is the Supreme transcendent truth... Gaudapada.

There is no independent universe, without borrowed existence, consciousness & bliss (Brahman). The pure being Brahman is neither changable nor partable, hence the question of creation does not arise... ajatavada.

Yet the universe exists to the senses & in transactional experience. Thus the provision of a relative vyavarika, is not to establish the relative reality; but to establish the eternality of the nondual Brahman & the ephemerality of the phenomenal universe. A process of superimposition of attributes on the attributeless Brahman, then negating it subsequently (adhyaropa -apavada).

The relationship of Brahman & Universe is unresolved because-

1. The instrument of understanding (mind), functions in relativity; while Brahman is absolute(beyond relativity).

2. Relationship, is between two things which exists. In this context. one (jagat) disappears, when the other is (Brahman).

Yet theories of creation (avidya. In ignorance); have been given as superimpositions on Brahman to create the adhyaropita jagat, only to negate it (apavada); so as to reveal that in reality Brahman alone is & in reality there is no creation.

Such one theory= In the beginning Brahman alone was as consciousness. The nature of consciousness, is to know & since there was nothing else to know, the infinite knowing itself as the finite is an error. Also it was afraid & sorrowful of loneliness due to error of knowing (when one is one alone, what is there to be afraid of?.. one aloneness being perceived as loneliness). Thus to get experience of transactions to tide over loneliness & sorrow, it projected from & in itself - the Jagat; without loosing it's own nature. Such an appearance of one as another, without loosing it's essential nature; is Maya (mirage on sand/ snake on rope).

As is the ocean in all waves, so is Brahman in creation; pervading it totally & not in parts.

Often creation is ascribed as a play or Leela, arising from the fullness & bliss nature of Brahman. Thus all of creation is born of, sustained with & dissolved in bliss.

Yet we suffer, because of forgetting our essential own nature of Infinite existence consciousness bliss. The jagat is a play in transactional roles, different in temporal & causal relations, yet one's real nature as Brahman remains as substratum. When a tired actor gets the call of being the self; one quits the play & becomes a seeker of the forgotten self, which is ones own nature.

Maya is just a statement of fact- that in ignorance, the infinite nondual Brahman, appears unexplainably as the finite multitude of jagat. There is no explanation, why the silver & snake, appears in the shell & rope. It is only misapprehension, since there never was a silver in shell or a snake in the rope.

The finite mind, being a product of Maya, is unable to fathom it's origin. This is not a futile knowledge, but a realization of profound mystery in the heart of reality. Maya is the power of Brahman, in Brahman & nondifferent from it in origin. It being akin to ignorance, is beginning less but ends with knowledge (atma/Brahma Gyan).

It is of three gunas, The Rajas (energy) & Tamas (inactivity), opposing each other. While Sattwa (spiritual qualities) balances.

Attachment to gunas is bondage (jeeva). The conditioned Brahman/ Iswara, though associated, has full control over the gunas (gunadhipati). The unconditional Brahman is beyond the gunas (gunatita)- liberation itself.

When the gunas are in equilibrium, the universe is potential - in dissolution. When the equilibrium is disturbed, with any preponderance of guna, the kinetic creation of universe begins.

From the subtlest Brahman, there appears Aakash(sound), then Vaayu (touch), Agni (sight), Water (taste), finally Earth (smell). Then by panchikaranam of these subtle panchatattva, matter evolves. Maya is the material cause of universe & Brahman, pervades all. Thus does the transcendent singular Brahman, become the immanent multitude of jagat.

The quest of Brahman is the highest knowledge (paravidya), knowing which all is known in essence. Though pure being Brahman, is unknowable as an object of knowledge, as it is the Subject alone, hence when there is knowledge of what one is not, one is Brahman. The knower of apavada of adhyaropa is Brahman.

The Brahmagyani is not deluded in Maya.

To such a being, in every name form & transaction (creation); it was -is & will be Brahman alone.

Hari ॐ.

60

WHAT IS REAL FREE WILL OR DETERMINISM

Evidences based on Biophysical, Psychological, Mathematical, and Theological law of Karma - "There is no free will."

*BIOPHYSICAL events of body and brain are all governed by laws of cause &effect. Hence are all predetermined, without a free will.

*MATHEMATICALLY & STATISTICALLY, the PAST is beyond control (free will), except in science fiction.

The PRESENT is the state between the past & future, which is already a past at the next instant & the next to the next is future. Hence the present is just a concept & in reality is actually a flux & absent. Vartamana Abhava, as in indic philosophy & in nyaya sutra of Gautama.

FUTURE, in our hands?, with free will.

Every future outcome is either, will or will not happen. There is no other option of both will & will not, happen together- the law of excluded middle. Thus future is predetermined between only two outcomes.

*KARMIC LAWS-All future outcomes are the resultant of past karmas, even the choice of Shreyas over preyas, is determined by past good karmas. Hence no free will.

The outcome of today, is due to the Karmas of yesterday & that of yesterday due to those of day before yesterday, & so on... regressus ad infinitum.

Suffering due to karma, karma due to desire, desire from duality, & duality due to ignorance of Self/Atman. This ignorance is beginning less. Hence no free will.

The desire to have knowledge of Self, is also due to past Sadhanas.

Determination & absence of free will, will lead to fatalistic & justification of evil, as Duryodhana had said- "you Krishna reside in me,& make me do evil."

Also if there is no free will, what is the use of Sadhana & spirituality?

Yet in practical life we see evidence of man overcoming natural obstacles by efforts of free will?

There are also numerous teachings in Shruti smriti, which encourages to do Self effort towards the goal of self realization.

Free will is a concept or thought in mind. Mind is consciousness & thoughts. Thoughts are in time space. Time space is Maya in vedanta, that which appears but not is.

Thus free will appears to be, but is not real; a transactional concept in maya/ignorance. While the real Self/Atman is ever free.

For a jivanmukta who has transcended mind, the pure consciousness is ever free, after the will has sublimed along with the mind. For an avtara/Iswara, who is in full control over Maya, there is the free will of creation.

For a jeeva, free will appears to be as Maya, but is not present. Yet the appearance of its presence gives the sense of doership & enjoyed ship, & it sustains dharma & censure adharma.

So in transactional life as jeeva, is to accept the illusion of Free will as real (dream of a charging lion), to wake up to realization, which is Freeness itself.

This illusion of free will is best used, in willing submission to the Supreme, as it's instrument (trusteeship of action) & accepting the outcome as the prasadam of the Supreme.

The illusion of free will, being used to be the Self, which is ever free.

There is none in bondage, no body a seeker, none liberated. That is the eternal truth of one, as the Self/Atman.

Hari ॐ.

61

VEDANTA AS DAILY LIFE

Spirituality is the lens of philosophy through which one can experience a blissed life.

The ultimate goal of every life is "dukha nivritti; Ananda prapti."

Daily samsaric & religious activities are all directed towards this ultimate goal.

The use of invocation & worship of God, to fulfill one's samsaric design, is conventional religion. While using ones body mind intellect, in the service of the Supreme, is spiritual religion.

There are four classes of devotees,

Arta (praying for removal of sorrow & pain).

Artharta (seeking gross and subtle excesses, wealth-fame-power.)

Jigyasu (seeker of knowledge of fundamental of jeeva-jagat & the Supreme.

Gyani (established in self knowledge/Brahma Gyan).

The Arta & Artharta devotees are in Pravritti dharma, guided by dharma -artha-kama guidelines.

The Jigyasu & gyani devotees are in Nivritti dharma, towards mokshya.

The outcome of all karmas (good & bad) are finite. The origin of karma is due to desire, desire is due to duality; while duality is due to ignorance. The remedy of ignorance is knowledge (Atmagyan).

\# Vedantic practice, leads wrongly to develop, ESCAPISM FROM SAMSARA. So long as one is not a Naiskarmasiddhi gyani, there is karma for chitta Siddhi. Which along with Shraddha (bhakti) & mind control, should be done in a spirit of karma yoga (trusteeship & Prasad buddhi; eg. without egoistic doership & without attachment to the outcome of the effort; accepting the outcome as the Prasad of divine design). This karma is to be done, holding on always mentally, to the absolute truth- "holding on to me/Atman, do your swadharma".

The wheel of karma moves on rotating, yet has to remain pivoted to the kuthasta.

The Supreme Brahman, is transcendent essence of all - "Isa vasyam idam sarvam".

The God realised in samadhi & meditation while being absent in samsaric transaction, is not transcendent, but a limited God. After all what ever one sees with open or closed eyes, is Brahman in essence.

Searching for gold, After throwing away the ornaments is just as futile as searching for Brahman After throwing away the samsara.

Similarly one ignorant of gold & revelling in the name forms & transactions of ornaments, also misses the gold, just as a samsari plunged in the multitudes of finite samsara, misses its eternal essence- Brahman. Vedanta enables to realise the essence (Brahman), in all, as the only one, at every moment; as a daily life.

The immediate result of such a practice, results in divinisation of worldly relations by gyan- (a penetrative view, which transcends, name- forms, and rests in recognition of the divine essence in one & all.); and humanisation of divinity in bhakti (as a son-bal gopal; as sakha- Krishna, as mother- kali, as grandsire- Bramha, as father/beloved/master...).

Vedantic spiritual practice & daily life can not compartmentalize. Then it is spirituality, that is neglected at the others expense; while life becomes a suffering without spirituality. Thus daily life should be based in vedantic spirituality at all times.

In Vedanta the essence of everything is the Supreme Brahman, (the Brahman alone is, the Jagat is an appearance in Brahman). To a seeker, not yet a gyani. One's relation, to anything or any one of Jagat, whose essence is the Supreme Brahman, is a relation of worship- Yagya. The form of such worship is seva. Such a mindset is bathed in thankfulness, on being blessed in performance of seva. "When I close my eyes in contemplation of gyan, I am at peace. When I open my eyes to samsara- what can I do for one & all?".

DEALING WITH OPPOSITION & FRUSTRATION ON THIS PATH=

1. Initial seekers to practice with guru gurukul or in private, without advertisement. It is one's private bliss.

2. Once established, on this path, the facts of opposition helps to sharpen & test one's self control, forbearance, yearning, steadfastness.. all which like the fire, which shines the gold.

3. There should not be any frustration or hopelessness in this path, as some life time shall be the time of self realization of all. Moreover there are many masters who realised the self. There is also the Shruti pramana, whence lord Krishna says "efforts on this path is not in vain, one starts from where one has left."

4. Once started on this path, there are no comebacks, one can not find peace without it.

5. Such a life of spiritual practice may or may not yield atmagyan in this life, yet the life lived in such a way, is life divine, giving bliss in present transactions.

RECONCILIATION OF SUFFERING WITH VEDANTA

1. For a GYANI, established in atmagyan. Who is not the body, not the mind. There is no mental or physical suffering. It is only expending prarabdha.

2. for the SEEKER, who is not yet a gyani, it is better to hold on to bhakti (surrender) along with gyan (contemplation). When gyan alone feels

inadequate, there is always the divine to surrender unto, with the Prasad buddhi of karma phala.

To keep on doing karma's in dharma, with single pointed concentration & cent percent dedication, cutting off all distractions; in the spirit of yagya or worship, dedicated to Brahman/Ishwara.

Till the living realization of Brahman doing for Brahman, by Brahman.

Hari ॐ.

62

SEARCH FOR ONE'S OWN NATURE

"Kasturi kundal basey, mrig dhoondey van Mahi.
Jyon ghat ghat Ram Hai, Dunia dekhey nahi.".

... Like the proverbial search of musk by the deer in woods, whereas all the while it was within itself only.

One's basic nature is divine, eg. existence consciousness bliss, expressed as peace/silence, happiness and love. Life is divine, with human experience & not the reverse.

The vision of a pure sadhaka sees the divine in all & also in oneself. Spritual progress is transcending individuality, into totality. Holding onto plurality is bondage in Maya.

The functioning in microcosm is Jeevahood, while it is Ishwara in macrocosm.

From birth till death, every life form is in search for endless Peace, Happiness & love. This is the commonest target & the least fulfilled.

ON PEACE

Struggle for peace is the striving of each jeeva. However a Struggle can not achieve, peace; which is it's antithesis. Similarly doing nothing, can not achieve peace. Peace, like self is not something achieved; it already exists as one's nature. It is the substratum on which functions the flux of dualities of emotions. To get peace, it is only needed to remove the obstacles that hide it as ones real Self.

And the obstacles are Desire, Attachment, Ahamkara (Ego), Mamakara (myness).

DESIRES lead to thoughts & imaginations along with planning to aquire, then karma to effect it. If it is unfulfilled- there is sorrow, if obstruction- then anger, if fulfilled -then trepidation to hold on to it. Thus leading to mental & physical disturbance, which is the antonym of peace.

ATTACHMENT leads to worries & anxiety, out of imaginations, thus agitating the mind. Not peace.

EGO leads to expectations. It's fulfillment or unfulfillment is the cause of further assaging of ego or the germination of anger & hatred. All being the graveyard of peace.

MYNESS leads to struggle & planning to aquire, horde & protect. A success, leads to geometric progression of the Struggle. While a failure is a cause of despair & anger.

The SOLUTION, to the above detractors of peace are-

1. Sakshi bhava- observing the cause of mental agitations & identification of oneself as the observer.

2. Ambassadorship -Working without Ego of doership, as an instrument of Supreme.

3. Prasad vritti- doing work without attachment to results.

4. Loving all as manifestation of Iswara.

ON HAPPINESS

Every jeeva seeks permanent happiness, from objects and beings; who are themselves impermanent. Thus the happiness so obtained from objects are impermanent, also when the cause of happiness ends - there is intense sorrow.

Sorrow is due to this delusional search, of permanent in the impermanent, of the seeker. Every experience is the interaction of subject(asmat) & object (yusmat). Objects as such does not create permanent joy or happiness. Thus the experience of permanent happiness is the nature of the subject(asmat/self). Yet one is in sorrow, due to ignorance of ones true nature.

Happiness is inside oneself & not outside, as evidenced by-a) closing one's eyes in moments of extreme happiness. a) happiness is intuited in deep sleep, when there is an objectless experience.

The way to permanent happiness is to know one's nature-The Self, by removing the obstacles eclipsing it. The path of Atma gyan.

ON LOVE

Love in pure form is one's subjective nature, unexplainable, independent, beyond time -space-object. Endless to sum up. There in more joy in giving love, than being loved. Para Prem is pure love & apara Prem is transactional love (a trade- available on reciprocation).

The apara/transactional love is between two (duality). It is laced in selfishness,& available to reciprocation. Induces hatred, fear & insecurity, by exclusion -for those opposed to the beloved. It ends with end of the object of love. It is a microcosmic transactional love between two. One falls in this love-Fell in love.

The Para Prem is selfless. The duality of Lover & beloved becomes one in essence (advaita). This is transcendence of love from microcosm to macrocosm. This love penetrates the transient name & form, to rest in the essential self of being. This love is not a need, nor a desire, neither a thirst. It is a fulfilled completeness, where the TAT dissolves int TWAM. One rises or grows in such a love - not falls in it.

(From teachings & discourses of Gurudev Swami Chinmayanand ji & Swami Swaroopanand ji.)

Hari ॐ.

63

WAKING UP TO IGNORANCE

A jeeva is body- mind- consciousness. The body prana mind intellect, is objectifiable =IDAM. This idam, is the "apara (lower nature) prakriti".

The consciousness is non objectifiable. It is purely subjective, hence one's swaroopa= AHAM. This aham, is the "para prakriti (higher nature).

The Aham, is intuited only & not perceived.

The Idam is perceived. Jeeva is Aham Swaroopa.

One's own nature or SELF, is infinite.- para prakriti. In duality, there is limitation of any other by me (the body mind) & me by the other, thus finite. So if one's nature is infinite, it has to be "me, as all & all as me."

In Dream of waking, one feels limited in gross, time space & object, as the Body mind intellect; as a finite jeeva.

In the dream of sleep, one feels limited in subtle time space & object. There is search for happiness & also fear in sorrows; in both dreams (sleep & waking).

In susupti (deep sleep), there is no limitation of oneself as objective body mind, nor is there limitation of objective dimensions of time & space. It is infinite in true sense - the para prakriti of one's self. In susupti one is just self-Nirvishesham; the Unmanifest. Mano buddhi ahamkar chittani na hum....

The ignorance of Self & the superimposition (adhyasa), of me, as gross body mind in waking dream & subtle body mind in sleep dream, is both transcended in deep sleep. One has no (adhyasa) superimposed gross or subtle. One is just Self (Aham), yet unknown; the pure subject can not be objectified (known). This is beyond all limitations, beyond all dualities of emotions (the greatest joy & sorrow is transcended in it). There is no search of joy, neither is there any fear of any sorrow, in susupti.

This is Ananda of sat Chit Ananda; not joy but Infiniteness. Infiniteness is only eternity & eternity is bliss unlimited.

The intuitive realization of, having not felt anything in susupti, is not a proof of nothingness, but rather a proof of objectless Aham alone.

Susupti is not a state of ignorance, since there is no time space object to be ignorant about.

There is no ignorance in sushupti, but there is ignorance about sushupti; which is ones para prakriti. This ignorance of ones nature(self), is the Avarana. Then this non perception leads to false perception as projection (vikshepa) of one self as gross, in the so called waking(dream) & the projection of subtle, in sleep(dream).

The waking dream & sleep dream is a projection in the nondual objectless consciousness, viz. Susupti. There is no waking up from sushupti, it is waking up in sushupti - in ignorance of waking dream or sleep dream.

Hari ॐ

(As perceived from Swami Prabuddhanand jis discourse on Bhagavad Gita Ch. 7. Discourse 77.)

64

KAIVALYA NAVANEETA

THE CREAM OF EMANCIPATION:

THE PITFALLS IN SELF REALIZATION

   & IT'S REMEDY =

1) IGNORANCE (Abhavana)- corrected by Shravana (hearing from Shruti-smriti & Guru.)

Ignorance veils the truth of "Ayam Atman Brahman & Aham Brahmasmi".

2) UNCERTAINTY (Asambhavana)-

It is the harbinger of confusion due to lack of Shraddha in the Shruti & Guru; which proclaims "Tat Twam Asi".

It is corrected by Sraddha &contemplation & analysis-Manana by self & in satsang.

3) WRONG KNOWING (Viparita bhavana)-

It is the illusion that the world is real & the body-mind- intellect is the Self.

Instead of the truth that "Brahma sattwi jagat mithya; jeevho brahmaiva naparah".

It corrected by meditative steadfastness of truth as Niddhidhyasana.

A constant effort in such SRAVANA- MANANA & NIDIDHYASANA; is to be practiced, so long there is sense of Knower - Knowing & Known as being present.

At such an end called Gyani/Jivanmukta; no further effort is needed.

THE GYANI

In order of merit, are of 4 types-

Though the bliss of liberation/Self is same in all. They are-

BRAHMAVID, VARA, VARYA, VARISHTA.

A) BRAHMAVID- Realized as Brahman & continue to perform swadharma as per shastras, as the will of lord. That is for worldly good; though the the performance of the gyani is, by the self- for the self & in the self. Without wavering from the Supreme state. Living in the silent all pervasive oneness of infinite inclusiveness. Though completely unaffected by personal or worldly happenings, since all is the self. Such a being accepts all that comes unsolicited without sankalpas. The fructifying prarabdha (body mind) of such a being may differ due to past life actions as a tapasvi, wandering mendicant, Guru, samsari, vaisya, kshatriya- raja or even as a cartman. (Shudra-Raikva- Jabala/Vaishya/Kshatriya/Brahmin).

B) The other three classes- VARA, VARYA, VARISHTA; all remain in SAMADHI.

THE VARA- has remnants of concern of basic, bodily needs & maintenance (food water).

THE VARYA- needs reminder by others about basic bodily needs.

THE VARISHTA- is oblivious of basic bodily needs by oneself or even at being reminded by others.

The SANCHITA KARMA of a Gyani, is burnt away in the fire of atmagyan, like roasted seeds. Never again to germinate in prarabdha of rebirth.

The AGAMA karma of present body of Gyani, is borne by the body-mind of - the followers & sishya, as to the merits. While the demerits pass on to the detractors.

AS of the present PRARABDHA of the Gyani, as gross, subtle & causal.

The GROSS exhausts itself back to the panchabhutas at death.

The CAUSAL ignorance, is burnt to ashes in the fire of gyan.

The SUBTLE body of mind intellect; dissolves itself, in it's substratum- the pure non objective consciousness- the Self.

Which is ever present as ones nature of eternal attributeless existence consciousness bliss- Without an origin- sustenance or an end.

Thus appears that -; as newly achieved.

The Self, that was ever there.

As a Pura api nava - ancient, yet new.

By the seekers of Atmagyan.

To dream a better dream, for the end of nightmares.

"There is no dissolution, no birth, none in bondage, None aspiring for wisdom, no seeker of liberation & none liberated."

As it is Brahman alone, that appears as all.

"Pragyanam Brahman".

"Aham Brahmasmi".

Hari ॐ.

65

THE SPIRITUAL PATH

For spiritual initiation, the earlier the better in life; as it reduces formation of impure mental vasanas, while providing the maximum time possible to attain the end. For those without spiritual tendency in active life, there is rarely such, after retirement.

Good past life deeds, induces the quest of spirituality. The grace of supreme, creates the desire to strive for it. The utmost effort in free will of viveka & vairagya, leads to the result of spiritual finale.

In the initial stages, one should avoid objects of desire & attachment, along with thoughts of lower propensities. The mind should be filled with Vedantic thoughts till one falls asleep or, the body drops off.

Even in samsara, a part of the mind intellect, should constantly hold onto the Supreme. Every physical/mental/intellectual, karma should be, as an oblation (yagya) to the service of the supreme. The result, what so ever (good/bad), to be accepted as prasadam of yagya, in same mindedness.

This path is for the fearless, who is ready to sacrifice ones entire I ness & My ness, of this & also of the heavenly worlds.

The motto is only striving for, discrimination, renunciation & knowledge.

The spiritual traveller, should have a healthy body, so as to minimise the body consciousness of the mind. As it is seen that a sick person, is most attached in thoughts of body consciousness.

Repeated hearing of the vedantic truths & repeated contemplation, followed by gradual progression from the objective limited Avatara & saguna brahman; into the final infinite, attributeless, transcendent & immanent subjective Self, as the end & means of meditation. will ultimately help to drop the limited upadhis of name forms & transactions, which one has superimposed on oneself, out of ignorance. In the dawn of self knowledge, one becomes the Self.

Daily hearing, reading & contemplating vedanta, along with some daily practical spiritual practice; is a must for a seeker.

A life of such a seeker is one of purity, meditation, spritual discipline & mental control. Gradually the viewpoint of all transactions become based on the living realization of divinity in one & all, as the Self.

Thus when all is the Self, what else is there to desire & what is there to renounce?

Hari ॐ.

66

THE DESIRE OF, THE DESIRELESS
(THE BONDAGE OF THE EVER FREE)

Desire is a feeling to acquire; arising from a feeling of incompleteness, in the absence of another being or thing.

The creation of Iswara; of a being or thing is essentially complete in itself. Hence in essence every person or thing, being complete in itself; is desire less.

THE BEING: The essential nature of a being is the choiceless attributes namely is -ness, knowership & enjoyership.

The isness is existence, which though being apparently transformable, yet is indestructible. The knowership is on the substratum of consciousness, which transcends all states of being (waking-dream-deep sleep & transmigration), thus eternal & complete.

The enjoyership is based on the substratum of bliss, which is choice less for every being.

Thus every being in essential nature is existence-consciousness-bliss (sat chit anand); ones real identity. Which is complete in itself, hence there can be no desire to complete the already complete.

A VEDANTIC STORY: There was once a prince separated at early childhood from parents. Taken care of by a tribe of nomads, from whom the lost one learnt the ways of life & considered oneself as a nomad. Then later the wise minister saw & recognized him.

There was the dilema of a) ignorance of the reality by the prince, who thought himself as nomad or

b)   some one else of mistaken identity.

COROLLARY OF THE STORY & THE TEACHING:

The life of a being, is a case of both ignorance(Avidya) & mistaken identity(adhyasa/superimposition).

Though our real identity is sat chit anand (the desireless). Yet in avidya one forgets it.

Then arises the superimposition of the thing on the being.

The characters of a thing is isness, knowable, & enjoyed. All being traits of object & not the subject.

The knowable thing is the body (healthy, sick, young, old); so are the pranas, an object known(energetic or tired), thus a thing.

The mind is also an object of perception(peaceful. angry, desirous..), thus a thing. The intellect is also an objective percept (dull, bright..), thus a thing.

Though I am the subject & i perceive the objects of my body, my prana, my mind, my intellect, my house.

Though one says that this is my house & i am not the house. Yet out of ignorance & mistaken identity, one says I am sick/tired/depressed or dull; due to :

1.   ignorance of ones real identity as sat chit anand (avidya).

2.   Superimposition of the thing (body, prana, mind..); on the being (sat chit anand).

This leads to desire of body as health, of the mind as riches & fame, of the intellect as acceptance..... and results, in karmas to fulfill desires, resulting in karmaphalas & transmigration.

Similarly a thing is complete in its isness, knowableness & in being enjoyed. Yet one says sometimes, this house (thing), needs (desires) a paint. The thing (house) does not, only when the being (owner), superimposed his identity on the thing, there appeared the desire (of paint).

CONCLUSION: Desires arise from ignorance of ones real nature of being or thing & a mistaken identity of the thing on the being or by the being on the thing.

This is the teaching of vedanta : removal of ignorance of self (avidya) & removal of mistaken identity (adhyasa).

Hari ॐ.

67

THE MERGING OF IGNORANCE IN GYAN.. OF FINITE DUALITY, INTO INFINITE SINGULARITY

.. Katha. Up. 1. 3. 13

yacchedvāṅmanasī prājñastadyacchejjñāna ātmani |

jñānamātmani mahati niyacchettadyacchecchānta ātmani || 13 ||

A vivekin is to merge the speech in the mind; the mind in the mahat(cosmic mind); the mahat in the pure non dual consciousness/Brahman.

1. MERGING THE SPEECH IN THE MIND=

It is the initiation into practice of meditation/nididhyasana, for a person with discrimination, possessed of four fold qualification, prepared by sravana and manana of shruti-smriti, on having approached a brahmanistha guru, with shraddha.

The speech is taken as a representation of all organs of sense and actions.

It is a natural tendency of vikshepa, to attach thoughts on external objects and thus getting drawn in thoughts of external world. This has to be turned inwards.

The sense organs are the seer of objects, to this; one has to focus, thus defocussing the objects.

The mind is the seer of sense organs, as without attention, a visible sight or audible sound is not perceived. Then to shift focus from sense organs to mind, which is the more subtle.

2) MERGING THE MIND IN THE TOTAL MIND=

The individual minds are like waves, in the sea of total mind, from which it rises, plays in transactions and dissolves back into it.

The individual minds are a flux of thoughts, good and bad. The thoughts of individuals are due to the notion of duality, which gives rise to selfish motifs, underlying every thought process and its subsequent karmas.

The total mind is singular without duality, thus sans selfishness, hence pure.

The waves of individual minds are the effects of the cause of total mind, without which, the individual has no existence.

The individual is a limited part of the more subtle and pervasive totality, when viewed in duality.

The individual identification is laced in false ego and selfishness. However established in totality, dissolve the ego and selfishness.

Such totality of identification, makes one to realize as - one in all; and all in one. The result is absence of affinity or repulsion, only love of all as the self.

It is the self which is loved most, and all are identified as the self.

3) MERGING THE TOTAL MIND IN PURE CONSCIOUSNESS=

The total mind/Hiranyagarbha though more pervasive, yet is with upadhis. It reflects the light of self effulgent pure consciousness/Brahman.

Thus total mind is the dream state of Virat (total body), which is seen in the self effulgence of Brahman, thus akarya (effect), of the karana(cause); which is Brahman.

When the total mind is perceived as effect, the search for its cause, establishes one in Brahman.

When total mind is seen as an object, the seer is Brahman.

Thus total mind is neither the ultimate seer, nor the ultimate karana; which is Brahman/Atman - the seer and karana, beyond which is none. The self, uncaused, unborn, self effulgent, unseen and unknowable.

Thus is one established in the Self, the subject which is never objectified.

*MERGING is the process of nididhyasana after sravana & manana.

It is not an action, it is just awareness & knowledge of "Who am I?"; till the duality of jagat becomes the non dual self/Brahman. It is Gyan(knowledge of self) Yoga(yuj of the limited in the infinite).

It is undressing oneself from the false, upadhis of being, as a body-mind-intellect-ego; & embracing the real nature of being-The Atman/Brahman.

It is the realization of adi Guru Shankara's; Nirvana shatakam. By negating in logiq; that one, is not- the jagat or the panchakosha. One is the sat chit anand-Atman.

Merging is moving from fear of death to immortality. Just as a rain drop fearful of loosing its limited identity while falling into ocean; is actually becoming the limitless ocean, by giving up its limited drop identity.

The gradual understanding of merging; leads one from-gross to subtle; ignorance to knowledge; finiteness to infinite; mortality to immortality; unreal to truth; duality to nonduality.

Merging is like near photography; where the tele lens of mind, projected & enmeshed in the multitude of jagat is transformed into a lens to enquire the nearest and innermost self. This Is by defocussing the effects (karya) & objects(seen). While focussing & realizing the cause(karana)&subject(seer).

Merging is both voluntary (nididhyasana/meditation)& involuntary(deep sleep & dream sleep).

Involuntary merging is seen in dream sleep, when the gross world of objects merge in the subtle world of thoughts. A pain ful body might enjoy a blissful dream.

Involuntary merging is also seen in deep sleep, when the gross & subtle world, merges in the causal experience of nothingness. But in both these involuntary merging, one is not aware of its initiation & it ends. Thus laced in ignorance, since there is veiling of self.

Voluntary merging is a practice of nididhyasana, as to remain established as the cause of effects or as the sakshi, seer of all those seen. Till one is established in the pure consciousness without upadhis; when there remains no effects & nothing to be seen (drysa). A state of Deep sleep in wakefulness.

Merging the individual gross(viswa), in the cosmic gross(virat); the individual subtle mind, in the cosmic mind(Hiranyagarbha); the individual causal ignorance in the cosmic Maya of Iswara & finally Maya into the indescribable Brahman; is like a road map of self realization, as in Mandukya up.

*METHODS OF MERGING

TWO ways of merging as:

1. Karya Karana viveka

2. Drg drsya viveka.

1. KARYA KARANA VIVEKA= Karya (effect) & Karana(cause); are to be discriminated. The effects are to be de focussed, so as to concentrate on the cause. The cause is always more pervasive & subtle, than the effect. Gradual & progressive discrimination leads one to the subtlest self which pervades all. This is the cause which is not an effect, abidance in this, which is pure existence consciousness; defocusses every effect. The individual is a part of totality in transaction; both in physical & mental aspect.

Such an enquiry, into body leads to the panchabhutas, of which the earth element, arise fromwater, the water from fire, fire from air, air from space & space from total mind, total mind from unmanifest Iswara, which is the illusory effect of consciousness existence/ Brahman. Brahman is unborn & without a cause.

The discrimination into the cause of every thing, being and action; brings about a change in reaction of oneself. When the cause of every effect is realized as the Atman/Brahman.

The cause of external world (karya) perception, is the sense organs(karana). The sense organs are the karya(effects) of the mind(karana). The mind is the effect of the cause of total mind(Hiranyagarbha). Focussing & abidement in total mind, absolves individual mind, which is laced in selfishness. Thus the mind becomes pure, free from likes & dislikes.

2. DRG DRSYA VIVEKA= Is the discrimination between the seer & seen. Based on the following principles of experience-

    1. The seer(drg) & the seen (drsya), are different. Not the same.

    2. Seen are many & seer is one.

    3. The seen are changing; while seer is relatively stable.

    4. The seen/objects, are experienced by senses.

    5. The seer is unseen/unexperienced.

Following the viveka of seer & seen, in any experience. There is gradual focussing & abidement in the more subtle & nondual, from the less subtle duality. Such as; from the many seen objects to the sense (seer). The senses are seen by the seer mind. The mind is seen by the intellect. The intellect is seen in the causal ananda of ignorance, the reflected pure consciousness; which is same in all (nondual); without upadhis & indescribable (the self is unseen as an object; yet that is what one is - the Subject.

A form of this method is the panchakosa viveka. The body & prana (seen), can be observed by mind(seer). The mind is seen by intellect; the intellect is seen in the light of pure consciousness; which is only, the seer. Never seen. The witness consciousness-self.

***OUTCOME OF MEDITATION (NIDIDHYASANA) AND ITS EFFECTS IN DAILY LIFE=**

Outcome of meditation-

1. Meditating in the viveka of seer and seen, makes one realize the sakshi chaitanya state of real seer, by negating the false body mind seer.

2. Meditation in panchakosha viveka, leads one to shift the ignorant ego from the gross body, to the less gross prana, then the subtle mind, then subtler intellect, then the more subtler anandamaya and finally to the subtlest self as Atman, in knowledge.

3. Meditating on the karya karana viveka, leads ones identification, from the limited(finite/mortal) effects, to the unlimited (infinite/immortal) cause.

"asatoma sadgamaya, tamasoma jyotirgamaya, mrityorma amritam gamaya."

Effects in daily life-

1. The effects are of knowledge from ignorance. The world of transactions do not change, there is only a change of view point.

2. Realizing the cause, brings about a change in response to any effect. Realising hunger to be the cause of theft of bread, changes ones attitude to the act of theft and its retributions.

3. The transactions of body, work, hunger etc. goes on as usual, but the element of anxiety, fear, sorrow or feverishness towards such acts; and of changes of decay, disease, old age and death, vanishes with understanding.

4. One becomes equanimous of praise and castigations, as all these pertain to the body-mind, which one has realized as not me.

5. In duality, there is fear of another, desire of another, selfishness about body mind ego. Merged in nondual meditation, is the end of fear, desire and selfishness.. this is love of all as the self.

6. The mind, intellect, gyanindrias and karmendriyas are stilled in full awareness, as in deep sleep. The Sleepless Sleep. The Supremes Peace.

Hari ॐ.

68

EXPOUNDING THE SUBTLETY OF SELF/BRAHMAN

indiiyebyah para hayartha,

arthe bhyas ca para mmanah,

manasa stu para buddhi,

buddher atmama han parah,

mahatah parama vyakta ma vyaktat purusah parah,

purusanna param kincitsa ka stha paragatih…… katha upanishad.

The sense organs are considered to be the instrument of perception & the first step in the spectrum of gross to subtle. The sensory objects in form of smell, taste, sight, touch & hearing are more pervasive than the sense organs. The mind is the next subtle as it is more pervasive, since it can perceive in subtle, in spite of absence of gross objects. The intellect is more subtle as it capable of discriminating the thoughts of mind. The vyasti intellect is apart of the samasti intellect, which is more subtle & pervasive. The total intellect which is the samasti subtle, is created out of the unmanifested causal Maya/Iswara; which is more pervasive. The substratum essence, of the unmanifested is the supreme Purusa. Which isinfinite fullness & the resident consciousness of all. The pinnacle of subtlety, beyond which there is nothing. It is unexplainable neti neti. But is not (neti), eg. nothingness or shunya.

SENSE OBJECTS ARE SUBTLER THAN SENSE ORGANS

The sense objects are considered in terms of their sensory essence as smell, taste, sight, touch & sound.

Under such a consideration, the sensory objects or stimulus are more pervasive, than the perceiving sense organs (which are less subtle).

The visual stimulus is a vast spectrum of cosmic, ultraviolet, visual, infrared & microwaves. The sense organ, eye; can perceive a limited range of VIBGYOR, amongst the entire available range.

Similar is sound, comprised of ultrasonic, sonic & subsonic. Of which the ears perceive only the sonic range.

In taste also, there is perception of sweet, sour, salt & bitter. There are many more tastes not perceptible to human tongue.

Similar are the states of smell & touch.

If there was no stimulus of sensory objects, there would be no sense organ for such; as there is no sense organ of chemical perception in humans, as found in snakes.

The sense organs are only an instrument for the objects, which are thus more pervasive & subtle.

Hari ॐ.

69

MAYA AND THE UNIVERSE

THE WORLD AS SEEN AND PERCEIVED:

Is principally governed by

1. Cause and Effect.

2. Change in Time and Space.

CAUSE AND EFFECT

There can never be anything out of nothing. Thus for every effect there has to be a cause. The debate is-

Is the cause basically same as the effect or are they different?

Satkaryavada- The effect is already potentially existing, in the cause. Like ornaments (effect) in gold(cause). Curd in milk, Jagat in Iswara, pots in clay. Though some effects can revert back to the cause and some may not, yet there is nothing in the substratum of effects, which is not the cause. Thus logically the effects are in essence, the cause. True logically, but the experience is contrary.

Asatkaryavada-The effect is different from cause, as it has different properties and the functions (vyavara) of effects are different from the cause, which is perceptible by experience. The function of ornament is different (wearable/ornamental) from gold, which is not a wearable experience. The function of jagat is experience of life while Iswara is not. Curd has different properties than milk, pot can be used as container, while clay can not. There is a CHANGE. When the cause gives rise to effect, which can be experienced by senses. True by experience, but not logically.

Thus both appear true, in different perspective. ANALYSIS OF CHANGE IN TIME AND SPACE:

The truth of experienced world, is the change in time and space.

ANALYZING TIME- Time is a continuum of Past, Present and Future. When did time begin?... regressus ad infinitum... Unknowable.

So lets analyze the time of ones experience.

Past is that, which is before Present.

Future is that, which is after Present. Then what is Present Tense?

The Very moment, one calls as present, is already, a past. The next is future, a continuous flux from past to future, without a real present tense, which is just a concept and intuitively transcient experience. Thus without a real present tense.

Both past and future, which by definition are so dependent on present, for experience are logically unreal.

Thus the very basis of Asatkaravad, which is time, in the temporal world of change, is just a concept for transaction and not a reality.

In every object and Jeeva, there are NAME, FORM, TRANSACTION, that is experienced.

And there is the pure Just EXISTENCE and pure, just CONSCIOUSNESS, without conditioning, which is undeniably present (but not experienced readily) as I AM. The I ness is consciousness; when without an upadhi. The AM ness without upadhi, is the proof of existence, which may change in the illusory time, but is ever there as the infinite, timeless (immortal).

This phenomenon of (Jagat), as effects appearing different from cause, with change in time and space, for transaction. Which is true in experience, but untenable in logiq. Is neither true (by logiq), nor untrue (by experience). This is Mithya or MAYA. Jagat mithya.

The pure unconditioned Existence, Consciousness; which is veiled, yet the true substratum of all these names, forms, changes and transactions, is timeless infinite.

This veiling is due to mithya jyana(false dristi) & not a positive entiety. This goes away with right knowledge (samyak jnana).

Thus It Is Immortal Bliss(infinite is bliss).

Sat (existence), Chit(consciousness), Anand(bliss)=Brahman.

That is the logical truth of every being.... Brahma sattwa Jivo brahmaivo naparah.

Brahma sattwa.(the only truth). Jagat mithya (Maya).

jivo brahmaivo naparah (TatTwamAsi).

Hari ॐ.

70

SILENCE & SOUND

Sound (vak) is perception by senses. Silence is not perceived by senses, it is an experience of background (substratum).

Sound is a creation, that which is created is bound to die. Silence cannot be created, it is the background on which sound is created; it is unborn, thus unending-eternal.

Sound is the experience of disturbance in silence. Silence is not the absence of sound but rather the experience of non disturbance in it self.

Sound can be thought of; Silence cannot be thought of. One can only be it (Silence). Since one can only be it, It is ones essential nature; the Self.

Everything with name, form & transaction (MAYA), can be expressed by the sound of voice & language. These are the effects which can be acquired, purified, modified & destroyed by karma(action).

That which is attributeless pure existence & consciousness (Brahman); is non describable by vakya vritti (sound & language). It is the pinnacle of silence unreachable by sound (language); but one is that silence, when the superimposing name forms of language has ceased to be.

Sound is the kinetic movie of life (jagat), on the silent potential screen (Brahman). Without the screen, the movie is not.

Yet to reach the awakened potential state of silent self, from the dream of kinetic name & forms; one needs the supporting pole of language of shruti. This language of shruti is also in ignorance; but only the last vestige of ignorance. Like the pole of a pole vaulter which has to be let asunder at the end, so as to soar in the heights beyond it.

Hear not that, which is not that penultimate sound(Shruti), beyond which is the bliss of silence of infinitude.

The culmination of all sounds & language is the source of all, AUM. Beyond is the bliss of silence of self.

Hari ॐ.

71

RECONCILIATION OF SUFFERING WITH VEDANTA

1. For a GYANI, established in atmagyan. Who is; not the body, not the mind. There is no mental or physical suffering. Life is only expending prarabdha.

2. for the SEEKER, who is not yet a gyani, it is better to hold on to bhakti (surrender) along with gyan (contemplation). When gyan alone feels inadequate, there is always the divine to surrender unto, with the Prasad buddhi of karma phala.

To keep on doing karmas in dharma, with single pointed concentration & cent percent dedication, cutting off all distractions; in the spirit of yagya or worship, dedicated to Brahman/Ishwara.

Till the living realization; of Brahman doing for Brahman, by Brahman.

Hari ॐ.

72

BONDAGE THAT LIBERATES
(LOVE OF A TRUE FRIEND)

Practically friends can be-

1. of pleasure.

2. for utility &

3. for virtue (satsang).

Sarcastically speaking-best friend, guest friend & pest friend.

Arjuna addressed his friend Krishna, as Sakha/Bandhu. Bandhu derived from bandhan/bondage.

In many a Rabindra sangeet, the supreme is addressed as bandhu.

The word bandhu is one of the earliest sanskrit words found in the Naisadiya suktam of Ryk Veda.

B. Gita on friend-"only the self can be the friend of the self."

Panchatantra on friend-"a friend is one who can not bear to be apart. "Seen in relative measure in parents, spouse, siblings, progeny, worldly friends yet when one departs; time heals, though with scars over varied periods... yet it heals, to bear the parting, ultimately. Thus relative friendship only, in transactional jagat.

The one who is used or of use, is a relation of convenience & not a friend. The one who is not of any use is useless & not a friend.

One can either be of use or non use, then is there no real friend?

A real friend is that which never forsakes one in any time- space & circumstance (be it good or bad, dharmic- adharmic).

Aristotle-"a friend is one's second self."... a paradox; Self is a first person, how can the second be the first person?

Bhagwat Gita-(ch. 6)-a true friend is like a Yogi, who treats the joy and sorrow of others as one's own.

Mundaka up.- sharing the same prana (essence), is being Sakha (true friend).

Two birds sitting on the same tree, the lower bird being the ego of doership enjoying joy and suffering sorrows. The higher bird being the Unattached (so called witnessing) consciousness, or Atman- the real self. The lower ego self, realizes and says to the higher Witnessing self/Atman - "You are Me." Which is the same in all as the principle of consciousness or existence- Brahman/Atman. Thus the You, becomes Me... The second self, becomes the first person Self. Not apart from one, at any time, under any circumstance. A true friend. A state of total identification with the Self/Atman, which is the ultimate culmination of Bhakti/Love. A love not limited by the distinction of Lover or Loved, but only Pure Love itself. This binding (bondage) of one's ego self, to the Only Self/Atman, is realization, which dissolves the ego self in the only Atman/Brahman."Brahmavid brahmaiva bhavati."

The paradoxical bondage that liberates."The true friendship of Self Brahman."

Hari ॐ.

73

THE KNOT OF IGNORANCE

"bhidyate hrdayagranthi, chidyante sarva samasayah, ksiyante casya karmani, tasmin driste paravare.".. Mundaka. Up. 2. 2. 8. explain the prayojana of (anubandha chatushtaya), Brahmavidya/Upanishad.

1. Cuts the knot of Hridaya Granthi.

1. Removes all doubts.

2. Removes bondage of karma into Naiskamyasiddhi. For one with aparokshanubhuti of Atman.

THE KNOT OF HRDAYA-GRANTHI

Is the three knots of AVIDYA-KAMA-KARMA. THE KNOT OF IGNORANCE =

Hrd-ayam is Hrt (supreme atman/consciousness) + ayam (this body). The Atman is real & eternal, whereas the body is mithya & ephemeral.

The avidya (ignorance) of the immortal self (as Atman) &

the adhyasa of the mortal body as the self is the greatest ignorance. The ignorance of self; or one's real nature.

As to, since when is one ignorant of self? Since times eternal (beginningless).

But ignorance ends with knowledge. Self ignorance ends with Atmagyan.

When the body mind intellect, is considered as the self due to ignorance of the immortal Atman as ones real self; there is the initiation of enjoyership of desires, with subsequent karma to fulfill it.

Thus in the triad of avidya- kama- karma. a jeeva is led into the mirage of karta- bhokta buddha of jagat as a samsari. In the tree of jagat, the root is the ignorance. The trunk & branches of desire arise from it. From the branches of desires, there arise the karmas & karmaphals as flowers & fruits with seeds, to give renewed embodiment.

Ignorance is thus the root (main cause), of binding of the hrt (eternal atman) with the ephemeral (ayam/body).

THE KNOT OF DESIRE (KAMA)=When there is superimposition of the body mind intellect, as the self; instead of the blissful & infinite Atman (as self), due to ignorance. There arises the second knot of bondage. Atman which is full & infinite bliss, needs no desire, to be full or to be happy. Whereas the avidya adhyasa of body mind is finite, & thus desires for fullness & joy; for body in gross & the mind in subtle arises. The thoughts of desire arise in mind like series of waves which induces body into action. The sea of mind made turbulent by waves of desire, makes the jeeva restless & loose it's tranquility, till the desire is apparently fulfilled. Only to give rise to another desire in a geometric progression. The objects of desires in vyvarika are themself finite & its fulfillment is incapable of giving infinite lasting joy. The thoughts of desire reap transient joys on fulfillment, yet there is creation of imprints of vasanas in the causal body which are long lasting & emanates new desires later, to aggravate desire with dissatisfaction... in repeated bonds (knots), of transmigrations.

THE KNOT OF KARMA=Any action is for aquisition, modification, purification or destruction of any object in gross or subtle. Desire is the initiator of all actions. Ignorance is the initiator of desire.

Every outcome of karma (karmaphala) is to be exhausted, be it sanchita, prarabdha or agama; in this or later embodiments. Thus karma is the knot of transmigration experienced as doership (kartabodha) & enjoyership (bhokta bodha). The enjoyership may be in joy/sorrow or a mixture, but it creates vasanas in the subtle, which is a progenitor of further desires & further karmas.

The avidya of one self as the body mind is the root cause of karma.

The atman which is ones real self (nature), is all pervasive- hence non aquisible; is without upadhis- hence non modifiable; is ever pure- hence non purifiable; is unborn, thus eternal- hence indestructible. Thus there is no karma in the paramarthika self (Atman).

Hari ॐ.

74

ARISE AND AWAKE (FROM DREAMS)

There are two dreaming stages, for embodied beings. The dream of waking stage and the dream of sleep.

The dream of waking is a projection of name and forms in gross and subtle (body-mind). The dream of sleep is a projection of nama roopa in subtle.

Waking from dream happens in either of the three ways:

1. Waking at the end of a full sleep.

2. Dream interrupted by ecstasy or nightmare.

3. Forceful arousal from sleep.

Life is alternation between dream (waking+sleeping) and deep sleep.

The deep sleep is the state of ones being without projection in either gross and subtle, it is the nearest state to ones self. Only, one does know this state as ones self and reverts back to dreams which are superimposed on it.

The natural ways of waking up from dreams are used in the teachings of Vedanta; to wake up the jeevas from samsara to the state of one's real self-so called liberation.

The long natural path.

The way of natural awakening. At the end of a full sleep, one wakes up naturally-fully satisfied. In the journey of transmigration, when one body mind had its full of transient desires, sorrows and enjoyment. Then it tries to fathom the means of permanence of bliss and of immortality. The end of varna ashramas induces one to viveka-vairagya ofvanaprastha and sanyasa by the gradual vedic teachings (karma kanda) into Vedanta (gyankanda), in self realization by the long path.

The Middle Path

Sometimes the dream is interrupted by a nightmare (falling into a gorge) or ecstasy (jumping up in joy). The nightmare and ecstasy of dream are as false as the dream, but are a means of awakening from the falsity of dream. Similarly, though the upanishads are the teachings of the teacher to the taught (concept in duality, thus mithya)- while in adwaita, the teacher - teaching - taught are one without a second. So a mithya (nightmare/ecstasy), is used to annul another greater mithya(dream). To awaken oneself to one's hidden real being- The self. Once awakened, the vedanta/dream, has no further purpose.

The Shortcut

Right here and now.

A forceful sound or jolt helps, to be awakened from dream and sleep (of ignorance). The slow whisper" pragyanam brahman".

Interrupts the dream into a murmur of melodious consciousness "ayam atman brahman". Finally into the banshee of arousal, in awakening by "Tat TwamAsi".

The embodied is awakened to the disembodied state of"Aham Brahmasmi".

That what one is; only deluded in dreams of waking and sleep, in the name of so called life or leela.

Hari ॐ.

75

DESIRES OF BEING

A Jeeva even in ignorance, is actually seeking the Nondual Brahman. Only it knows not what, how and where.

The three desires of every being=

1. Long life.

2. Knowledge which is power.

3. Happiness (free from sorrow).

The desire for life is existence. For this, one turns to physical upkeep and medical science, which helps to prolong it. But immortality is far from being achieved. This existence is SAT (Satyam) of vedanta, knowing which one realizes one's self as immortal existence (Anantam).

The desire of knowledge as power is a never ending mirage, drawing a jeeva into vortex of karma and desire. The Vedantins search of knowledge is "what is that, by knowing which, all is known-that there is to know".

This is consciousness itself or CHIT (Gyanam).

The search of happiness and avoidance of sorrow is the continuous striving from birth to death. Yet never achieved. The vedantin finds it in nonduality, which is bliss. To transcend the emotions of duality is the secret. If there is joy, there is sorrow. If birth, then death..

This nonduality is one's Atman in vedanta, which is ANANDA swaroopa.

The search for "Satyam Gyanam Anantam" or Sat Chit Ananda Brahman. For both the one in ignorance or for a seeker, the quest is the same. Only the direction differs.

Hari ॐ.

76

CAN BHAKTI OR KARMA LEAD TO ENLIGHTENMENT?

Veiling(ignorance) of self by projecting superimposition of non self as self is the cause of bondage.

In adwaita, liberation is the realization of self as the nondual substratum of all, in gyan.

Karma is to gain or reject another entity, which is a notion in duality, thus avidya. Avidya which is ignorance, can not remove ignorance. Thus never a cause of enlightenment, as darkness cannot remove darkness.

Bhakti or upasana is worship of another supreme lord, separate from one self. Thus also anotion in duality. Duality which is ignorance can not be the cause of nonduality hence no liberation.

In the epitome of karma yoga, when there is no sankalpa, no doership-enjoyership, nor is there attachment to outcome. Then; is not the doer, doing and done; fused into nonduality? By Brahman, through Brahman, for Brahman.

In the epitome of Bhakti, the ego of the devotee is dissolved to naught. There remains only the Iswara. Then as the worshiped- worshiper & the act of worship dissolves into the one alone supreme;-then on, dual saguna Brahma, merges into the non dual Brahman.

Is it not non duality in a different light?

If a false (ignorance) dream of roaring lion can wake up one from the falsity of dream.

If the duality of teachings -taught (gyan), can remove ignorance of non dual self.

Can, not Karma and Bhakti which are notions of duality in ignorance. Remove duality into adwait enlightenment?

Hari ॐ.

77

USE OF MIND IN ATMAGYAN

A microbe is not seen by telescope and a distant star is not seen by a microscope. When there is the choice of wrong instrumentation.

The senses are instruments to perceive the gross. The mind is the instrument to perceive the subtle (thoughts and emotion).

The intellect is the instrument of discrimination (good/preferable). The sences are the gateway of projection.

The mind by indulging in avidya is the cause of veiling of vidya/self.

Using the intellect sharpened in sadhana (viveka-vairagya and the shat sampatti), to rule over the mind, so as to control the senses as well. Leads to erasure of projection and veiling (Maya nullified). The state of sthita pragya/manonasa or no mind.

The self reveals itself (swayamprakasha), when the veils and projections of superimposition have been removed.

The mind intellect is not an instrument to know the self (as the eternal subject is unknowable as an object).

The utility of mind is only to remove the Ego/ahamkara (body-mind-intellect complex), which superimposes itself as the pseudo self over the real self.

Hari ॐ.

78

THE DECLINE OF SANATAN DHARMA

"yada yada hi dharmasya glanir bhavati bharata abhyutthanam adharmasya tadatmanam srjamyaham."

Whenever there is decline of dharma and the concurrent rise of adharma, the supreme principle determines its destruction and annihilation by all means.

The hindus of the day, supposed to be followers of the sanatan Vedantic lofty philosophy, steeped in fearless action and universal love of all beings as a non dual soul.

Are today, alas an ignorant lot, cultured in a false notion of religion, which is the antithesis of what it is supposed to be.

Intoxicated in superstitions, false notions of distorted religion, divided in castes by birth, ignorant about the ethics and values of real dharma, false belief of gender discrimination and the final death knell of selfish materialism.

Added is the systematic suppression of educational information of vedantic truths by projections of years of religious malpractice of the brahminical society, leading to self doubt, distrust and hatred. The cause of rampant conversions out of need, fear or greed.

The so called present upholders of hindutva are mostly due to hatred of other faiths rather than love of one's faith. An unity of hatred is a castle of cards, to be blown away at theslightest whiff of selfish desires. It also gives rise to timidity and its projection as pseudo secularism, to mask one's own ignorance and fear. If really there is any truly secular philosophy, it is Vedanta. About which most hindus are unaware of in ignorance. And instead of upholding it, take to oppose it in mistaken and fear laced logiq.

It is an irony that the opponents of sanatan dharma, in the name of secularism, oppose the very secularism; that is espoused in the upanishads and Bhagavad Gita. How many of them have read these? If at all there was a little of such knowledge, there would have been, no opponents of Vedanta.

The greater irony is the lack of such Vedantic knowledge and query amongst the so called upholders of religion, who are blinded in ignorance of scriptures and enticed in the falsities of religion, to use it to develop a following for political, material, or gain of name and fame. The lofty philosophy of a way of living in a view of universal love, Universal oneness and good; thus is rotten at its roots out of ignorance, apathy, mal education and the tree of vedantic living is crumbling from the roots.

Nothing shall thrive in falsehood and hate arising out of ignorance of one's roots and principles. Most present hindus are ignorant of one's basic tenets of Vedantic faith and neither have any inclination nor will to know about it.

How can such a falsehood, considered as religion by obviating the true values, survive? It is bound to disappear in the sunset of ignorance and materialistic atheism.

Like a forest fire, so necessary in destruction, to give way to new growth of freshness.

This falsehood is passing into the fire of oblivion, from that shall arise again, new buds nurtured in sap of true vedantic values.

The destroyer shall become the originator and then the sustainer. So shall it go on.

Everything shall pass in decay with age, to give way to the new anew.

So is it in religion.

Hari ॐ.

79

LIFE AS AUM

Every life, be it cosmic or individual is AUM....

AUM, analyzed is :

A=waking state.

U= dream sleep.

M=deep sleep state.

These are the three acts of movie in which every jeeva is leading the so called life. This movie is however projected on a background substratum/screen,.. Brahman, in vedanta.

This substratum is -

1. pure consciousness, beyond the triad of knower, knowing and known.

2. pure existence, which is unborn, unending and which is the truth for every being and thing, in spite of transition and transformation of name and form.

3. bliss pure, which is beyond the dualities of joy/sorrow, love/hate. A state unexplainable by words of experience. Since once in that state there is only the melody of nondual silence.

HOW CAN DAILY LIFE CONFORM TO SUCH PHILOSOPHY?

Only by repeated reading, hearing, contemplation, practice and faith in the truth of shrutis and smritis.

Daily life as a yogi, in the bhakti, karma and jnana yoga, cleanses the mind and enables it to be attuned to the higher transcendence.

WAKING LIFE FACTS

Self realization, is Brahman realization, which is being Brahman. This is actually un realization of oneself as this gross name and form of body, or the subtle mind and intellect or the causal ananda, which are all changing and transient. To be one with that which is the substratum or self, which was and is unchanging through all transmigration.

Transmigration or rebirth, is due to karma phala of karma; karma is due to desire, desire is for, the false my and mine (the false ego).

The false ego that, i am this body/prana/mind/intellect or nothing but an accident, is all due to ignorance of what one is in essence.

The self ignorance.

Wakeful and dreaming life is a continuum of karma in gross physical and subtle mental forms. Karmas are driven by desire and sankalpa (planning), thus affected by anxiety of doership and its fruits, thereof.

The doership and its results can be absolved completely by bhakti and karma yoga with agyan of the real me/the self.

In vedic teachings, every being and thing is divine in essence.

Living in these principles, there is no need of special time, place or mental frame for worship or meditation. The whole life can become a pious act of worship-yajna and meditation. Every person, jeeva or object that one comes across in transaction is actually the eternal principle (Brahman), in different names and forms of appearance. A living conviction of the essence of Brahman, in every name and form thus unifies the doer to the done. There is only Brahman appearing as doing to Brahman by Brahman. Absolved of doership in every act of eating, drinking, breathing, earning and all other daily actions. The actions become an oblation/yajna to Brahman, and are thus of maximum excellence since it is not ensnared in dualities of mental emotions, which reduces the excellence of action. Realizing Brahman/God in every being and thing, is the outcome of gyan. Manifested as the epitome of bhakti, where one sees the Iswara in every object and being as the immanent appearing form of the transcendent.

Next is the surrender of fruit of karma. Every outcome is accepted by the karma yogi as the prasadam of the supreme Iswara. The good and the bad outcomes are all prasadam and is always good for a seeker as it is a means to absolve the ego from sanchita prarabdha (which is a cause of rebirth). The complete detachment to fruits of action, then ushers a state of non accumulation of agama karma.

The seeker is thus born in the luminosity of gyan yoga, to find who really am I? and what is this jagat?

The shruti - smriti and the guru, kindles the lamp of vedanta. From the unreal, never is a real born.

The real can never become the unreal.

The real is eternal, unborn and unending, which is existence-consciousness-bliss=Brahman.

The unreal is not false but illusory mithya, which has a birth, death and transition in between. The entire jagat and jeeva belongs to this category. It only appears, but is not it, in eternity. It is Maya or ignorance. The essence of every being, which is the self, the only one; -same in all..

Hari Om.

PRACTICAL OM MEDITATION

1. To sit in a solitary, clean space at a quiet time, in comfortable posture.

2. To control senses by withdrawing mind in self, in a mental state of sanyasa and unwavering seeker of truth.

3. With sraddha & obeisance to guru & Iswara, seeking their blessings for a pure undisturbed mind.

4. Meditate on self using Om as support. Since Om represents Brahman/Atman in absolute. The Iswara & prjna in the unmanifest causal. The Hiranyagarbha & taijasa in the subtle & the Virat - visva in the gross.

5. First meditate on A, of AUM, the individual gross body; viswa waking state with which we identify most, then the cosmic gross as Virat, inclusive of all the gross bodies of the creation. To observe this as a witness (I am not the body).

6. Then meditate on the subtle individual mind/intellect as the dream sleep of individual taijasa or the cosmic Hiranyagarbha, represented by U of AUM. As a witness(thus not the mind intellect).

7. Then meditate on M of AUM, representing the causal bliss of ignorance of individual as prajna & Iswara of cosmic as its witness (i am not the anandamaya).

8. To meditate with low chanting of Om or mental chanting in this process till a time, when there is focus on the silence after AUM (amatra); to finally detach from the desire of chanting to establish in the absolute silence of infinite joy. Released from being the witness as the state of subject only. Turyia.

Hari ॐ.

80

THE PATH OF WORK KARMA YOGA

LAW OF KARMA.. IS IT ONLY FATE?

Karma is only in realms of pratibhasika(dream) or vyavarika(waking), so long as there is doership & enjoyership.

Karma is the basis or substratum of future embodiment, to start with. But it is bondage, only with karta bhokta bodha, when there is mind intellect... the double edged sord.

Doings of lower life forms, without enjoyership doership, entails no agama karmaphala, it is only exhaustion of sanchita karma. A progress in the evolutionary path of consciousness.

With advent of mind intellect of human birth; there is doership enjoyership with free will.

The karmic substratum at birth (body mind), is like a material to work upon with free will.... mud, marbel, gold or stone or cow dung.... But is not the final end. With free will and present karma, a Michaelangello will make a master piece of stone, more precious than gold. While in hand of Iconoclast, a priceless creation will become rubble. Thus very evident like said in Vedanta, that karma though gives the substratum to start the transaction, is modifiable by free will and color of mind (varna), at the time of transaction.

Atman is in the realm of paramarthika, non transactional. Neither a witness nor a dispenser of justice, but the unbiased consciousness which envigors both the enjoined & nissiddha karma, like the light of sun which equally lights up the the karmas of shankara & hitler.

The result of karma may or may not be instant. It is a complex interplay of fructifying past sanchitas & the mental element. Thus is explained different outcomes for same effort by different people at different time frames.

The atman is a pure non doer, like light. It is the reflecting or refracting media of mind, colored by gunas due to fructifying karmas of past & free will, that is the doer & enjoyer. This mind intellect since is the one with karta bhokta bodha(subtle), based in ignorance(causal); is the one that has to dream the dream of life, in transmigration.... to dream a better dream in free will(atmagyan).

The gross body, is just an instrument without karta bhokta bodha, like the weapon of a killer, thus spared the outcome of karma phala, in transmigration... so left behind to the panchabhutas.

Thus in the law of karma, the entire gamut of future outcome of work & embodiment, is for the doer enjoyer mind intellect (subtle), (causally) ignorant as the superimposed self or false Ego. Such a mithya Ego alone is responsible for ones karma phalas, no Iswara or Atman, is responsible for it.

Yes, Manonasha, dissolves the objective mind intellect, in subjective pure consciousness, by Atma gyan, to transcend vyavarika into paramarthika.

Karma, since it pertains to Maya, is not False(in vyavaharika), nor true(in paramarthika).

It is neither True nor False, it is Mithya.

KARMA YOGA

***

Karma yoga is the yoga of action or work; specifically, karma yoga is the path of dedicated work: renouncing the results of our actions as a spiritual offering rather than hoarding the results for ourselves, in doership & enjoyership.

As karma is both action and the result of action. What today is; is the result of our karma—both good and bad—created by our past actions. This chain of cause and effect created by oneself, can be stopped by karma yoga:

like using a poison, to make an antidote, we use the sword of karma yoga to cut the chain of cause and effect bondage. By absolving the ego, from the work process; by offering the results up to a higher power—whether a personal God or to the Self within—we stop the whole cascade.

Knowingly or unknowingly, all of us perform actions all the time. Even thoughts are action. Since action is inevitable, while being alive, we need to rephrase it into a path to God-realization. As we read in the Bhagavad Gita-"Whatever your action, Food or worship; Whatever the gift

That you give to another; Whatever you vow

To the work of the spirit... Lay these also

As offerings before Me."

All of us work with expectations in mind: we work hard in our jobs to get respect and appreciation from our colleagues and promotions from the boss. We clean our yards and make them lovely with the hope that our neighbors will be appreciative if not downright envious. We Work hard in school to get good grades, anticipating that this will bring us a fine future. We cook a splendid meal with the expectation that it will be received with plaudits and praise. We dress nicely in anticipation of someone's appreciation. So much of our lives is run simply in expectation of future results that we do it automatically, unconsciously.

This, however, is a perilous pattern. From a spiritual viewpoint, all these expectations and anticipations are pitfalls that will bring us misery either sooner or later. Misery is inevitable because our expectations and desires are endless and insatiable. We will live in sorrow from death to death because our motivation is to gratify and enlarge the ego; instead of breaking the bonds karma, we are forging fresh chains.

Whether we are devotional, intellectual or meditative by temperament, karma yoga can easily be practiced along with the other spiritual paths. Even those who lead a meditative life, can benefit from the chitta suddhi of karma yoga. As thoughts can produce bonds just as physical actions.

Just as devotees offer flowers and incense in their loving worship of God, so can actions andthoughts be offered as divine worship. Knowing that the Lord exists in the hearts of all creatures, devotees can and should worship God by serving all beings as his living manifestations.

"A yogi," says the Bhagavad Gita, "sees Me in all things, and all things within Me."

The highest of all yogis, the Gita continues, is one "who rejoice with the bliss and suffers the sorrow of every creature"within his or her own heart.

Jnanis take a different but equally effective tack. They know that although the body or the mind performs action, in reality they do no work at all-Naishkarmya. In the midst of intense activity, they rest in the tranquil stillness of the Atman. In the attitude of witness, jnanis continually remember that they are not the body, not the mind. They know the Atman is not subject to fatigue or anxiety or excitement; pure, perfect and free, the Atman has no struggle to engage in, no goal to attain.

The point of all the yogas is to spiritualize our entire life; instead of compartmentalizing our days into "secular" and "spiritual" zones. Karma yoga is particularly effective at this since it won't allow us to use activity as an escape. By insisting that life itself can be holy, karma yoga, gives us the tools of everyday life to cut our way to freedom. To quote again the Bhagavad Gita Regarding Karma Yoga:

Thus you will free yourself from both the good and the evil effects of your actions. Offer up everything to Me. If your heart is united with Me, you will be set free from karma even in this life, and come to Me at the last.

DOERSHIP =TO WORK AS AN INSTRUMENT OF SUPREME.

ENJOYERSHIP = TO ACCEPT THE OUTCOME AS THE PRASADAM OF THE SUPREME.

Hari ॐ.

81

BHAKTI YOGA THE PATH OF LOVE, OF SHRADDHA, & OF DEVOTION

DEVOTION & LIBERATION

Devotion is a must accompaniment of any means chosen to attain atmagyan.

There has to be sraddha in shruti, guru & astikavada; which is a form of bhakti.

True devotion is complete identification of oneself in one's sakara Iswara.

Under such a state, the supreme Iswara, out of compassion & love for the bhakta; kindles the lamp of knowledge (buddhi yoga), in the heart of devotee. Who thus knowing him, becomes one with him (Iswara).(B. Gita-10. 10-11).

It is also declared, that with single minded devotion, one Knows the supreme & enters unto it.(B. Gita. 11. 54).

Thus Bhakti can be the bow, to launch the arrow of gyan; which strikes the target of Atman, to become one with it. Gyan is thus needed ultimately. Even a long association with Iswara as sakha, could not give Arjuna respite from moha. Sri Hari had to deliver the knowledge of atmagyan in Kurukshetra, to make him realize.

The supreme Iswara can give the knowledge of Atmagyan by any means, as-

1. Just a look, glance, touch or grace as was to Ahalya or Dhruva.

2. Iswara can give gyan as a guru directly to a bhakta, as Krishna to Arjuna & Uddhav rishi, so as to be realized. Here such gyan becomes means of gyan for the future of mankind.

3. Iswara can guide and send the devotee to gain self realization, as in case of sant Namdeo. who was sent to guru Vishoba Khechar by lord Vitthala.

4. Iswara can send the guru to the disciple to be enlightened in Atmagyan, as the divine mother had sent Totapuri ji to Ramakrishna, from a far away Puri to Dakshineswar.

5. Iswaras grace through the Guru(Sankara) gave instant gyan to a simple devotee- Giri, who instantly was blessed in Atmagyan, to be one of his principal disciple- Totakacharya.

Though the grace of leela of the Iswara for a bhakta(disciple), may vary; yet it ultimately is, his direct or indirect grace of gyan that makes "Tat twam asi"; a living realization of "Ayam Atman Brahman".

THE FALSEHOOD OF SAMSARIC LOVE

Spiritual yearning (mumukshutva) occurs to either-

1. One in deep sorrow resulting in vairagya (aversion to worldly desires, knowing their impermanence.). Arjuna Vishad yoga.

2. One in absolute fulfillment (Triptata), having no other desire(vairagya). Like raja Janak.

3. For those in partial sorrow or joy, there is an enticing thought, of desire to improve by karma, thus karmaphala & transmigration. The yearning of emancipation remains dormant.

Samsaric transaction is laced in falsehood, when one proclaims love for child, spouse, parents, friends, society or country. A little discrimination (viveka), bares the falsehood.

A)   One says -" I love my child, my wife, my work, my parents, my country.. etc." If in all these proclamation, the MY, is substituted by OTHERS, the love lessens or vanishes. Thus the love for MY, is the utmost. Others are just a projection to hide MY and MYNESS.

B)   If one's best of all desires are fulfilled, having the best of life, family, child, spouse, parents, country, work... then there remains no more desire to improve upon them, by karmas to attain better karmaphala in future life forms. Such a being naturally would seek only liberation, from this going & coming back in the play of samsara. Vairagya & Mumukshutwa is natural for such a being.

If traces of unfulfilled desires remain in any samsaric transaction or relationship, there is vasana & yearning to improve, thus rebirth; the path of karma in samsara.

Of the two initiators, eg. VISHAD OR TRIPTATA;

there is a greater (Titiksha) forebearance to dualities of emotion in those initiated by Triptata (completeness). Since such a one is so absolutely complete as the self, there is no provision to gain(desire) or loose (relinquish).

Whereas in those initiated by Vishad, a change of worldly fortunes might waver the steps on the seekers path, to the enticement of Samsara. For them is needed, constant sama, dama & nididhyasana (sense control, mind control & contemplation); so as not to fall from the lofty heights of sadhana, into the mundane jagat.

THE YOGA OF LOVE

The epitome of Love is total identification of one self with the beloved.

For those more emotional than intellectual, bhakti yoga is recommended. Bhakti yoga is the path of devotion, the method of attaining God through love and the loving recollection of God. Most religions emphasize this spiritual path because it is the most natural. As with other yogas, the goal of the bhakta, the devotee of God, is to attain God- realization— oneness with the Divine. The bhakta attains this through the force of love, that pinnacle state of emotions.

Love is for everyone: we all love someone or something, frequently with varying intensity. In love, one forgets oneself; in the single pointed focus on the beloved. The ego sublimes as we think of our beloved's welfare more than our own. The single pointed focus, gives us concentration: even against our will, we constantly remember the object of our love. Love creates the conditions necessary for a fruitful spiritual life; by creating sinle pointed determination & sublimation of ego.

Vedanta guides one to use this powerful force for God-realization. We must remember that when we love another we are really responding— though unconsciously—to the divinity within him or her. As we read in the Upanishads, "Atmaneyeshu kamayae atma Priya bhavati."; "It is not for the sake of the husband that the husband is dear, but for the sake of the Self. It is not for the sake of the wife that the wife is dear, but for the sake of the Self." Our love for others becomes unselfish and motiveless when we are able to recognize divinity in them.

However our love is misplaced, as a superimposition of one's idea of perfectness on whatever is loved in the finites. It is God alone, however, who is True, Perfect, and Beautiful. Vedanta therefore says: defocus from finite love to refocus on infinite love. Put the emphasis back where it belongs—on the divine Self within each person that we encounter. That is the real object of love.

The idea is to divinise one's worldly relations & humanise one's Godly relationship. Thinking of God as our Master or Father or Mother or Friend or Child or Beloved. The determining factor here is, Which attitude feels the most natural to me and which attitude brings me closest to God?

Jesus looked upon God as his Father in Heaven. Ramakrishna worshipped God as Mother. Many great saints have attained perfection through worshipping God as the baby Jesus or the baby Gopal. Many (Mira) have attained perfection through worshiping Krishna as the beloved. Others have attained perfection through worshiping God as their master or friend- sakha (Arjuna).

The point to remember is that God is our own, the nearest of the nearest and dearest of the dearest. The more our minds are absorbed in thoughts of Him—or Her as the case may be—the closer we are to the goal of human life, God-realization.

Many people are drawn to worshipping God through love and devotion. Yet other spiritual aspirants are more motivated by reason than by love; for them, bhakti yoga is the wrong spiritual path. Those who are endowed with a powerful and discriminating intellect may be better suited for the path of jnana yoga, striving for perfection through the power of reason.

Hari ॐ.

82

RAJ YOGA

The Path of Meditation

Raja yoga, is the royal path of meditation. As a king maintains control over his kingdom, socan we maintain control over our own "kingdom"—the vast territory of the mind. In rajyoga we use our mental powers to realize the Atman through the process of psychological control.

To whom, the disturbed mind; is an obstacle to self realization. For them is this path of meditative mind control - Raj yoga. If the mind can be made still and pure, the Self will automatically, instantaneously, shine forth. Says Bhagavad Gita:

When, by the practice of yoga, the mind ceases its restless wanderingsand becomes still,

the seeker realizes the Atman.

The state of mind is like water of reservoir; that is tainted in dirts of ignorance, turbulence of thought ripples, flow of desires, floods of passions & whirlpool of doubts. The residing substratum of Self is completely veiled by such a mind.

The minute we stop thinking one thought, another jumps in with greater force. When one tries to sit still for meditation, there are a flood of thoughts that inundates the mind.

Most of the time we remain unaware of the mind's turmoil because we are habituated to giving our minds free reign; in being ruled over by the mind: we've never seriously attempted to observe, let alone train the mind. Instead of one, using the mind, the mind uses us. Our lack of mental discipline has created the turbulent, ill-behaved minds that have given us endless difficulty. Without psychological discipline, the unruly mind becomes the ruler that enslaves one; instead of the other way round. And all of us, sadly enough, have suffered mental agony because of it.

Mind control-

While we may have grown accustomed to living with an uncontrolled mind, we should never assume that it's an acceptable, if not inevitable, state of affairs. Vedanta says that we can master the mind and, through repeated practice, we can make the mind our servant rather than being its victim. The mind, when trained, is our truest friend; when left untrained and reckless, it's one's nemesis.

Now, instead of the polluted lake we previously envisioned, think of a beautiful, clear lake. No waves, no pollution, no tourists, no speedboats. It's clear as glass: calm, quiet, tranquil. Looking down through the pure water, the bottom of the lake is crystal clear. The Bottom of the lake, metaphorically speaking, is the Atman residing deep within our hearts. When the mind is pure and calm, the Self is no longer hidden from view. And, Vedanta says, that mind can be yours.

The Bhagavad Gita, says how-

Patiently, little by little, spiritual seekers free themselves from all mental distractions, with the aid of the intelligent will. They must fix their minds upon the Atman, and never think of anything else. No matter where the restless and fluctuating mind wanders, it must be drawn back; to submit to theAtman alone.

The mind is cleansed and made tranquil through the repeated practice of meditation and the practice of moral virtues.

There is no way to meditation without the foundation of moral virtues. Any contrary effort is like a castle of cards.

For such an unsurmountable task as realizing the Self, all areas of the mind must be fully engaged. We can not compartmentalize our life into secular (in which we can live as we please) and a spiritual area. Just as we can't cross the ocean in a leaky boat, so we can't cross the ocean with two legs in two different boats. We must fully integrate all aspects of life and direct our energies towards Self realization.

This doesn't mean that one must totally renounce the world and live in a cave, monastery or convent. What it does mean is that all aspects of our daily life must be spiritualized for God-realization. Not to throw away the name & forms of ornaments in search of Gold; but to realize Gold as the essence of all ornaments of name & forms. Because raja yoga is the path of meditation, it is—when practiced exclusively—generally followed by those who lead contemplative lives. Most of us will never fall into that category. Raja yoga is, however, an essential component of all other spiritual paths since meditation is involved in the loving recollection of God, mental discrimination, and is an essential accompaniment to Karma yoga.

Meditation

As for directions on how to meditate and what to meditate is an intensely personal matter; only a genuine spiritual teacher can accurately gauge the student's personal tendencies and direct the student's mind accordingly.

THE GURU

Further, spirituality is caught, not taught. A genuine spiritual teacher ignites the flame ofspirituality in the student by the power of his or her own attainment: the student's candle is lit by the teacher's flame. And cannot be lit by books or by unqualified teachers who speak religion without living it. True spirituality is transmitted:only Pure, unselfish teachers who have achieved some level of spiritual awakening can enliven our own dormant flame. The shotriya Brahmanistha is a Guru.

THE METHOD

That said, some basic guidelines can be given: any concept of God—whether saguna or nirguna —that appeals to us is helpful and good. We can think of God as being present either outside of ourselves or inside. Ramakrishna, however, recommended meditating upon God within, saying "the heart is a splendid place for meditation." Repetition of any name of God that appeals, is good; so is repeating the holy syllable "Om." It's helpful to have regular time for meditation in order to create a habit; it's also helpful to have a regular place for meditation that is quiet, clean, and tranquil; away from sensory distractions.

Hari ॐ.

83

JANA YOGA

The Path of Knowledge

Is not knowledge in the intellectual sense— but knowledge of Brahman-Atman and the realization of their unity. Where the devotee of God follows the promptings of the Guru & Self. The jnani uses the powers of the mind to discriminate between the real and the unreal, the permanent and the transitory.

Advaita Vedanta, affirm the sole reality of Brahman. All Vedantins affirm the sole reality of Brahman. The distinction here is in spiritual practice:while all Vedantins are philosophically monistic, in practice those who are devotees of God prefer to think of God as distinct from themselves in order to enjoy the sweetness of a relationship. Jnanis, by contrast, know that all duality is ignorance. There is no need to look outside ourselves for divinity: we ourselves already are divine.

What is it that prevents us from knowing our real nature and the nature of the world around us? The veil of maya. Jnana yoga is the process of directly rending that veil, tearing it through a two-pronged approach.

An Unreal Universe

The first part is negative, the process of neti, neti—not this, not this. Whatever is unreal—that is, impermanent, imperfect, subject to change—is rejected. The second part is positive: whatever is intuited to be perfect, eternal, unchanging—is real in the highest sense.

Are we saying that the universe that we apprehend is unreal? Yes and no. In the absolutesense, it is unreal. The universe and our perception of it have only a conditional reality, not an ultimate one. To go back to our earlier reference to the rope and the snake: the rope, i. e., Brahman, is perceived to be the snake, i. e., the universe as we perceive it. While We Areseeing the snake as a snake, it has a conditional reality. Our hearts palpitate as we react to our perception. When we see the "snake" for what it is; as the rope, we laugh at our delusion.

All the worldly inputs, through our senses, our minds, our intellects, is inherently restricted by the very nature of our bodies and minds; which is limited & finite. Brahman is infinite; it cannot be restricted. An Error, is the outcome of explaining the infinite by finite means. That error is Mithya. Space, time, and causation— which is the universe of change; cannot be the infinite, all-pervading Brahman. Our minds are limited by every possible condition; whatever the mind and intellect apprehend cannot be the infinite fullness of Brahman. Brahman is beyond the realm of mind - thoughts & speech. It is the pure subject, that objects to objectification.

Infinite is one alone- nondual. There can not be a second infinite, as it limits the other.

Brahman is infinite, all- pervading, and eternal. Thus Brahman is non dual. There is nothing other than Brahman. What we see at all times can only be an appearance in Brahman. Any limitation is only our own misperception. Jnanis remove this misperception through the negative process of discrimination between the real and the unreal and through the positive approach of Self-affirmation.

Self-Affirmation

In Self-affirmation we continually affirm what is real about ourselves:The shatakam of Nirvana-" Mano buddhi ahamkara, chitta ni na hum.... Chidananda roopah Shivo hum Shivo hum." We were never born; we will never die. We are pure, perfect, eternal and free. That is the greatest truth of our being.

The philosophy behind Self-affirmation is simple: as you think, so you become. We have programmed ourselves for thousands of lifetimes to think of ourselves as limited, weak, helpless & mortal. An illusory self-destructive nightmare! If we think of ourselves as weak, or helpless sinners, we will act accordingly. If we think of ourselves as Spirit—pure, perfect, free—we will also act accordingly.

As we have over lifetimes, etched the wrong thoughts into our minds again and again to create wrong impressions, so we must reverse the process by hearing, contemplation & abidance of right thoughts—thoughts of purity, thoughts of strength, thoughts of truth. As

- "I am spotless, tranquil, pure consciousness, and beyond nature.

- All t his time I have been duped by illusion." Astavakra.

Jnana yoga uses our considerable mental powers to end the hypnotized limitation, to know that we are even now—and have always been—free, perfect, infinite, and immortal. Realizing that, we will also recognize in others the same divinity, the same purity and perfection. No longer confined to the painful limitations of "I" and "mine," we will intuit, the one Brahman everywhere and in everything.

Not to look at any one oranything, as other than God/Brahman.

It is not that "I am a human being with occassional spiritual experiences;

but I am a spiritual being, with human experience. "

Isa vasyam idam sarvam.

Hari ॐ.

84

THE DEAREST OF THE DEAR

ANANYA YOGA

"ye tu sarvani karmani mayi sanyasa matparah,
ananyenaiva yogena mam dhyanta upasate."

= Regarding the Self, as the supreme goal; those who renounces all actions as an oblation to the self, thus worshiping the Self, with single minded devotion (yoga).

The endavour of absolute mental harmony, to a state of perfection of a chosen ideal... is YOGA.

When in such an effort; the goal is one alone, without otherness (Ananya); it is Ananya yoga.

The guru of Bhagwat Gita, preaches the practice of Ananya yoga, for the divine... one alone goal of Self realisation; to every seeker.

THE best of devotees are =

1. Who has the Supreme Brahman as the only goal. 2). Who pursues the single goal with Shraddha & single pointed concentration. 3). Who has renounced all thoughts & activity as an oblation in the yagya of Supreme.

Meditation is not mearly a contemplation on a goal, but an active way of becoming one with the goal.

A person is the sum of thoughts (mind) & feelings (intellect).

The mind, is peculiar, in being unable to contemplate on anything, not conditioned by the senses.

Thus there is the initial need of using the MIND to meditate upon the sensory concept (saguna), of the attributeless (nirguna).

Then using the INTELLECT, to transcend the nama Roopa of sauna Brahman (Iswara); to stay established in the essence of its nature (nirguna Brahman).

MIND is the one that superimposes bondage & it is Mind again which realises, its own nature as the Self; to dissolve in it as liberation.

Mind control is a sine qua non, for a seeker of atmagyan. To control mind, it is imperative, not to identify oneself as the the mind itself & be led into a whirlwind of thoughts & desires projected as jagat.

But rather to stand apart from it as a Sakshi, to the mind & then to use the intellect, in discrimination of the Shreyas from Preyas; to rule over the mind rather being it's slave.

Until the living realisation, that the Sakshi, is also a mind construct, functional in the borrowed consciousness of Atman/Self.

There is neither a witness, nothing to witness & no act of witnessing; only pure non dual Sat Chit Anand......& that is the Supreme truth.

So long, it not a living realisation, there is the need of repeated practice of such contemplation (niddhidhyasana or meditation)- ABHYAS YOGA.

For the agitated, wandering mind; incapable of ABHYAS YOGA, it pointless to untimely force it, like opening a cocoon for a butterfly, as it will be destructive alone.

To such an extrovert of outward action, it is suggested to dedicate all actions as trusteeship or ambassadorship of the divine. THE SURRENDER OF DOERSHIP OR EGO.

When that also is impossible, in the highly egotistical rajasic & tamasic beings; is advised the SURRENDER OF ENJOYERSHIP (surrender of fruits of action). The present is the action; to which is the future of fruit. To brood over the fruit (FUTURE); results in imperfect action (PRESENT). This is inaction in action. KARMA YOGA.

Initiation is with Vedic Rituals & karmas of Purva mimansa, which pertains to the gross body- the annamaya purification, in this or past transmigration.

Pranayama & Hatha yoga purifies the pranamaya kosha, in development of control & focus.

A thorough knowledge of the spiritual practice & its necessity is a prerequisite for the success of yoga, achieved by sravana (removes abhavana) - mañana (removes asambhavana); thus purifying the manomaya kosha.

-Meditative contemplation/niddhidhyasana (removes viparita bhavana), of such teachings of Shruti smriti; purifies the intellect (Vigyanamaya kosha).

Such a pure being who has transcended the body- mind- intellect. Thus realising one's Self, as the Self in all - Atma Krida.

And the all in, the self of one- Atma Rama.

To such a being, to whom all is the self; there is no desire to gain, nor anything to renounce. Such a being is established in the one alone Self, beyond the dualities of physical- mental & intellectual constructs.

Is the dearest devotee; it is the(my) SELF itself... The dearest." Atmaneyeshu kamayae atma Priya bhavati."

Guru Krishna... Bh. Gita Ch. 12.

Hari ॐ.

85

EXPLAINING THE UNEXPLAINABLE

How is the color Red'; explained to someone who's blind by birth?

There are certain qualities which are perceived by one definite sense; out of the 5 senses. There are few qualities which are perceived by a combination of senses, such as form. While there are some attributes which are perceived by intelligence alone, like, name.

Yet there are sometimes situations, unexplainable yet existent & undescribable. That from which words and senses come back. Thus the unperceivable is not necessarily nonexistent.

The world of one blind from birth, is a world of touch, taste, sound, smell and thoughts. Redness is not touch, taste, smell, or sound; neti-neti. But is an abstract perception the mind of blind.

Redness to blind; is like Brahman to jeeva. Unexplainable, yet existent, in the veiling of ignorance.

The failure of explaining redness by upadhis and pramanas to a blind is an effort in futility. So is Brahman, which is beyond senses, as it is the substratum of senses. Indescribable.

Vedanta/Upanishads are the way to be the indescribable. Redness is described to one blind by; neti-neti.

Red is not the teeth, not the hair, not the bile, not the waters; it is the one that comes out from a cut as blood.

Red is not the sunflower, not the jasmine, not the leaf; it is that in a rose. Red is not the orange, not the cucumber, etc. It is the red apple.

This description leads to an incomplete or illusional sense of redness to the blind; based on the other senses of touch, taste, smell, sound; in the mind.

The world is a world of perception of projections by the senses. To some one with none of the five senses from birth; there is no world. To that person only the intellect functions as the I (ego); the mind devoid of objects is folded like in deep sleep.

The I sense of the intellect, in absence of the objectified mind; is due to reflected consciousness of the self effulgent Atman. This is what is the real I- the Atman/Brahman. This consciousness or Atman is beyond the senses(unobservable), mind (unexplainable) and intellect (imperceptible). But one realizes in knowledge, the essence of one's being as that, in spite of absence of senses and mind.

"Tat twam asi "of upanishads become the realization of Aham Brahmasmi.

Hari ॐ.

86

OM IN UPANISHADS

Om in Chandogyya up.(1. 1. 1)=

Om is Udgith, one should meditate on it.

Om in Taittiriya Up.(1. 8. 1)=

Om is Brahman, it is all that is. Established In this, one attains Brahman.

Om in Katha Upanishad=(1. 2. 15)

1. There is only one existing truth.

2. This truth is the only outcome of all prayers and tapas, as enjoined in vedas.

3. This truth is a representation of nirguna Brahman (unconditioned), the substratum of all. As well as saguna Brahman (conditioned/ Iswara), the cause of srishti, sthiti and laya.

4. The summary of this truth is AUM/ , a composite ek aksharam.

5. Since it represents both the saguna and nirguna Brahman, thus it is the most auspicious and supreme alamban of meditation of the supreme truth.

OM IN MUNDAKA UP.(2. 2. 4)

The art of Archery in Mundaka upanishad, is an elaboration of Brahma Atma aikyam, using Om as support.

1. The seeker is asked to take up the great Bow, provided as AUM, by the upanishads.

2. To prepare the forgotten arrow of self, covered in rusts of superimpositions by polishing and sharpening with sravana, manana and sadhana catusthaya. Then to mount the arrow of self on the bow of AUM.

3. To draw back the string of bow, towards the self, like drawing back from desires.

4. With single pointed mumukshutva aim at the one and only target of Brahman, without distraction.

5. Release The Arrow Of Self, so as to viddhi (pierce/realize), the target of Brahman.

6. Then the arrow (atman) and target (Brahman), becomes inseparable.

7. Ayam atman Brahman.

8. The distance the arrow flies to the target, is not a distance in time and space. It is the distance of ignorance of adhayasa. And the force required to travel the distance of ignorance is knowledge.

OM IN MANDUKYA UP

FOUR QUARTERS OF BEING- AUM.

This is analyzed from two viewpoints; of individual & cosmic perspective & its representation by aspects of Om (AUM).

Om (AUM), is ek akshara, but composed of A-U-M (matra) & the silence that follows (amatra); 4 components.

Life is perceived as the changing, Waking, Dreaming & Deep sleep states. The Mandukya up. points out a 4th dimension, which is the unchanging witness consciousness of these three states; in which arises- sustains & dissolves these three states; this is the 4th. Which is nothing separate but the continuous substratum of all these three states & also that beyond these states. This is both within & beyond the realms of time space. This is Represented by Om.

Which is Brahman, in cosmic/samasti, and the Atman or self in individual/vyasti.

A ripple in silence is sound. From the silence (amatra); arises the sound of AUM, which dissolves back into it. This silence which is the substratum of AUM (akara, ukara & makara); is the infinite existence consciousness-Brahman in cosmic. & Atman in individual parlance. The 4th. or Turyia.

When the absolute Brahman is overlapped in Maya, it becomes, the Iswara of the total/samasti. Akin to the unmanifested cosmic dissolution. This cosmic state has a parallel to the individual/vyasti, in form of deep sleep state called prajna. This is the third state; represented by M of AUM, the makara. This is the causal state of ignorance (avarana), without projection (vikshepa).

When the makara/causal is associated with the subtle mind & intellect; it becomes the state of dream sleep. Which is Hiranyagarbha of the samasti & taijasa of the vyasti. This is the 2n

state, represented by U of AUM, the ukara. There is avarana of Atman & projection in the subtle.

When makara (causal) & ukara(subtle) is associated with gross; it becomes the Viswa in vyasti & Virat of samasti. Represented by A of AUM, the akara. The 1 st. state fo being, akinto the waking of gross body & objects; with avarana of Atman & projection in both gross & subtle.

The cosmic totality of Virat, Hiranyagarbha & Iswara is Iswara. The individual totality of vishwa, taijasa & prajna is Jeeva.

The absolute of cosmic is Brahman; while the absolute of individual is Ataman. And Ataman is Brahman.

"ayam atman Brahman".

PRACTICAL OM MEDITATION

1.   To sit in a solitary, clean space at a quiet time, in comfortable posture.

2. To control senses by withdrawing mind in self, in a mental state of sanyasa and unwavering seeker of truth.

3. With sraddha & obeisance to guru & Iswara, seeking their blessings for a pure undisturbed mind.

4. Meditate on self using Om as support. Since Om represents Brahman/Atman in absolute. The Iswara & prjna in the unmanifest causal. The Hiranyagarbha & taijasa in the subtle & the Virat-visva in the gross.

5. First meditate on A, of AUM, the individual gross body; viswa-the waking state with which we identify most, then the cosmic gross - as Virat, inclusive of all the gross bodies of the creation. To observe this as a witness (I am not the body).

6. Then meditate on the subtle individual mind/intellect as the dream sleep of individual taijasa or the cosmic Hiranyagarbha, represented by U of AUM. As a witness (thus not the mind intellect).

7. Then meditate on M of AUM, representing the causal bliss of ignorance of individual as prajna & Iswara of cosmic; as its witness (i'm not the anandamaya).

8. To meditate with low chanting of Om or mental chanting in this process till a time, when there is focus on the silence after AUM (amatra); to finally detach from the desire of chanting to establish in the absolute silence of infinite joy. Released from being the witness as the state of subject only. Turyia.

MANDUKYA UP.(9-12)

METHODS & OUTCOME OF OM MEDITATION.=

The outcome of Om meditation depends on the extent of understanding & establishment in any of the four aspects of Om (A-U-M-amatra)... Prasna Upanishad.

1. A meditator established in the individual gross waking world of Viswa (the A of AUM in vyasti), is a jeeva with transient joys & sorrows of birth to death experience. A Samsari.

2. A meditator established in the gross cosmic waking Virat state (A of AUM in samasti); obtains all sensory objects of desire in the gross physical world. Such a one is a prominent person the finite world. But finite, all the same.

3. A meditator established in the subtle, U of AUM. Either as the individual (taijasa) or cosmic (Hiranyagarbha), attains to all that is subtle, pertaining to mind intellect. Less as in dividual & more as cosmic.

   Such a person is an inducer of knowledge with followings.

   Such a being is also equanimous, as U is between A & M. All are loved equally & impartially by such a being & is reciprocated to one also.

   The initiation of knowledge results in removal of abhavana of atmagyan/Brahman; in all the associates/family.

   Though there is progress yet the results are finite.

4. A meditato established in the causal, deep sleep state of individual prajna or cosmic Iswara as the M of AUM. The results being more in cosmic, than in individual establishment. Has no projection of duality, thus no fear.

   All has merged as one, thus realising oneself as the self of all in samasti & the anandamaya being the nearest to self, in vyasti.

   One knows the real nature of all objects. Yet with an end, thus finite.

5. The meditator established in the amatra of silence, the fourth of OM. Is merged in the non dual infinite consciousness existence. There remains no act of meditation, nothing to be meditated upon & no meditator. The jagat is revealed as mithya. There remains the

unexplainable state of immortal substratum, the eternal truth. The Brahma Atman aikyam. Turyia.

"Ayam atman Brahman.

Hari ॐ.

WHAT IS GOD/BRAHMAN?

A deduction based on the following Shruti/Smriti statements=

1. Satyam-Gyanam-Anantam Brahman.

2. Isavasyam Idam Sarvam.

3. I am in all and all is in me.

4. Pragyanam Brahman" and

    "Ayam Atman Brahman."

5. Tat Twam Asi

6. Aham Brahmasmi

For a nididhyasana on the above 6 statements, there are two supportive statements-

a) God is Omnipotent, Omniscient and Omnipresent.

b) The way one invokes me, I respond to that mind in that way.. Sri Krishna.

MANANA ON FIRST STATEMENT.

*Brahman means vast.

*Anantam is infinite

(# in space-omniscient,

#in time-omnipresent/eternal.

#in object-it is the essence of all objects and beings, without which, all is not= non dual.).

*Satyam is truth-which is existence (existence is an eternal truth for everything and being, transformable but indestructible).

*Gyanam is the principle, which illumines the triad of knower, known and knowing, thus it is Consciousness.

Thus the God principle or Brahman is all encompassing, Omniscient, eternal, non dual, existence, consciousness, knowing which there is neither sorrow or joy... only bliss.

Sat-Chit-Anand.

MANANA ON THE SECOND STATEMENT=

Every thing and being is composed of six components-

1. existence/sat,

2. consciousness/chit.

3. bliss/anand,

4. nama,

5. roopa and

6. function.

The first three elements are common to all and unchanging, thus fundamental & can be called ones innate nature. The last three elements are changing sensory perceptions. That which is unchanging is Sattwi/truth. That which is changing and impermanent isMithya (not Asat).

The Unchanging principle in every thing and being is the Godly principle/Brahman/Iswara.

The changing/impermanent principle in everything is Maya.

The changing principles may or may not be there, but the Sat Chit Anand, is there always and ever, for all.

Every thing and being, in essence is Brahman/Iswara only... isavasyam idam sarvam.

MANANA ON THIRD STATEMENT=

Brahman is in all and all is in Brahman. The ultimate statement on nonduality.

Brahman is like the space, the one and only.

But appears separate. like the space in the pot, the space in the body, the space in the atom etc. When the limiting boundaries which are transient and impermanent, breaks, the individual percepted spaces becomes one with the universal space. So does the individual consciousness(chittakash), merges into the universal consciousness (chidakash), ontranscendence of the limitations of body-mind ego.

All is in the universal existence consciousness.

Without the existence- consciousness in one; one is not.

MANANA ON THE 4TH STATEMENT

Every thing and being reflects the elements of existence- consciousness, in varying proportions, this is the Atman, which is same as Brahman.

MANANA ON 5TH & 6TH STATEMENT

That Godly principle/Brahman, is the essence in one and all, That is your essence- That thou art.

When a body mind realizes such a truth by analysis; as the Brahman is in me and also in all that is. Then all is one alone Brahman, none else exists in reality over the all times, space & causation.

Brahma swatti, jagat mithya, jeevo brahmaivo naparah.

"kase naman karu mai, jab sab hi Ram Ram Ram." - whom do I bow down to; when all is the supreme in essence.

Since the supreme is all powerful, it can be with and without form. Both transcendent and immanent. If it be said that God is only formless and can not exist as a form; is a limitation to the all powerful and all pervading nature of God, and vice versa.

The innumerable forms of gods, not prevalent in vedic periods (when only the five elements were worshiped), went on to be worshiped in different forms, representing a desire to be fulfilled in transaction.

In vedic tradition there is the use of the term yajna, instead of worship. Yajna is the one pointed dedication of doership, doing and outcome as an oblation to the presiding deity of desire, an act of karma yoga for pure mental state of transaction.

Till the time, when a body mind realises the impermanence of all (vairagya), and starts seeking Why, What, and Who am I? (by viveka, sravana, manana and nididhyasana).

To Realize Finally,

When one searches for God, one finds the self. When one introspects into the self, one finds God.

Hari ॐ.

88

SENSE ORGANS & IT'S RELATION TO INTELLECT

A] RELATION OF SENSE ORGANS IN ONE WITH CLEAR INTELLECT =

The sense organs are the horses of the chariot of gross body of the owner(jeeva), the intellect is the charioteer & the mind is the reins, to control the horses of sense organs, directed out in the path of objects of jagat.

If the intellect is clear in discrimination of the sreyas(eternal); from the preyas(ephemeral). Then the charioteer intellect, which is the driver of journey, knows the path & destination & also the purpose of journey of life.

Such a charioteer intellect, has trained & nourished the horses of sense organs by sama dama & sadhana chatushtaya, which follows its command lovingly, when conveyed by the mind reins.

The horses of sense organs of such a chariot, are disciplined & with intent of purpose, to end the journey of transmigration. The destination of Atman/ Brahman is reached, which is not a journey in space or time, but in realization of ones real nature, which was there always but covered in superimpositions.

B] THE SENSE ORGANS IN UNCLEAR INTELLECT An unclear intellect as charioteer, of the chariot of body & jeeva, is devoid of discriminatiin of shreyas from preyas. Thus One Chooses The Ephemeral Over The Eternal.

There is no intent of purpose of such a journey, steeped in ignorance of destination of Atma Brahma eyaikam. The journey of such a jeeva (owner of chariot), is an unending search for permanent bliss amongst, desire fulfillment of impermanent objects & jagat.

A dash from womb to tomb, again & again.

An impure rein, as mind steeped in immoral, criminal and dull thoughts; make the rein of control over the horses of sensory organs, weak, ultimately breaking to make the horses uncontrolled desire seeking agents of charvakas.

Such an ignorant, charioteer intellect, has no knowledge of the horses of sense organs & vice versa. The reins of mind are not controlled & are instead a whirpool of thoughts indesires, leading the horses of sense organs to run amuck, in the karma of samsara.

The charioteer (intellect) & owner (jeeva) of the chariot (body), is led by the wild horses (sense organs), in a purposeless & directionless journey (samsara); full of dangers of accident (birth-death). Which should have been the other way round.

Hari ॐ.

89

RESULTS OF UNCLEAR INTELLECT

1.   There is ignorance about the purpose of human life, which appears to be fulfillment of sensory pursuits rather than self realization.

2.   The horses of sense organs, lead the owner(jeeva) of chariot (body) & its charioteer (intellect), in a wild run amongst paths of impermanent objects. The owner & charioteer are enslaved by the horses, instead of being the other way round.

3.   The reins of mind are weak and this leads to an uncontrolled journey of life with no directions.

4.   A directionless and uncontrolled journey of life led by uncontrolled horses of sense organs is fraught with dangers of repeated accidents, inform of births & deaths.

5.   The destination reached (samsara); is not what is intended (self realization/Brahman).

RESULTS OF CLEAR INTELLECT

1.   There is knowledge of purpose of journey called human life, as self realization.

2.   The owner (jeeva) of the chariot (body), has as the charioteer a clear intellect, which has strengthened the reins of mind by sadhana chatushtaya & gyan, so as to have complete control over the horses of sense organs. The owner is the master & not the enslaved.

3.   The reins of mind are firm in control, thus guiding the horses of senses in a directed journey to destination of self realization.

4.   A controlled & directed journey, attains to self realization, the supreme state, from which there is no coming back in transmigration.

5.   Intended and reached destination is same-Brahma atman aikyam.

Hari ॐ.

90

THE STATE SUPREME IS PURUSA

"indriya bhyah para hyartha, arthe bhyas ca param manah. manasastu para buddhi, buddheratma manah parah.

Mahatah paramavyaktam, avyaktat purusah parah. purusanna paramkincit, sakasth asapara gatih."

... Kathaup. 1. 3. 10-11.

In the spectrum of gross to subtle, the sense organs with limited perceptions are the grossest. The sense objects with a wider pervasiveness beyond the limits of sense organs are the next subtle. Next in hierarchy of subtlery is the mind with a capacity to imagine & percieve even in absence of objects. The intellect is more subtle than mind, as it discriminates the thoughts of mind. The total cosmic intellect of Hiranyagarbha is more pervasive as it encompasses the total subtle. The unmanifested causal is the next more subtle, as it is unknown as the vasanas of Maya, of the creator Iswara. Beyond the unmanifest is the most subtle Purusa/Brahman/Parmatman/Visnu (not the Iswara swaroopa) (avyaktat purusah parah). This is the epitome of subtely, the supreme realisation beyond which there is nothing more to be realised. This is a positive state of subjective, objectless consciousness & not nothingness.

LOCATION OF THE STATE SUPREME (PURUSHA/VISHNU)=

"esa sarvesu bhutesu gudhotmana praksate.

drsyate tvagryaya buddhya suksmayasu ksmadarsibhih.".. Kathaup. 1. 3. 12. It is the very essence of being. Said to be in the allegorical heart.

Purusa means- PURNATVAT (complete fullness/infinite) or PURISAYANAT (resident consciousness, the substratum of being).

Visnu means- Visati sarvam (that which is in all.) or Vyapana silah (the al lpervading).

This is the very self of every being(nearer than nearest), ever present, yet unknown due to adhyasa of panchokosa (avarana) & vikshepa of outside jagat (farther than the farthest).

A mind intellect cleaned by karma yoga, purified by bhakti in shruti & guru, polished in gyan of sravana, manana & niddhidhyasana, is the harbringer of subtle and single pointed intellect; capable of dissolving in & as the Brahman.

Hari ॐ.

91

MITHYA OVER IMPERMANENCE

"ब्रह्म सत्यं जगत मिथ्या जीवोब्रमैहव नापरह"

Is a very profound & useful vedantic statement.

The world of objects & beings are known to be transient and impermanent. Yet the passion & desires for them does not cease to end for a samsari.

Though known by all, to be impermanent, yet the desire for tasty food & drinks, beautiful apparels, objects, places & relations are desired.

Actually the impermanent factor of things & beings; adds to the fervor of acquisition & holding on to it. Thus increasing desire & karma.

Along with the associated joy of aquisition & savoury, the anger and sorrow of faliure or loss & the anxiety of holding on to.... in a spectrum of emotional sufferings.

There is mental suffering & affliction in joy, sufferings, pain, loss, death, disease etc. When it pertains to oneself in doership & enjoyership.

However the same emotions are enjoyed in a movie of tragedy, love, adventures, horror, etc. Since it is known to be an illusion & appearance only, eg. Mithya (viveka).

One is not affected in the knowledge of it being an illusion/movie (unattached sakshi), not attached to the happenings in retrospect (vairagya), and only in blissed self.

Thus knowing Jagat to be Mithya, is more powerful than knowing it to be impermanent. As it nurtures the viveka, vairagya, unattached Sakshi bhava & to be blissed in all its play.

A state of fortitude & equanimity. The doorway to self realization.

A different logical contemplation of-

ब्रह्म सत्यम जगत मिथ्या

1.   Everything and being in the world ORIGINATES & ENDS.

2.   That which is EXISTENT,

     Does not ORIGINATE; as it was already existing.

3.   That which is NON EXISTENT, does not originate; as it is not there like the horns of Hare.

4.   That which is both Existent & Non existent, does not originate. As contradictions do not form a unity.

5.   Thus that which ORIGINATES (hence ends also); is neither EXISTENT or NON EXISTENT...... an APPEARANCE only.

6.   So from absolute standpoint, where EXISTENCE is the eternal truth.

     It stands, that NOTHING ORIGINATES.

     Hari Om.

     Hari ॐ.

92

AVIDYA -KAMA-KARMA

The cycle of Bondage.

Avidya is ignorance of one's true nature as the infinite, immortal Atman, and consideration of one self as the finite body mind jeeva.

There is veiling of the self & projection of the subtle mind, kindled by vasanas of causal; into finite external jagat.

This ignorance initiates thoughts of dualities, as likes & dislikes towards objects, which are desires. All desire is for the self & for happiness. A mistaken self identity due to avidya, results in misdirected desire of finites, instead of the infinite. Finite objects give finite joy, which are transient.

There arises waves of thoughts of desire in the mind, which becomes turmoil. There is action as karma to fulfill desires, with subsequent sanchita, prarabdha & agama karma phala.

The adhyasa of gross body, gives rise to karta bodha while the superimposed subtle body gives bhokta bodha, in all thoughts & action.

Though the outcome of desire & karmas are transient, yet they leave imprints of vasanas in the causal body, which are long lasting & creates new desires & karmas. A never ending seeking, of mirage water to quench thirst of happiness. A continous succession of birth to death embodied experiences in transmigrationThe bondage of samsara.

Ignorance is the root, in the triad of avidya- kama- karma, as the cause of bondage. The dispeller of ignorance is only by knowledge.

SELF KNOWLEDGE, is aparoksha anubhuti of a changed viewpoint.

Before; one feels as a human being with occasional spiritual experiences.

After; one feels as a spiritual being with occassional human experience; till then when the experiencer, experiencing & experienced, all merges into a nondual consciousness.

There is an end to the feeling of oneself as the body mind intellect & realisation of one & all as only the nondual unborn existence consciousness bliss itself.

The end of avidya. In such a realisation, when all in essence is the self; there remains nothing to be desired. No thought waves, resulting in no mind. In absence of mind, the vasanas of causal cease to manifest. The desires for happiness in objects end, with the realization of one's nature as bliss itself. The Desireless bliss.

With no desire, there remains no karma.

Karmas are enjoined with karmaphala, which one has to redeem in different embodied forms, thus a continnum of transmigration.

Karma is for aquiring, purifying, modifying or destroying. With self realisation as

"Atman"-

a)   which is the all pervading:thus there is no karma to aquire.

b)   which is ever pure; there is no karma to purify.

c)   which is attributeless; there remains no karma to modify that without attributes.

d)   which is unborn & eternal : there remains no karma to destroy. End of all karmas.

"bhidyate hrdaya granthi, chidyante sarva samasayah, ksiyante casya karmani, tasmindriste paravare.".. Mundaka Up. 2. 2. 8. explain the prayojana of (anubandha chatushtaya), Brahmavidya/Upanishad.

1. Cuts the knot of Hrdaya granthi.

Removes all doubts.

Removes bondage of karma into Naiskamyasiddhi. For one with aparoksha anubhuti of Atman.

THE KNOT OF HRDAYA- GRANTHI

Is the three knots of AVIDYA-KAMA-KARMA. THE KNOT OF IGNORANCE=Hrdayam is Hrt (supreme atman/consciousness)+ ayam (this body). The Atman is real & eternal, whereas the body is mithya & ephemeral. The avidya (ignorance) of the immortal self (as Atman) & the adhyasa of the mortal body as the self is the greatest ignorance. The ignorance of sel for one's real nature.

As to, - since when is one ignorant of self? Since times eternal... beginningless.

But ignorance ends with knowledge.

Self ignorance ends with Atma gyan.

When the body mind intellect, is considered as the self due to ignorance of the immortal Atman as ones real self; there is the initiation of enjoyership of desires, with subsequent karmas to fulfill it.

Thus in the triad of avidya- kama- karma. a jeeva is led into the mirage of karta- bhokta bodha of jagat as a samsari.

In the tree of jagat, the root is the ignorance. The trunk & branches of desire arise from it. From the branches of desires, there arise the karmas & karmaphalas as flowers & fruits with seeds, to give renewed embodiment.

Ignorance is thus the root(main cause), of binding of the hrt (eternal atman) with the ephemeral (ayam/body).

THE KNOT OF DESIRE (KAMA)=When there is superimposition of the body mind intellect, as the self; instead of the blissful & infinite Atman (as self), due to ignorance. There arises the second knot of bondage. Atman which is full & infinite bliss, needs no desire, to be full or to be happy. Whereas the avidya adhyasa of body mind is finite & thus desires for fullness & joy, for body in gross & the mind in subtle arises. The thoughts of desire arise in mind, like series of waves which induces body into action. The sea of mind made turbulent by waves of desire, makes the jeeva restless & loose its tranquility, till the desire is apparently fulfilled. Only to give risecto another desire in a geometric progression. The the objects of desires in vyvarika are themself finite & its fulfillment is incapable of giving infinite lasting joy. The thoughts of desire reap transientjoys on fulfillment, yet there is creation of imprints of vasanas in the causal body which are long lasting & emanates new desires later, to aggravate desire with dissatisfaction... in repeated bonds (knots), of transmigrations.

THE KNOT OF KARMA=Any action is for aquisition, modification, purification or destruction of any object in gross or subtle. Desire is the initiator of all actions. Ignorance is the initiator of desire.

Every outcome of karma (karmaphala) is to be exhausted, be it sanchita, prarabdha or agama; in this or later embodiments. Thus karma is the knot of transmigration experienced as doership (kartabodha) & enjoyership (bhokta bodha). The enjoyership may be in joy/sorrow or a mixture, but it creates vasanas in the subtle, which is a progenitor of further desires & further karmas.

The avidya of one self as the body mind is the root cause of karma.

The atman which is ones real self (nature), is all pervasive- hence non aquisible;

is without upadhis- hence non modifiable; is ever pure- hence non purifiable;

is unborn eternal- hence indestructible. Thus there is no karma in the (paramarthika) self (Atman).

Hari ॐ.

93

A JNANI

(Is not affected by Karma Phala).

Karmaphala manifestes as embodied experience of kartabodha(doership) of body(gross) & bhokta bodha (enjoyership) of mind(subtle); by manifesting as prarabdha; the vasanas of causal & sanchita karmas of past lives, with an added free will of agami karma(in human embodiment only).

Thus for law of karma to function, there is the need of-

1. Jeeva in ignorance of Atman as self.

2. The superimposition of body mind intellect as the self.

3. Karta & bhokta bodha.

4. The dualities of jagat for doership & enjoyership.

Karma functions as-

a) Sanchita- karmas accumulated in all past lives & unfructified karmas of this life which are added on.

b) Prarabdha-the part of sanchita karmas which has fructified, giving rise to the present embodiment.

c) Agami karma-karmas of free will of present human life only (some gives results in this life, some is added to sanchita).

The realization of a Jnani-

I am not the body, not the mind intellect.

I am of the nature of ever pure Atman.

The moment of this realization, negates the body mind as the superimposed self along with it's doership & enjoyership. There is nothing on which the sanchita karma can fructify, in the absence of body mind doer enjoyer.

Sanchita karma is burnt instantly in the fire of atmagyan.

As to agami karma, a jnani is without enjoyership & doership. Unattached to the outcome & means like the unwetted lotus leaf in water. Unfructified agami fails to be added on; as sanchita is already destroyed. The fructifying agami continues in the present prarabdha.

As to Prarabdha, it continues till the body lasts finally for the body to merge in the five gross,& subtle; to merge in the tanmatras.

But since there is no doership & enjoyership, the jnani is just a witness to the actions of prarabdha as a divine leela. Yet acts of papa & punya of present prarabdha are distributed respectively amongst the detractors & benefactors of the jnani. Till prarabdha lasts, thekarmas of jnani are those of a brahmanistha guru, to guide the seekers of atmagyan. Thus karma phalas do not accur to a self realized being.

STATE OF A JNANI

Akriyavan (Atma rati &Atma krida) is a jnani.

Established in "the self in all"; discriminating the ephemeral nama roopa from the eternal self (Atman), in all & negating the transient & ever established in the eternal Atman. Revelling incit. Atmarati. Action in inaction.

Established in"all in the self"; transacting in nama roopa as a leela/krida; yet remainingfirmly established in the essence of Atman in all. Atma krida. One continues being active in serving one & all as the self only. Inaction in action.

PRAYOJANA (OF ATMAGYAN/BRAHMA ATMA EIKYAM)

Positive Results Attained By A Jnani-

1. The knower of Brahman, attains the supreme Brahman.

2. Brahman is eternal bliss & it's knower attains to that eternal infinite bliss. It is that bliss from which one is born, in which one thrives & into it, one dissolves.

3. All desires are fulfilled instantly, since all is the self. There Remains Nothing To Desire

4. Crosses all sins & karmas of samsara, to be one with the Self (Atman).

5. All, in such beings linage, are seekers of Atma gyan.

6. Identifying the self as Atman (eternal) at all times. without doubt & negating the finite superimposed nonself body mind, as self. One realizes immortality as one's true nature.

Negative results of Janani-

There is no ignorance of self, the jagat appears but is not an eternal truth, there is no sorrow, delusion, fear, hatred, doubt, desire or desire prompted action. Since all is the self, there is no hatred, only love for all.

There is no duty left to perform, without the body mind intellect ego. State Of Complete Contentment.

There is no vivada as there is none to debate with.

Established in the silent language of nonduality.

Hari ॐ.

94

DOUBTS OF A SEEKER

DILEMMAS IN ADVAITA

1) IF BRAHMAN IS SUPREME, HOW COULD A GREATER POWER PUT IT UNDER ILLUSION?

BRAHMAN is Supreme, ever free pure consciousness beyond the attributes of Knower- knowing & Known.

Illusion pertains to a knower about anything known.

Thus BRAHMAN is beyond Illusion.

It is like the subtle space or light.(consciousness)... omnipresent. The presence of which, allows appearance of any thing that objects to it, eg. The mind intellect that reflects -refracts or transmits (transparent), it; as per it's make by past vasanas, into mirror-(plane, concave-convex) or

Prism or plain glass or space. Where the appearance changes, yet there is no change or modification to the substratum of light in presence of which all these appears.

It is the mind intellect of jeeva that is under Illusion when it becomes the knower and tries to know the infinite as finite perceptions. Mathematically when infinite is expressed in finite terms, it is an unexpressed error= Maya, the Illusion.

2) IF BRAHMAN HAS NO PARTS, HOW CAN THERE BE A BRAHMAN, THAT IS BOTH LIBERATED & IN BONDAGE?

There is never a rope & a snake both. The snake is only an illusory appearance.

BRAHMAN is partless & ever free consciousness that is ever existing. The rest of creation is just a dream appearance, that has no reality in absolute terms.

The reality is BRAHMAN that is, was & will be(ever free).

As to the bondage, it is the illusory dream. In Dream one found oneself once to be a king & again as bonded. From the waking standpoint it is false.

There is no one in bondage & none liberated.

3) IF THERE IS NO LIBERATED BRAHMAN, HOW IS LIBERATION POSSIBLE?

Liberation is not possible in reality. Since one was never in bondage. It is just an Illusion in ignorance, not known since when... like not knowing Sanskrit. But the knowledge (gyan) of it removes this ignorance & one intuits that which one was always.

Liberation is also a dream.

But a better dream that awakens to reality(nonduality), from the serenading dreams of samsara. The dream of a charging lion.

4) IF THE WORLD IS A DREAM; WHERE MANY A JEEVAS ARE, WITH MANY AN INDIVIDUAL DREAM; WHOSE IS THE DREAM?

The creation is a dream, where the innumerable created are with their individual dreams. These are the individual Taijasas -the vyasti; within the Samasti of Hiranyagarbha.

It is the dream of total mind.

Just as one can have a dream in a dream.

5) HOW COULD THE ATTRIBUTELESS BRAHMAN BE TAUGHT BY ONE?

FOR THAT; ONE HAS TO RECOGNIZE THE NEED TO TEACH.

WHICH IS ITSELF AN ATTRIBUTE IN DUALITY.

Once established in Brahma swaroopa, there is no perception of teacher & taught,... no guru - no sishya. The Brahma Swaroopa of Jeevanmukti.

Established in Brahman, yet with a body mind, that intuits the truth of advaita. Yet the body mind is & in prarabdha; that acts to teach those gross & subtle coverings of oneself (others to the ignorant), the bliss of non duality. Brahma Swaroopa of Jivanmukta. Like the nimitta karma of having a bath, where one cleans one's own parts which are unclean.

6)   Upanishad says that Brahman pervades the entire visible and invisible Cosmic manifestation. It's said that Brahman is without time and space.

If so, why the same is not reflectd in the inanimate/lifeless things and space?

Brahman pervades the universe as existence consciousness.

It appears, depending on what reflects it. A red rose will only reflect red color, not green.

The gross (inanimates) reflects the existence mainly.

The gross and subtle (Viswa & Virat, those with body and mind), reflects both existence and consciousness, in individual & cosmic level.

The subtle only; as Taijasa & Hiranyagarbha reflects only individual & cosmic consciousness.

The causal reflects the bliss of non objectification in individual(pragyana) & cosmic (Iswara).

All however is a reflection only of the effulgent Brahman, which is inapparent. Like the light in space, which is fully there but appears dark, till a planet, satellite or meteor reflects it, to make its presence observable.

Hari Om.

FROM DOUBTS OF IGNORANCE;

ARISE DELUSION

The DELUSIONS are of 5 types

1. THE WORLD IS REAL.

2. I AM, THE BODY MIND INTELLECT.

3. I AM A DOER & EXPERIENCER.

4. I AM SEPARATE FROM THE SUPREME.

5. THE SUPREME PURE EXISTENCE CONSCIOUSNESS BLISS; IS NOT I; BUT GOD.

Doubts arise because of-

1. The teachings of paramarthika by shruti & smriti; are contrary to that what is learnt in vyavaharika.

2. The reliance on pratyaksha pramana of senses is more than that of the paroksha pramana of shruti smriti which leads later to aparoksha pramana (difficult for a samsari).

Based on these, there arise three fold doubts-a) Of jeeva. b) Of jagat. & c) Of Iswara.

DOUBTS OF & ABOUT JEEVA

pertains to panchakosha, karya karana & states of being.

Panchakosha doubts

Annamaya doubts-

Doubts about how to maintain body, what to eat, how to live, what to achieve, duties to self, family, society, nation & world. As to what is dharma & adharma etc are all transactional doubts of gross body.

Pranamaya doubts-

Doubts & thoughts of bodily functions, disease- wellbeing etc. are dilemmas of transactional pranas.

Mano - Vignanamaya doubts-

Doubts about happiness-sorrow, love-hate, good-preferable, etc. are all transactional dilemmas of mind & intellect.

State of being doubts-

Doubts on dream & waking, as to what is true? The state of deep sleep & its nature. Are all dilemmas of the three states of being.

Karya - Karana doubts -

Karya karana doubts of where & from what has one come & unto what does one go? Ultimately ending in the final doubt about one self"what or who am I?"

One becomes a seeker, to be guided by mother shruti.

DOUBTS OF JAGAT-

What is this universe, what is its origin & its fate? How does it function in the micro & macrocosm. All these doubts leading into external exploration of material science as the big bang,-waxing waning -ever lasting theory.

The quantum & atomic theory of microcosm.

The theory of relativity of macrocosm. Ultimately to end in the Uncertainty principle & yet doubt remains.

Viewed poetically & philosophically, the passions of joy or melancholy give dualities to experience. Yet the final answer is far from achieved.

Delving into karana of jagat, one moves from gross matter to elements, then to molecules, atoms, subatomic particles, quarks, strings, waves &, into uncertainty of remaining doubts.

Thinking philosophically & spiritually into the cause, one proceeds from satkaryavada, asatkarvad, srishti drishti, drishti srishti to finally end in ajativada.

DOUBTS ON SUPREME/ISWARA-

Debates on the existence of Iswara/Brahman; amongst various lineage of thinkers. Amongst the astika darshanas, the sankhya & amongst nastikas all, do not believe in Iswara's existence.

There is bever a debate

 on some thing non existent.

Thus such a debate is proof enough of Iswaras existence.

Iswara is as real as the jeeva;

so long as the jeeva considers one self to be real.

For Science; to doubt Iswara; is scientific double speak. Science is based on cause & effect. Yet when it comes to the effect- universe, it is reluctant to accept, the cause.

DOUBTS FLOATING IN CONTEMPLATION

From Absolute standpoint =

1. The act of a knower, knowing a known is in the ambit of avidya.

2. To a realised being in & as pure consciousness; the standpoint of a knower in knowledge of a known is not possible.

3. There are instances of realised masters preaching the dream of charging lion, as Vedanta; to others who are seekers & supposedly in dream of ignorance.

Who is it that preaches & writes, for whom & about what?

4. In terms of Advaita the language of Brahmagyan appears to be the language of silence.

5. Is it then, that those who have preached or written; have done so in the penultimate state before dissolving into the silence of realisation?

6. If that be; then there is no Jeevenmukti of teachers & gurus.

Jeevanmukti is only when one goes into silence as Jada Bharata or an unheard sanyasi established in Brahmagyan.

Or only when such Gurus preaching at the boundary of ignorance & gyan; passes into Vidheamukti.

SELF REALIZATION (END OF

ALL DOUBTS)=

What Is That By Knowing Which, all is known?

That thou art;

As the substratum & eternal truth (as the Atman), in one & all.

Isa vasyam sarvam idam.

Knowing that Atman as existence-consciousness-bliss; the substratum of one & all; all isknown in essence. Nothing is left to know.

The aproksha anubhuti of "Aham Brahmasmi"; is revelation of one's eternal nature by removing the ephemeral superimpositions of body mind intellect, due to ignorance. The state of infinite fullness. Nothing Left to know-acquire or relinquish.

The doubter, doubting & doubt all dissolves into non dual consciousness -Brahman.

Hari ॐ.

95

MIS UNDERSTANDING THE PANCHAKOSHA VIVEKA

The tenth man on reaching the other side of river, counts his other nine companions.

Ignorantly oblivious of his own self. A void stares at him as the absence of one companion. Then he starts to grieve at an imagined drowning of the missing tenth person. Thus suffering.

A seeker using the discrimination of Nitya Anitya viveka, on one's bodily components;

In the PANCHAKOSHA contemplation, a) wherein; one is the seer of that which is separate, transient, observable & non conscious.

b) Whereas the observer is not the observed.

Realises progressively that, One (I); am=

1. Not the Body.

2. Not the Prana (life forces).

3. Not the Mind.

4. Not the Intellect.

5. Not the Causal bliss.

Finally to stare at a blank objective void.

Is this VOID/SHUNYA; the Self/Atman?

In the story of tenth man; - The seer of nine persons & the void; Is the tenth.

"You are the tenth", as pointed by an outsider (knowledgeable passersby).

In the PANCHAKOSHA viveki, the fallacy of Shunya/Void as the last remnant, as self/Atman; is due to a category error.

The error of search of the SUBJECTIVE Self, amongst the empty bag of five bodily OBJECTS.

The seer of Panchakosha & the seer of, end of the bodily objectives (the void/shunya); is the Self/Atman.

The void is the ultimate object of final discrimination, like deep sleep.

The consciousness in which this intuition arises -

1. Is the Sakshi which witnesses the experience.

2. The pure being Atman/Self when, sans the witnessing. In realm of silence beyond the triputi of knower- knowing & known.

The eleventh knowing passersby gives the indication to the ignorant tenth, to be the tenth. That he already was.

The eleventh to the viveki is the Shruti/Smriti or Guru, who Indicates the truth as "Tat Twam Asi".

Yet a living realisation is one's own unshakable intuition as "Aham Brahmasmi" & "Brahma sattwi Jagat Mithya".

Hari ॐ.

"A DIALOGUE IN THE DARK" EXPERIENCE

In a special restaurant, where the ambience is pitch dark. One is ushered by a guide who moved confidently and led the diner to the seat. The seat is felt by touch & a spatial orientation based on touch; of table, spoon etc. is arrived at. Co diners are percepted by sound of voices. The fresh flowers in the vase could be apprehended by its fragrance. The aroma ushered the servings of choicest food along with the sound of sizzlers. Yet all without sight.

The food was savoured by the feel of its texture & temperature; then by its aroma & finally by its delicious taste.

Initially one might feel an incomplete dining experience, without sight.

However at last when one was ushered out, guided by a staff, to whom it was normal. It was revealed, that all staffs there were visually impaired.

For the diners it was a tryst of visually challenged experience!

A little introspection revealed, that never before was taste, touch or aroma of dining so experienced, in presence of sight.

The absence of one or more senses, accentuates the function & experience of the other senses, so commonly seen in the animal kingdom. Thus withdrawal of senses, highlights the mind. Withdrawl of mind intellect, leaves the non dual consciousness alone.

The overriding outgoing senses, though being incomplete themselves; sum up in incompleteness, to give a transactional false sense of completeness. For example, the eyes perceive only a limited range of electromagnetic waves, the hearing is limited in auditory range, so is taste & touch.

All experiences are in consciousness, which enlivens the individual senses & mind intellect. The sensations & state of mind intellect is experienced; but consciousness isn't.

Advaitic enquiry by hearing, contemplation & niddhidhyasana (abidance/meditation), when leads one, unto constant abidance into the eye of the eye, ear of the ear, mind of the mind; is a state of pure, one & only subjective consciousness; without an object. When all the senses & mind intellect has withdrawn into the inner self/Atman. There remains only the consciousness, without the reflecting mind or projecting senses... the Manonasa. Ones own real, yet, so far unknown nature-The Self.

There remains no objective experience, except consciousness & one is consciousness (pragyanam) itself.

"Pragyanam Brahma".

"Ayam atman Brahman".

Thus-ayam atman pragyanam. The self is consciousness.

Hari ॐ.

TWO ASPECTS OF SELF REALIZATION

"SELF IN ALL (B. Gita Ch. 10- Vibhuti yoga).

& ALL IN THE SELF (B. Gita Ch. 11-Cosmic form).

In chapter 10, is explained as Vibhuti yoga, how the self is the substratum of all. The one in all - The clay, in all pots of different names, forms & uses. To realize the substratum (clay), in all (pots); one has to use the mind & senses alone, in knowledge. The plurality of all remains as a transactional reality & only an intuitive realization of the singularity, as the essence of all, is gained. ATMA KRIDA.

In chapter 11, of the Cosmic form, is explained "all in the self". All the dynamic multiplicity (pots); are potentially, existent in the clay. To have such a realization of all plurality (names & forms/pots), in the one total singularity (Clay); there is the need of detachment from the names & forms of multitude, along with a special gyan vision of the total singularity & unbroken abidance in it. The plurality becomes mithya, singularity (Brahman), alone is. Reveling in the one alone (Atman/Brahman)- ATMA RAMA.

Self realization is complete only when both Atma krida(self in all) & Atmarama (all in the self), becomes one's unbroken abidance.

Hari ॐ.

98

SYMPHONY OF MELODIES OF UPANISHADS

(SELF ENQUIRY)

स होवाच: न वा अरे पत्युः कामाय पतिः प्रियो भवति, आत्मनस्तु कामाय पतिः प्रियो भवति । न वा अरे जायायै कामाय जाया प्रिया भवति, आत्मनस्तु कामाय जाया प्रिया भवति । न वा अरे पूत्राणां कामाय पुत्राः प्रिया भवन्ति, आत्मनस्तु कामाय पुत्राः प्रिया भवन्ति । न वा अरे वित्तस्य कामाय वित्तं प्रियं भवति, आत्मनस्तु कामाय वित्तं प्रियं भवति । न वा अरे ब्रह्मणः कामाय ब्रह्म प्रियं भवति, आत्मनस्तु कामाय ब्रह्म प्रियं भवति । न वा अरे क्षत्रस्य कामाय क्षत्रं प्रियं भवति, आत्मनस्तु कामाय क्षत्रं प्रियं भवति । न वा अरे लोकानां कामाय लोकाः प्रिया भवन्ति, आत्मनस्तु कामाय लोकाः प्रिया भवन्ति । न वा अरे देवानां कामाय देवाः प्रिया भवन्ति, आत्मनस्तु कामाय देवाः प्रिया भवन्ति । न वा अरे भूतानां कामाय भूतानि प्रियाणि भवन्ति, आत्मनस्तु कामाय भूतानि प्रियाणि भवन्ति । न वा अरे सर्वस्य कामाय सर्वं प्रियं भवति, आत्मनस्तु कामाय सर्वं प्रियं भवति । आत्मा वा अरे द्रष्टव्यः श्रोतव्यो मन्तव्यो निदिध्यासितव्यो मैत्रेयि, आत्मनो वा अरे दर्शनेन श्रवणेन मत्या विज्ञानेनेदं सर्वं विदितम् ॥ ५ ॥

THE GREATEST LOVE- Is the love of self. Everything loved is for the sake of self (Brihadaran. up). Every work is for the self.

Any one will say, "I love my work/love my family/love my parents/love my country etc..

However if said that, one is allowed love of work/family/parents/country; except ones own. It is unpalatable. Thus if the common factor MY, is taken out of My (work/family/parents/country); the love vanishes. In fact love for everything is for the sake of Myness (self).

THE CHOICE & LOVE OF DESIRES-

The greatest desire is for the greatest love.

The greatest love is for the self.

The greatest desire & love is uncompromising, unpartable, without a choice of giving up- choiceless.

Thus the love & desire for Self is choiceless.

In the happiness for an object, the objects are with a choice, changeable & finite. The happiness itself is however choiceless. The desire & love of any object is for hapiness. As choicelessness is the greatest love or self. Thus happiness or Bliss is the nature of Self.

Any desire or love limited in finiteness of time space, is choicable, with provision of increment or change. However when limits of time space is removed, then it is love for infinite. This is an ultimate desire & the ultimate love, which does not have a choice to improve or change. Choiceless. Self is choiceless, thus infinitude is the nature of self.

The desire to exist in a relative existence of God, beings of different realms, human, as a particular professional, as a son/daughter, parent, spouse... are all finites, relative, changable & with a choice. But pure existence itself (be it matter/energy/consciousness), is choiceless. Choicelessness is self, thus Existence pure(attributeless) is the nature of self.

The perception of name, form, & the entire creation of panchabhutas are through manifestation of the senses. Hearing as waves from space. The added touch from air, the added sight from fire, the added taste from water & the added smell from earth. The sensory perceptions are all with a choice, changeable & finite. However the substratum or background on which senses & mind intellect functions, eg pure consciousness is a choiceless necessity or love. Choicelessness is self. Thus pure consciousness is the nature of self.

The nature of self is Bliss(Ananda), Infiniteness(Anantam), Existence pure without attributes (Sat), pure Consciousness (Chit/Gyanam).

Satyam gyanam anantam is Brahman.

Atman (Self) is Sat Chit Anand.

This (ayam), Self(atman); is Brahman.

Aham Brahmasmi.

Hari ॐ.

(from teachings of Yagyavalkya through adi guru Shankaracharya, by Chinmay swami, Atmapriyanand ji, Prabuddhanand ji.

99

ON NATURE OF SUPERIMPOSITION

Experience is of Absolute(paramarthika), Vyvarika(gross subtle) & pratibhasika(subtle) types; in decreasing order of experience of reality.

Superimpositions(adhyasa), can happen in a similar background of experience(gross on gross) or a lower form of experience(subtle on gross or gross on absolute).

EXAMPLES OF ADHAYASA=

A) Adhayasa of lower form of experience

1. Snake on rope.

2. Silver on Shell.

3. Mirage water on sand.

    These are superimposition of subtle on gross(pratibhasika on vyavarika). These superimpositions are easily understandable as non existing superimpositions, by enquiry in knowledge; thus of the nature of ignorance only(which is removed completely by knowledge). The ease of erasing this adhyasa is due to an aparokshanubhuti of the relative higher experience, which here is vyavaharika (gross subtle); leading to removal of ignorance in pratibhasika(subtle).

4. The creation on Brahman

5. The Jeeva on Atman.

    Here the superimposition is of vyavarika, the lower experience on the Absolute(Paramarthika); this becomes difficult to abide, since there is no aparokshanubhuti of paramarthika till self realization. While on being self realized, there is no differentiation between the knower, knowing & known. This is thus a state of being, but not an expression in language or thought.

B) Adhyasa in same level of experience-

1. Ornaments on Gold.

2. Pots on clay.

3. Waves, foam on ocean.

Here the superimpositions are in nama roopa of same form of experience of gross(ornaments, pots, waves) on the same gross substratum(gold, clay, ocean).

Enquiry into nature of such superimpositions in same level of experience, removes the ignorance of permanence of nama roopa, into transience. While the substratum remains.

In the first group(superimposition of lower experience on a higher one), the superimpositions are not of the nature of substratum & vanishes totally with gyan. The jagat vanishes in Turiya(ajativada).

In the second group(superimposition of same realm, on substratum of same level of experience), the nama roopa transaction becomes mithya on enquiry of transience, but the substratum of experience in that relm of consciousness remains, jagat remains- only view point changes(mithyatva).

In reality of Advaita, the experience of the self realized, is from a higher experience of paramarthika, into analysis of vyavarika or pratibhasika, which thus vanishes. Ajativada is more logical than mithyatva & existing.

Asangatwam leading to mithyatwam, leading to ekatvam(ajatam).

Hari ॐ.

100

THE DESIRE OF, THE DESIRELESS

(THE BONDAGE OF THE EVER FREE)

Desire is a feeling to acquire; arising from a feeling of incompleteness, in the absence of another being or thing.

The creation of Iswara; of a being or thing is essentially complete in itself. Hence in essence every person or thing, being complete in itself; is desire less.

THE BEING: The essential nature of a being is the choiceless attributes namely is -ness, knowership & enjoyership.

The isness is existence, which though being apparently transformable, yet is indestructible. The knowership is on the substratum of consciousness, which transcends all states of being (waking-dream-deep sleep & transmigration), thus eternal & complete.

The enjoyership is based on the substratum of bliss, which is choice less for every being.

Thus every being in essential nature is existence-consciousness-bliss (sat chit anand); ones real identity. Which is complete in itself, hence there can be no desire to complete the already complete.

A VEDANTIC STORY: There was once a prince separated at early childhood from parents. Taken care of by a tribe of nomads, from whom the lost one learnt the ways of life & considered oneself as a nomad. Then later the wise minister saw & recognized him.

There was the dilemma of a) ignorance of the reality by the prince, who thought himself as nomad or

b) some one else of mistaken identity.

COROLLARY OF THE STORY & THE TEACHING:

The life of a being, is a case of both ignorance(Avidya) & mistaken identity(adhyasa/superimposition).

Though our real identity is sat chit anand (the desireless). Yet in avidya one forgets it.

Then arises the superimposition of the thing on the being.

The characters of a thing is isness, knowable, & enjoyed. All being traits of object & not the subject.

The knowable thing is the body (healthy, sick, young, old); so are the pranas, an object known(energetic or tired), thus a thing.

The mind is also an object of perception(peaceful. angry, desirous..), thus a thing. The intellect is also an objective percept (dull, bright..), thus a thing.

Though I am the subject & i perceive the objects of my body, my prana, my mind, my intellect, my house.

Though one says that this is my house & i am not the house. Yet out of ignorance & mistaken identity, one says I am sick/tired/depressed or dull; due to :

1. ignorance of ones real identity as sat chit anand (avidya).

2. Superimposition of the thing (body, prana, mind..); on the being (sat chit anand).

This leads to desire of body as health, of the mind as riches & fame, of the intellect as acceptance..... and results, in karmas to fulfill desires, resulting in karmaphalas & transmigration.

Similarly a thing is complete in its isness, knowableness & in being enjoyed. Yet one says sometimes, this house (thing), needs (desires) a paint. The thing (house) does not, only when the being (owner), superimposed his identity on the thing, there appeared the desire (of paint).

CONCLUSION: Desires arise from ignorance of ones real nature of being or thing & a mistaken identity of the thing on the being or by the being on the thing.

This is the teaching of vedanta : removal of ignorance of self (avidya) & removal of mistaken identity (adhyasa).

Hari ॐ.

(my pranams to swami Prabuddhanand ji for the clear insights).

101

MANANA ON WAKING -DREAM & DEEP SLEEP

A) A DOUBT

A question for all, If I create this entire universe with my mind & the waking world is a dream, what about "other" people who can see the SAME universe with "their" minds. The stars I "create" are exactly the same seen by others.

Analysis of Dream=

In your dream, suppose three of you are visiting Alaska to see the northern lights. All three will see it & will also transact between themselves. This will be a true (sleep dream) experience for all three characters of the dream. It will have only subtle & causal elements, in the taijasa, experienced by the viswa nara.

The Dream of total mind(Hiranyagarbha)=

All elements of the dream, has the same experience(just as the dream of viswa nara) of stars, rivers, jagat.. only to realise its falasity on waking to the next higher state of consciousness(Turyia).

The dream of Hiranyagarbha, executed through Virat; includes gross, subtle & causal elements.

The waking, is a dream no doubt. But is not my(body minds) dream. I (body mind), is a part of a dream of the cosmic total mind(hiranyagarbha), of which you are also a part, so we all see the same stars.

Hari Om.

B) IGNORANCE IN DEEP SLEEP

(Truth or Myth?)

In deep sleep, the experience, rather intution of a jeeva is-

1. No experience of body mind intellect as self.

2. No experience of sorrow or joys, even pertaining to the waking or dream experience of the same day; moments ago.

3. No experience of relation, attachment, desire or sankalpa(planning).

4. No objective experience, rather Experience of objectlessness. The subsequent recollection of having felt nothing, on waking up.

5. It is not a drop out void, in the time zone of ones intution of existence. The continum exists, hence is a positive factor, not a void.

6. It is a state of nonduality, from which one wakes up to duality.... the jobs & taxes after the temporary nonduality.

7. The absence superimposition (adhyaropa of jagat, body, mind, intellect) is everyones intuition in deep sleep. There is no doer, nothing done nor the doing.

8. Since nothing is perceived, it is taken as ignorance. While since jagat comes back on awakening, it is considered as seed of ignorance (avidya).

Doubts

a)   One who knows or attains to Nondual Brahman, becomes one with... not to return.

Then how the jagat after deep sleep.

b)   Mandukya - if deep sleep be the Nondual, why the mention of viswa, taijasa, prajna(deep sleep) & Turiya- the fourth, separately?.

c)   If deep sleep is Brahman, then one needs only sleeping pill or General anaesthesia or coma, to be enlightened.

The shrutis (Mandukya included); are the penultimate adhyasa, before the apavada of itself, into the intuition of self. The means of adhyasa as a tool for realisation by apavada, is applicable only for the waking state. Thus the shrutis are for waking contemplation of the unrealised. And the deep sleep as prajna, is, in the shruti, a description from the unrealised waking view of the deep sleep. Since the seeker is as yet unrealised, hence the deep sleep ends in duality of waking, since the self akin to deep sleep is not known till then.

For a jeevan mukta, realized in nonduality.... there is no, knower- known & knowing, only Pure existence consciousness or Self. A state of perpetual deep sleep in both, wakefulness and sleep.

Regarding action done by jeevan mukta, after non duality, it appears to be like inertia of motion of past samskaras : which ultimately ends.

Hari Om.

C) WHO IS IT, THAT AWAKENS TO REALIZATION?

IF ALL IS A DUALITY & MITHYA, OF WHICH THE SEEKER IS A PART.

The mind is an absolute reality, when perceived in its true nature of unobjectified consciousness= the SELF.

THE DREAM mind, oscillates between being, as a subject & also as object. To create a creation of duality by illusion, which is real so long as it lasts, or so long as it is not judged from the next higher state, eg. waking state.

(similar is the waking state, when viewed from a realized state -a dream.)

In the dream of sleep, there is mind as consciousness alone., in its true nature. While there is subtle duality in absence of gross. This is illusory when viewed from the waking state.

Here the mind is the entire duality, in dream.

So long as the mind is present, there is duality.

When the mind is absent as in deep sleep or in the state of Manonasa (realised being); there is no duality.

When one awakens to the realisation, that the Self -alone is & the rest are all transient name -forms & transactions; then there is no more any imagination or thought - No Mind. Thus an absence of any object of realization or any one realized. Only the knowledge is.

The knowledge, which has the absolute as its object, is the absolute itself; non different from it. As heat is to fire.

"In duality, one sees another.... knows another. When all has become Atman alone, then whom could one see, with what........ also, whom could one know & by whom or what?"... Br. Up. 4-5-15.

Hari Om.

D) WAKING UP TO IGNORANCE

A jeeva is body- mind- consciousness. The body prana mind intellect, is objectifiable =IDAM. This idam, is the "apara (lower nature) prakriti".

The consciousness is non objectifiable. It is purely subjective, hence one's swaroopa= AHAM. This aham, is the "para prakriti (higher nature).

The Aham, is intuited only & not perceived.

The Idam is perceived. Jeeva is Aham Swaroopa.

One's own nature or SELF, is infinite.- para prakriti. In duality, there is limitation of any other by me (the body mind) & me by the other, thus finite. So if one's nature is infinite, it has to be "me, as all & all as me."

In Dream of waking, one feels limited in gross, time space & object, as the Body mind intellect; as a finite jeeva.

In the dream of sleep, one feels limited in subtle time space & object. There is search for happiness & also fear in sorrows; in both dreams (sleep & waking).

In sushupti (deep sleep), there is no limitation of oneself as objective body mind, nor is there limitation of objective dimensions of time & space. It is infinite in true sense - the para prakriti of one's self. In sushupti one is just self-Nirvishesham; the Unmanifest. Mano buddhi ahamkar chittani na hum....

The ignorance of Self & the superimposition (adhyasa), of me, as gross body mind in waking dream & subtle body mind in sleep dream, is both transcended in deep sleep. One has no (adhyasa) superimposed gross or subtle. One is just Self (Aham), yet unknown; the pure subject can not be objectified (known). This is beyond all limitations, beyond all dualities of emotions (the greatest joy & sorrow is transcended in it). There is no search of joy, neither is there any fear of any sorrow, in susupti.

This is Ananda of sat Chit Ananda; not joy but Infiniteness. Infiniteness is only eternity & eternity is bliss unlimited.

The intuitive realization of, having not felt anything in sushupti, is not a proof of nothingness, but rather a proof of objectless Aham alone.

Susupti is not a state of ignorance, since there is no time space object to be ignorant about.

There is no ignorance in sushupti, but there is ignorance about sushupti; which is ones para prakriti. This ignorance of ones nature(self), is the Avarana. Then this non perception leads to false perception as projection (vikshepa) of one self as gross, in the so called waking(dream) & the projection of subtle, in sleep(dream).

The waking dream & sleep dream is a projection in the nondual objectless consciousness, viz. Susupti. There is no waking up from sushupti, it is waking up in sushupti - in ignorance of waking dream or sleep dream.

Hari Om.

(As perceived from Swami Prabuddhanand jis discourse on Bhagwat Gita Ch. 7. Discourse 77.)

E) THE MAGIC SHOW (That which is not)

ILLUSION is a wrong or misinterpreted APPEARANCE, eg. preception of a sensory experience, of that which is not.

For any illusory appearance there are three factors= 1) APPEARANCE OF.. 2) APPEARED TO.... 3) APPEARED ON...

ON "THE APPEARANCE OF" - The appearing appearance can not be real, as it is a superimposition on one that is the real. It has no independent existence, without that truth, on which it appears. The snake is unreal & is not- without the rope.

ON "THE APPEARED TO"- It can not be the same. The witness(appeared to) & object witnessed (appearance), are different. The Appeared to (witness), is not affected by the distinctions of the appearances.

In every conscious experience of appearance, there is a changeless principle of consciousness, witnessing the gross- subtle & causal. It is impossible to point out differences in the witnessing consciousness of different beings, hence accepted as the ONE witnessing consciousness in all- The ATMAN. The world (object); appears before it (subject), & is thus not identical with it.

ON "THE APPEARANCE ON"- An illusiory appearance, is never on a void, or without a substratum. Never is an illusion, sans the substratum (no snake, without rope). The illusion is a pseudo (false appearance), on a reality. Thus the illusory appearance is not identical to that which is the truth (substratum). Nor is it (appearance), determinably different from it (the Truth/Substratum), since it is invariably linked to the truth, in ignorance. Only knowledge separates it.

"The entire cosmic manifestation is pervaded by me, in my unmanifested form. All beings dwell in me, but i do not dwell in them."

To the entire illusion/appearance, I (Atman/Truth), is the substratum, without which nothing is.

Yet, I (Atman/Truth) am not of the nature of illusion (appearance/jagat).

"maya tatam idam sarvam jagad avyakta murtina,

mat- sthani sarva bhutani na chaham teshvavasthitah."... B. Gita. ch9-4.

Hari Om.

F) WAKING DREAM & DEEP SLEEP

OF WAKING & DREAM SLEEP

The waking bias is the root of ignorance, into the analysis of waking & dream. In casual viewing, the waking appears real, as to the unreality of dream. Mainly because-

1. Waking objects remain as it is at a later time, while dream objects vanish with dreams end.

2. The world & environment of me & others are shared & same in waking. While dreams are different for different persons.

3. Waking transactions follow a set pattern, while dream transactions are random without a pattern.

4. Waking objects are of use, while dream objects are not.

5. Waking world is stable, dream world is unstable.

6. There is doership in waking, with free will; there is no free will in dream.

This entire common experience is due to an error of reference.

*) To determine truth or falsehood in any concept, there is the need of evaluation of that entiety, by a standard which is more stable/higher or truthful, in comparison to it.

The dream is unreal, only when viewed from the higher waking standpoint.

The waking on the contrary is analysed from same waking standpoint only & not from the higher standpoint of Realisation (Turyia).

The dream, while it lasts; is as real as a waking experience.

There is no difference between WAKING & DREAM, both are the same.

Only, the sleep dream is individual jeevas dream (Taijasa).

While the waking, is the dream of cosmic mind (Hiranyagarbha) & not the jeevas dream. Thus is refuted, the truth of waking reality-

1. As does the dream world vanish at dreams end of Taijasa, so does the waking world vanish at dreams end in Hiranyagarbha (in cosmic dissolution).

2. The environment of all the jeevas is same & shared as a part of the dream of Hiranyagarbha in one universe.

    So is the environment of dream, same & shared for all the participants in the dream of a Taijasa.

3. The set pattern of waking experiences appear normal since it is viewed from the waking perspective only & not from Turyia. Whence it would be as absurd as dream experience viewed from waking viewpoint.

    While in dream, while it lasts; the experiences appear perfectly normal.

4. Waking objects are of use, but in waking conditions only. As are dream objects. The water of waking world is of no use in a dream thirst.

5. Stability is also a myth. The stability of waking world, is stable in time proportions to the dream of Hiranyagarbha; as is the proportional stability of Taijasa dream world in the dream time of jeeva.

6. The ONLY DIFFERENCE OF WAKING & SLEEP DREAM; is the so called freewill or the karma, that makes it's effect of viveka vairagya; to manifest. Thus providing the choice of Shreyas to Preyas.

    Making the Waking to be the one only state, when Self realization & liberation is possible. In dream there is only the expending of minor karmaphalas, as good & bad dreams. There is no new acquisition of sanchita karmas.

7. In the dream of Taijasa, the jeeva goes to a dream sleep & dreams; a dream within the dream & wakes up from that sleep in the dream, as a FALSE AWAKENING.

In the dream of Hiranyagarbha, the jeeva in so called awakening (Viswa); goes to sleep inside the Hiranyagarbha dream & wakes up to awakening (also a) FALSE AWAKENING.

The Natural Waking experience of a jeeva in ignorance, is of SRISTI -DRISTI vada. The creation (sristi) already exists & on waking, one sees (dristi) it as experience.

The natural dream of a sleeping jeeva, is of DRISTI -SRISTI vada, where the visions & impressions of mind experiences (dristi) are already in mind, which projects it as a created world of dreams. The elements of this creation are subtle only with no gross elements. Since the creator is a jeeva in mixed gunas.

The dream of Hiranyagarbha is also a DRISTI -SRISTI, which is this jagat of us. The mental impressions of past creation in terms of residual karmas of jagat at cosmic dissolution is the experience (Dristi), which leads to the dream creation (Sristi). The elements of this dream are gross as well as subtle, since it's creator Hiranyagarbha/Brahma, is beyond gunas.

DEEP SLEEP

Deep sleep of Hiranyagarbha is the cosmic dissolution, where the entire creation is absorbed back.

Deep sleep of jeeva is Brahmanand. Where the mind intellect is folded back, with no objective experience, even of one's body.

There is prana alone that functions. There is not an absence of experience, rather an experience of nondual objective absence. Even the greatest of mental & physical sorrows as absent in this. This is the pure non objectifiable subjective state of Self. Yet on waking up, one is drawn back into samsara. This is due to the the call of prarabdha that binds till then. On waking up there is a moment of transition in bliss, then the calling of samsara is back. The deep sleep is the gateway to dream & waking. The projections of mind is totally absent. This Brahmaswaroppa is not recognised by most, as there is incomplete chitta suddhi, which is a prerequisite to be established in Brahmagyan.

When DEEP SLEEP is recognised as ones basic nature, & not as a state of being; this is the so-called fourth. Turyia.

Hari Om.

G) "LIFE IS BUT A DREAM"

THE DREAM OF SLEEP = In the mind of a single being in dream, there appears multitude of objects, beings, time- space perceptions & transactions; all, so real while it lasts. This is without any change in the essential nature of the one dreaming. This dream is, not unreal while asleep. Also not real, while seen from waking standpoint.

THE WAKING DREAM =The waking world is also, not unproven, as not a dream. It is also of objects, beings, time- space perceptions & transactions, that appears real while the waking lasts. But this is not the dream of an individual. The individual being a part of the dream itself & the dream being the dream of the cosmic (total) mind - Hiranyagarbha.

This dream (effect) too appears in the Absolute total consciousness, without causing any change in it (the cause). This dream is also not unreal as a waker & also not real from the absolute standpoint of Turiya.

That - NOT UNREAL & ALSO NOT REAL, is MITHYA.

"Brahma Satyam, Jagat Mithya."

Hari ॐ.

102

SHREYAS & PREYAS

The desire is the governor of mind, led by the senses, which goads the karma indrias into action.

Desires can be with choice or choiceless.

Those with choice are variable, transient; hence impermanent.

The choicelessness of a desire is because, it is ones own basic nature.

The choiceless desire of a sencient being are of three types-

1.   To exist everywhere & at all times.(infinite existence= Sat)

2.   To know everything & at all times.(infinite consciousness=Chit).

3.   To be happy always & under all circumstances.(infinite bliss= Ananda).

Brahman is "Satyam gyanam anantam Brahman".. Tait. Up. That is Sat Chit Ananda.

Thus ones own basic nature is Brahman..."That thou art".

Every BEING is Existing, Knower & Enjoyer.

Every THING is Existing, Knowable & Enjoyable.

The existence of a thing & being is same & the common Panchabhuta.

The common factor in knowership & knowableship is consciousness, without which it is not. This discrimination is due to Ego, which transmigrates.

The common factor in enjoyership & enjoyedship is bliss, again discriminated due to the Ego.

The entire basis of the asmat & usmat jagat is thus the same existence consciousness & bliss. The common factor of which, like the root of a tree is existence, which apparently branches out the total consciousness into individual knowership & knowableship; while the infinite bliss into finite enjoyership & enjoyableship.

This superimposition of finiteness on infiniteness & individuality on totality, is though apparent & experienceable; yet untenable mathematically, logically & spiritually. It Appears but Not Is(Mithya not false). This is the power of Maya, the creator of Ego.

In essence Me, You, That, This... is the same Brahman. "Sarvam Brahma Mayam."

Hari ॐ.

103

TO WHOM OR WHERE IS NESCIENCE?

Shankara- "In truth, there is no nescience."

It is affecting the ego sense of the person who asks the question on nescience.

Then if, one accepts being affected by nescience; to such a one, nescience is a perceived object or posession. The subjective Self, remains unaffected, yet appears to be affected.

Time is not a reality & bondage- liberation, are not real events or two separate real states of being.

Nescience never affects the subjective Self.

Nescience affects all that is perceived (objective), to afflict.

Enlightenment does not destroy nescience.

It only reveals that nescience never was.

Hari ॐ.

104

THE SIMILARITY IN THE MAKE UP & THE JOURNEY OF A JEEVA

STAGES IN LIFE=(Journey of life)

1. INFANCY- main desire is food.

2. CHILDHOOD- Incessant physical activity is the predominant element.

3. YOUTH- Mental likes & dislikes in & about the world.

4. MIDDLE AGE- Discrimination of hard facts & finding conclusion to life activities, present & past.

5. OLD AGE- Peace & Rest.

See how they relate to PANCHA KOSHA (Make up of a being)

1. Outer Annamaya-food.

2. Pranamaya- activity.

3. Manomaya- mind sheath.

4. Vijnanamaya/Intellect sheath of discrimination.

5. Anandamaya sheath of bliss.

Striking semblence.

Hari ॐ.

105

WHY THE HUMAN EXISTENCE?

It is a stage of evolution, in the scheme of transaction.... in the game (leela) of finding who am I.

In the beginning there was Brahman (the god principle without form) alone.

Brahman is ever(eternal)=existence, consciousness.

The nature of consciousness is to know.

Since it is the only one with none else, its knowing power can know only itself by false projection of itself.. the projecting power.

But to give a sense of reality to the projection in the self, it has to forget its real self identity (Brahman).... the veiling power.

The combination of this veiling and projecting power is MAYA (ignorance), in vedanta.

Since Brahman(God), is infinite in capabality, its projection and veiling is also infallible.

The Brahman projected itself as the objects and jeeva and forgot its real self as Brahman.

Since then one is in the game of finding "Who am I?".

Since the cause of this game is Maya/ignorance.. the solution to this problem of ignorance is the gyan of who am I.

You will ask when did this begin?

Ignorance is beginningless. Suppose you are asked since when do you not know japanese language?The answer is= for ever.

But once you learn japanese. It ends then and there.

In vedanta, the universe is beginningless (Roger penrose.. the waxing and waning theory of universe.)

But with self realization of Brahman(god),

there is only it and all is an illusion.

(Brahman is the only truth eternal, rest is all transactional illusion, and you (the self), is Brahman.

From the amorphous(subtlest=Brahman), came the slight less subtle= space, from it the next less subtle air, from it the next less subtle fire, then the water and finally the gross Earth. The pancha bhutas.

The space element is akin to frequency, symbolised by nada/sound and its sense of hearing, which is first to come and last to go... it is in fact the first sensory perception in any life form. It is also the last sense to leave body at time of death.... the importance of chanting divine names and mantras at time of death.

The air element is akin to touch, the next tactile sensation... in all life forms and is the penultimate one to go before death.... the importance of holding a deathbound by some one loved. Interestingly the air element other than the new touch also conveys, the previous elements sense of sound.

The next is the fire, with previous features of sound, touch an an addition of vision, represented by eye.

The next in line is Water with previous senses of sound, touch, visibility with an added taste perception.

The final is the evolution of the grossest Earth, with the previous sound, touch, sight, taste and the addition of smell.

Correlate these with biology of present century, this is the very sequence of evolution of senses amongst living organism, finally epitomized in primates with fully evolved 5 senses. In death the reverse order is the way one goes back to the panchabhutas.

Absolutely scientific deductions from a civilization, ages ago...

Scientific evolution from unicellular to mankind is the same. It is the evolution of consciousness, not body. Otherwise dianos would have been the topmost creation.

The creation and evolution in Vedanta is explained scientifically by the law of cause and effect. This is the law of karma.

If i say the scorpio car happened just by itself without a cause, you will say mad. But the same scientific mind says, the universe and humans happened by chance, without a cause. This is scientific hypocrisy.

THE LAW OF KARMA(CAUSALITY)

If god is all merciful and loving, how can it create some blind, some with vision, some dull, some intelligent? All the world is an interplay of duality.... The falacity of abrahamic faiths... unexplained.

In vedanta Brahman is non transactional, neither responsible for the good or the bad.

It is a continuation of the balance sheet of our past karmas, that has landed us where and who one is. None to blame, only can be modified by present karmas.

Karmas are

1. sanchita.. accumulated not expending now (fixed deposits).

2. prarabdha.. present karmas that has to be expended as this body of this life time.. cash in hand.

3. agama karma.. ones sankalpa/future plannings.. recurring deposits, which is going to be added to the sanchita/fixed deposit, to be used as prarabdha in next lifes.

So long as there is karma, there is karma phala.. equal reaction, hence rebirth with its joy and sorrow.

To sum up=

Why am i in sorrow?

because of transmigration.

Why transmigration?

because of karma and its phala.

Why then karma?

because of sankalpa/desire.

Why the desire?

because of considering the transient and changeable as the infinite and eternal.

Why this delusion?

Because of ignorance of the eternal.

What is the eternal?

That Thou Art... you are the Brahman as the atman.. and not the body mind that you consider yourself to be.

This holds true for all beings and things.

"ayam atman brahman."

"sarvey idam brahman".

Every being and thing has 5 qualities=

existence, consciousness, bliss, nama, roopa.

The first three are ever existent, indestructible =Brahman.

The last two are transient, changing and finite= Maya.

With vedanta, the world does not change, but with gyan the focus of viewpoint changes to behold the eternal in everything, by forsaking the mortal Maya elements.

"asato ma sat gamaya,

tamaso ma jyotir gamaya,

mrityor ma amritam gamaya."

And all is shanti, shanti, shanti AUM.

Hari ॐ.

106

THE SPIRITUAL PATH

For spiritual initiation, the earlier the better in life; as it reduces formation of impure mental vasanas, while providing the maximum time possible to attain the end. For those without spiritual tendency in active life, there is rarely such, after retirement.

Good past life deeds, induces the quest of spirituality. The grace of supreme, creates the desire to strive for it. The utmost effort in free will of viveka & vairagya, leads to the result of spiritual finale.

In the initial stages, one should avoid objects of desire & attachment, along with thoughts of lower propensities. The mind should be filled with Vedantic thoughts till one falls asleep or, the body drops off.

Even in samsara, a part of the mind intellect, should constantly hold onto the Supreme. Every physical/mental/intellectual, karma should be, as an oblation (yagya) to the service of the supreme. The result, what so ever (good/bad), to be accepted as prasadam of yagya, in same mindedness.

This path is for the fearless, who is ready to sacrifice ones entire I ness & My ness, of this & also of the heavenly worlds.

The motto is only striving for, discrimination, renunciation & knowledge.

The spiritual traveller, should have a healthy body, so as to minimize the body consciousness of the mind. As it is seen that a sick person, is most attached in thoughts of body consciousness.

Repeated hearing of the vedantic truths & repeated contemplation, followed by gradual progression from the objective limited Avatara & saguna brahman; into the final infinite, attributeless, transcendent & immanent subjective Self, as the end & means of meditation. will ultimately help to drop the limited upadhis of name forms & transactions, which one has superimposed on oneself, out of ignorance. In the dawn of self knowledge, one becomes the Self.

Daily hearing, reading & contemplating vedanta, along with some daily practical spiritual practice; is a must for a seeker.

A life of such a seeker is one of purity, meditation, spiritual discipline & mental control. Gradually the viewpoint of all transactions become based on the living realization of divinity in one & all, as the Self.

Thus when all is the Self, what else is there to desire & what is there to renounce?

Hari ॐ.

107

STEPS IN VEDANTA (FIRST STEP) BHAKTI

The world is a composite cognition of nouns & adjectives, through the five senses & the cognition of abstract (love, honesty...) by the mind. In cognition of the abstract, the mind even tries to give a form, name or transaction; to the formless abstract. That is the way of vyavaharika life.

In the story of appearance of creation, there is the appearance of less subtle (pervasive), from the subtlest or all pervasive.

The all pervasive Brahman appears as the Akash first, with its sensory character of vibration; represented by sound (hearing).

From this, the Vayu with sensory representation of touch added to the already existing sound.

Then the Agni, with added sight to the previous sound & touch.

Then Water, with taste added to the previous sound, touch & sight.

Finally Earth with smell added to the previous sound, touch, sight & taste.

To realize the supreme all pervading subtlest Brahman, there is the need to hold on to any or a combination of sensory perception & then analyze its subtle to subtlest essence.

The jeeva being a slave of various senses in combination & the mind, is governed in perception by sensory combination.

The first step of Bhakti is just that guide, unto the path of nondual realization.

For the seeker established principally in the realm of Aakash or sound sense, there is the hold on to the pranava; AUM or Mantras & then to analyze by gyan yoga, its substratum or pervasion by Brahman.

For the one predominantly in the realm of touch of Vayu Tatwa, there is the representation as softness or hardness of a child (bal gopala) or the Shiva linga.

For one in the Agni tattva of sight. there is the resplendent form of mind enchanting smiling bal gopala playing flute. Serenading the sound, touch & sight of seeker.

For one in Jal tattwa of taste, the gentle bal Gopala holding out the butter laddu. serenades the seeker enslaved in the sensory combination of taste, sight, touch & sound.

The seeker ensnared in all the five senses of Earth element, is brought into focus after being weaned away from the jagat of senses, into the beatitudes of bal Gopalas garland of fragrant flowers.

The deity may change depending on the seekers faith.

Then introspection into the successive subtler element of ones worship leads unto AUM.

Then introspection of panchakosha viveka, leads the seeker to realize ones own essence as AUM also.

Such a bhakta & gyani, may be in the appearances of senses, yet is ever established in the thing or being, that pervades all.

Such a scientific way of weaning the senses from the gross to subtle & then the subtlest.

The essence of form worship, in Vedas.

Hari ॐ.

108

ROAD TO HOME COMMING

The samsaric world is an interplay of I ness & myness, along with superimposition of the thing on being (i am this fat body) & the being on the thing (this house needs a paint, the house does not; the owner does).

The I ness arises out of a feeling of limitedness (separate from another).

The myness arise from a sence of incompleteness of body, mind or intellect; as one perceives oneself to be, (eg. oneself will feel complete in possession of another thing or being).

Superimpositions arise out of Avidya (ignorance).

INITIAL STAGE= (I am this)

There is complete overlapping of thing on being & I ness predominating in such a scenario. I am pained by the troubles of my family/country etc.

FIRST STAGE OF VIVEKA=(This is mine)

When the thing is perceived differently from the being.

a)   The family/country/planet; is not me. It is mine(possession).

b)   The body is not me. It is my posession.

c)   Similar introspection with mind & intellect.

In this stage, Myness predominates over I ness. There is resulting desire & karma to keep the possessions in good state & make good use of it(avoiding unwanted & improper use). The stage of control.

Myness predominates over I ness.

SECOND STAGE OF VIVEKA=(This is yours)

The stage of trusteeship.

The body belongs to the Panchabhuta Earth elements.

The smell to the Earth, the taste to water, the sight to fire, the touch to air & the sound to Aakash. And all these to individual Devas & Ishwara.

The individual mind belongs to the total/cosmic mind (Hiranyagarbha).

Even the mindless state of prajna(individual deep sleep), belongs to the total objectless consciousness, which is a positive entity.

The things of jagat are similarly from the panchabhutas. There is nothing objective, that is mine. All are the creations of Iswara by Maya, who is the owner.

This one is its trustee only.

THIRD STAGE OF VIVEKA=(You are this).

The stage of realisation, when it is experienced that the supreme Iswara itself appears as the body, senses, mind, intellect, pranas, jagat & the jeevas.

FOURTH STAGE=(You alone are, none else).

The entire creation of names, forms & transactions have no independent existence.

Are only reflected consciousness & are capable of giving transient joys & sorrows.

It appears, but not is.

It is mithya (neither existent, nor non existent).

It all appears on borrowed existence, consciousness & bliss; from Brahman, which is the only infinite existence consciousness & bliss.

The self is in all that appears- Atma krida.

All that appears is in the Self- Atma rama.

Hari ॐ.

USE OF MIND IN ATMAGYAN

A microbe is not seen by telescope and a distant star is not seen by a microscope.

The choice of wrong instrumentation..

The senses are instruments to perceive the gross. The mind is the instrument to perceive the subtle (thoughts and emotion).

The intellect is the instrument of discrimination (good/preferable).

The sences are the gate way of projection.

The mind by indulging in avidya is the cause of veiling of vidya/self.

Using the intellect sharpened in sadhana (viveka-vairagya and the sat sampatti), to rule over the mind, so as to control the senses as well. Leads to erasure of projection and veiling(Maya nullified). The state of sthitaprajna/manomasa or no mind.

The self reveals then itself (swayamprakasha), when the veils and projections of superimposition have been removed.

The mind intellect is not an instrument to know the self (as the eternal subject is unknowable).

The utility of mind is only to remove the Ego/ahamkara (body-mind-intellect complex), which superimposes itself as the pseudo self over the real self.

Hari ॐ.

110

MIND & DUALITY

The mind assumes duality as imaginations.

Or; The duality imagined by mind is mind itself.

The proof of agreement & difference (anvaya - vyatireka).

**A) When mind is present; duality is present

1)   Duality of dream objects appearing in the individual Taijasa dream..

2)   Duality of waking objects appearing in the cosmic hiranyagarbha mind.

**B) When mind is absent; duality is absent.

1)   In individual vyasti deep sleep when mind is shut down- Prajna- no duality.

2)   In cosmic samasti deep sleep- Iswara.

3)   When mind has become no mind (manonasa); by viveka vairagya & atmagyan.

Vision of duality is ignorance/Bondage.

Vision of unity is knowledge/Liberation.

Hari ॐ.

SADHANA & PRAYOJANA

SADHANA

TYPES=

1. BAHIRANGA (external)

2. ANTARANGA (internal)

3. SAKSHAT (instant).

1. Bahiranga

For any activity there has to an ambient external environment for proper outcome along with internal environment.

Ignorance is the root cause of all bondage. Knowledge is the only antidote of ignorance. For the best outcome of learning, the mind has to be clean, tranquil, with single pointed focus & with faith in the teacher & teachings, without doubt.

For an unclean mind (karma yoga)=

With the mind enmeshed in the vagaries of jagat with endless distractions of desires; it is imperative that the result out weighs the action. To clean the mind of such distraction is the need of karma yoga, so as to work as an oblation & accept the result as the prasadam for Iswara. Then finally to absolve oneself completely from the result. A process of chitta suddhi.

For distracted unfocussed mind (rajyoga)=

The need is dhyana, & japa, so as to remove distractions & make the mind single pointed, in it's aim.

For a doubting faithless mind (bhakti yoga)=

The need is faith/shraddha/bhakti; in the apaurusheya sayings of shruti, smriti & its conduit, the Guru.

All these constitute the bahiranga sadhana, towards realizing the fullest of subsequent gyan.

2. Antaranga Sadhana

Is essential to remove the maladies of abhavana, asambhavana & viparitabhavana.

The complete abscence of knowledge of liberation (abhavana); is removed by hearing/reading from scriptures, about it. This is sravana.

The impossibility(asambhavana) of achieving liberation, even after sravana; is removed by logical contemplation & discussion. This is Manana.

The contrary feelings (viparit bhavana), arising after sravana manana; is removed by practice of meditation. In a life abiding in the truth, realised in sravana manana. This isniddhidhyasana.

All these constitute the antaranga sadhana of gyan yoga, in acquiring the knowledge of self realization or liberation.

Sakshat Sadhana= The realized abidance in the knowledge of"all in Self & the Self in all."Is the point of liberation. This is not something realized in course of time(gradual); in any place (such as heaven) or in particular body (of future transmigration). It is instant -right here & now-Sakshat; not that the world changes or disappears. Only there is an instant change of viewpoint, where the transient transactional world is neither true, nor untrue. Only the essence of all is the truth, which is the eternal, indescribable Self.

Abiding knowledge is the sakshat means of liberation; to which other sadhanas are essential contributes.

TWO TYPES OF GOAL (of Sadhana)

1.   APRAPTA

2.   PRAPTA =

The Aprapta Goal

To get & achieve something else, which is considered not mine or me.

This is a goal only in the realms of duality; when one considers oneself as a separate identity, in time, place or object (animate/inanimate); then there is desire for that which is considered separate.

This goal is principally based on the notions of, me & mine.

Such goals maybe places to go, things to aquire for need, enjoyment or hoarding., or relations & transaction with other jeevas.

The origin of such a goal is due to ignorance of the self in all; thus giving rise to desire to acquire. Then there is the need of transactional knowledge of the object of desire & the knowledge of the means to acquire it.

Following such a knowledge, there has to be a sankalpa (planning), in the mind; which then initiates the body into karma (action); so as to fulfill the apraptata by acquisition.

Aprapta goals are all the desires of transactional world, like food, clothing, house, enjoyments, family, progeny, money, fame, places to visit, time management, care of body mind & even satwik desires of benevolence, charity, education & even the desires of different lokas, after death.

For fulfilling an Aprapta goal, there is thus knowledge followed by karma; always. The Prapta Goal=

That which one is & is already in and as, oneself; but is hidden from the body mind, due to ignorance.

For such a type of desire to be fulfilled, the explanation or knowledge; that it is already achieved or fulfilled; is enough.

There is no need of any further karma to acquire it, since it is already in one self as the; all in the Self.

Seeking of such a goal is seen as in-

a) finding the missing tenth man, by the tenth man himself; while forgetting to count oneself.

b) searching of specs or ornament while wearing it.

c) A prince living from childhood with other non royal group feels himself to be one such commoner; until being told of his real birth status.

d) searching for gold as something separate, yet while all ornaments are lying in front.

e) searching for Brahman in jungles & caves in seclusion after rejecting the creation; while Brahman being right there in all as its essence.

f) searching for liberation from bondage, due to misconception of oneself as jeeva; where as there is none in bondage & none to be liberated, as one is the ever free Atman.

In the above Prapta type of goals & desires, to be fulfilled; there is only the need of knowledge of truth. No subsequent karma or action is needed for its fulfillment.

"KNOWLEDGE IS THE ONLY MEANS OF LIBERATION".

Is not a statement of fanaticism. Fanaticism is a view, which is believed without proof & reasoning, along with acceptance of ones view only, while rejecting others. Such notions may even go contrary to normal experience. It also gives rise to conflict & hatred towards others.

That knowledge is the only means of liberation, is a statement based on proof & experience. Moreover it accepts other means of karma, bhakti, meditation as essential prerequisites to the establishment of knowledge, in daily life; without any conflict or dogmatism, depending on the frame of the mind of seeker.

It is a logical conclusion; that Sorrow of death & transmigration is due to karmas; karmas are due to desires; which are due to vasanas; vasanas arise in duality; duality is due to ignorance of the self in all & all in the self(nonduality). Thus ignorance is the root cause & knowledge is the only remedy for ignorance. This is a proven fact of experience.

The knowledge of nonduality, is knowing that by which allis known as the essence (Atman). And that essence, is the essence of all (Brahman). Brahma Atman aikyam.

Just a knowledge of such a concept, makes one a philosopher, while a living realization, is liberation.

The conduit from philosophy to realisation, is through mind intellect; which is tainted in vasanas & desires, lacking in conviction of liberation & wandering in the dualities of jagat. To cleanse the tainted mind is the need of karma yoga (for chitta suddhi).

To remove the lack of conviction, is the need of sraddha & bhakti, in guru & scripture. After all one has to have faith in Physics books & Einstein & do the experiments in person, when one wants to learn relativity.

A wandering mind, can be made focussed by meditation.

Vedanta does not negate different means of sadhana, but considers them as prerequisite for

a living realization of Atmagyan. How can such a teaching be a fanaticism?

Knowledge is like light. As light enters a dark cave, shrouded in darkness for ages; darkness ends then & there, instantly. So does the dawn of knowledge, ends the beginningless ignorance, then & there. There is instant realization of self as liberation. Like, if it be said that, eyes are meant to see, not ears. It is a statement of fact of experience & not a franatical dogmatic saying.

Moreover there are shruti pramanas which states that there are no other means, other than living realisation of knowledge as means to liberation. "sarva bhutastham atmanam sarva bhutani c atmani, sampasyan brahmapram amyatinanyen ahetuna."Kaivalya Up. 1. 10= Realization of one's self in all & all in the self, one attains the supreme Brahman & not by any other means.

In Bhagwat gita, Sri Krishna says that

"for one in absolute devotion to him, he out of love & compassion, bestows buddhi yoga to the bhakta so as to make the one with him. The Iswara becomes or sends a guru, for realization of the bhakta. (B. Gita-10. 10-11)

Thus gyan yoga is the only ultimate & penultimate means of Atmagyan/ liberation.

Hari ॐ.

KNOWLEDGE ALONE IS THE DIRECT MEANS OF LIBERATION...

As revealed in the Upanishads=

1) Kaivalya Up.(1. 3)-

Not by work, progeny or wealth. It is only by renunciation, that one attains to immortality or liberation.

Work is to acquire, modify, purify or destroy. Liberation which is realization of self as Atman, which is all pervading, attributeless, ever pure & eternal. Thus a complete antithesis of outcome of karma. Similarly progeny & wealth are means to achieve & fulfill needs & desires of this & other worlds, all which are finite. The eternal liberation is unachievable by these.

To realise the ever pure eternal Atman as self, which one already was & is. There is only need to renounce the adhyasa of body mind intellect, as the self. This renunciation is actually a knowledge, which gives intuitive realization of one's essence of immortality.

1. Mundaka Up.(3. 2. 6)-

    Established in the teachings of Upanishads along with a mind purified by the yoga of renunciation (of body mind intellect ego); one attains to the supreme Brahman.

2. Svetasvatara Up.(1. 11)-

    With knowledge of Brahman; all bondage is snapped, ignorance is removed, all sorrows end in the finality of liberation.

With self realization or Brahmagyan, when the self is a reality in all & all in the self, there remains none else. The ignorance of self as body mind is erased, thus all bondages are cut. From the finite jeeva, one is enlightened to one's real nature as immortal Atman.

3. Kaivalya Up.(1. 10)-

By realization of the Self in all & all in the Self, one is liberated; not by any other means. A direct statement about knowledge, as the only means of liberation.

4. Svetasvatara Up.(3. 8)-

also Purusha Suktam(20)-

Knowledge of the self effulgent being as the self, which is beyond darkness & ignorance (of the superimposed non selves as self), is the Atman. The eternal immortal, that what I am, liberated right here & now. There is no other way.

5. Kaivalya Up(1. 17)-

That consciousness that illuminates the waking, dream, deep sleep & beyond; is Brahman. That I am. Knowing this, one is liberated.

Hari ॐ.

VIRTUES NEEDED FOR SELF REALIZATION

Mundaka-upanisad mantra (3. 1. 5) "satyena labhyastapasā hyeṣa ātmā samyagjnanena brahmacaryena nityam. antahsarire jyotirmayo hi subhro yam pasyanti yatayah kisinadosah".

The 4 virtues helping progress, in the path to self realization; as per Mundaka Up.(3. 1. 5)=

1. SATYAM (truthfulness)-Transcendental truth is possible only to one who is truthful in transactional. The vision of truth, is not possible to one, who views the world through spectacle (viewpoint), tinted in colors of untruth. It is the most important virtue, as various shrutis have upheld truth as the abode of Brahman. It is also said that truth alone wins & falsehood never wins. Thus to be a winner in the spiritual path, truth is the basis. Not only should the spoken but also unspoken mental clatter, should be truthful. A spoken word, is a matter of honor, never to fall back unto.

2. TAPAS (Single pointed mental focus)-When the scattered thoughts of mind, which scatters the mental energy into dissipation, are brought to focus, by control of the ambling sense organs & mind, into a single focus of Atmagyan. Such Tapas, not only is progenitor but also conserver of energy. Tapas also indirectly promotes love. Since lack of concentration is due to lack of love of the subject. This is the highest austerity amongst all spiritual practice.

3. SAMYAG JNANA -Right perception, by knowledge & thinking.

    This is a requirement for both transactional & spiritual realm, at all times. This is Viveka or the power of discrimination, so very essential to a seeker. It is the function of a proper intellect, which helps to control the mind & subsequently, the senses. This is also the factor, that helps to choose the shreyas from the preyas. This practice, helps to discriminate between the seer (Brahman) which is attributeless truth, from the seen, which are with attributes & are neither the truth or untruth (mithya)... this is the supreme knowledge (Samyag jnana).

4. BRAHMACARYA-CELIBACY- (of mind)-includes two aspects,

   a) Extreme longing for Brahman & nothing else- Mumukshwatwa (to such a being, is the grace of Guru/Iswara/Atman.)

   b) Celibacy of sense organs, mind & vasanas, from anything, that is an object with attributes; while being fixed to the attributeless-existence consciousness bliss, principle or substratum of all.

A constant and unbroken abidance in these 4 virtues, (eg.- nityam), at all times; is the surest path to self realization.

FACILITATORS & DETRACTORS IN THE PATH TO SELF REALIZATION =

According to the Kaṭha- upaniṣad mantra (1. 2. 24)

"nāvirato duścaritān nā śānto nā samāhitaḥ",

the factors that stands as impediments in the path to Self-realization=

The factors, retarding the progress in the path to self realization according to the Katha Up. mantra-1. 2. 24 are=

1. Bad Conduct (duscarita) -in the physical level, has its effects of uncontrolled senses, vasanas in mind out of raga dvesha, Such a being is impure with vices; the opposite of the pure Atman.

2. Lack of sense control (indriya loluptah)- uncontrolled sense organs are like unreined wild horses, running amuck in pursuit of endless external objects & desires. Resulting in a mind in turmoil.

3. Asanta manasa- The outcome of the endless pursuits of uncontrolled senses, is a mind with successive waves of desires, in likes & dislikes. Such a turbulent mind obscures, the inner self, like the river turbulence, where the bottom remains invisible.

4. Asamghita (lack of focus)- in intellect, is the outcome of an agitated mind.

5. Desire for quick result- is lack of patience. Lack of patience is the pitfall in the path of forbearance (titiksha).

6. Indulgence in fruits of labor at gross level, is about material result while at subtle level is about appreciation. Both of which causes mental distraction.

HariOm.

Mundaka Upaniṣad (1. 2. 23) "nayamatma pravacanena labhyona medha yana bahuna srutena.

yameva iṣavṛṇutetena labhyaḥta syaiṣ aātmāvivṛṇutetanūṁsvām."

Atmagyan is not possible by only sravana, manana.

Atmagyan is possible to the one, who chooses Atmagyan alone & nothing else. To such aseeker, Atman reveals itself by grace.

A single pointed focus & the solitary yearning of the Self alone, which has absolutely destroyed all other desires, into this one & only desire of self, is the key to the door of atmagyan.

That unknown, which is one's actual subjective true eternal nature & the conscious essence of all objective knowledge, is being tried to know. The fallacy of object, trying to know the subject, in vain. Yet in the process, the object dissolves in the absolute subject (Self); being one with it, as it always was & is.

The revelation of Atman/Self, to such a seeker, has three ways of explanation, leading to the same Atman, appearing as either the Self or Iswara or Guru tattwa. Such, guiding appearance depends on the spiritual practice & evolution of the seeker.

ATMA KRIPA-The atman chooses, the seeker; to reveal itself

ISWARA KRIPA-The Iswara chooses the devotee, to reveal the Atma gyan.

GURU KRIPA-A brahmanistha guru having verified, the state of adhikarin, of a seeker, who has dully approached for Atmagyan; is imparted the lofty teachings.

When a mumukshu seeker after having chosen Atmagyan, over everything; makes effort in sadhana chatushtaya with single pointed dedication of a purified mind. Such a being comes under the grace of Guru kripa or Iswara kripa, to be led away from the illusion & sorrow of duality of jagat; to be one with the supreme nondual essence, which is the one & only Self, in & as; all. This is Atma kripa.

Guru/Iswara/Atma kripa= same thing, accepted by a seeker, depending on ones mental frame.

Hari ॐ.

114

CONTEMPLATION OF THAT; BEYOND CONTEMPLATION. (BRAHMAN)

The knowledge which deals with the Absolute, as its object. Has to be absolute itself. Non different from it, like light is from sun.

For the ignorant mind devoid of discrimination, the Self is hidden & the jagat alone exists. When discrimination alone supervenes, the Self alone is.

The Self is unborn & so is its knowledge.

It is its own nature, not different from it.

The atman (self), is the atmagyan (self realization).

Hence not acquirable, creatable, modifiable, destructible or purifiable.

It is itself already and ever that.

Tat Twam Asi.

Hari Om.

A] UNKNOWABLE YET KNOWN, IS THE SELF=

(APRAMEYA - yet - JANYATE)

While objects change from past -present to future; the self (pure consciousness) remains same.

The nature of self is to exist eternally in the present alone. This nature is continnual, even when the body falls. Since its existence is eternal, it is not an effect.

To know anything as an object, the knower has to remain as a separate identity. This is not possible with the self, as it is ones essential nature. Thus there is no determinate knowledge of the self..... Unknowable,(APRAMEYA).

The Vedic revelations are mainly negative (neti-neti), in character. These negates the ignorantly accepted false attributes (superimpositions), taken as the so called self. With sadhana chatushtaya, sravana, manana & nididhyasana on the vedantic revelations; there is a living realisation.

As to when the selfhood is no longer applied to the non self (body-mind-intellect); one comes to the intuition that the Self alone is - it is figuratively known -JANYATE.

Though in such a state, when all is the Self; What is the knower, by what is anything known or what is there to know.

Hari Om.

B] KNOWLEDGE OF THE ABSOLUTE

Is mainly negative in character, neti neti; in the upanishads.

Language can not objectify the eternal subject, the Self.

Every one is already familiar to the existence of ones self, but not in actuality.

There is no rule, that superimposition can occur only on that, which is known as an object.

Superimposition can occur on that substratum, which is not known clearly.

The various means of knowledge eg. perception, inference or revelation are-

* Not needed for self realization as the self is self evident.

* Incapable of revealing the self, as all that these means can reveal, are objects; while the Self, is pure non objectifiable subject.

Vedanta is not a teaching about the Self. It is a teaching to remove the false notions, superimposed on the self, as the false self.

Thus Vedas & Vedanta are also extensions of nescience, like a dream within a dream. But a better dream, that weans one from the dream of samsara, to awaken into pure non objectifiable consciousness.

At the event horizon of all negations (neti neti); is the Self, which is permanent & self affirming- thus not subject to negation.

Hari Om.

C] ALL THIS IS BRAHMAN

The light of absolute existence -consciousness (BRAHMAN); when viewed through the prism of =

1.   Intellect; is perceived as thoughts.

2.   Mind; is perceived as feelings.

3.   Body & Senses; is perceived as objects.

The totality of thoughts, feelings & objects, is the Jagat.

Thus in essence all is BRAHMAN.

"sarvam khalvidam brahma."

"Isavasyam idam sarvam."

Every animate being is an appearance in the eternal consciousness.

Every inanimate thing is an appearance in the eternal existence.

Every wow !!!, is an appearance in the eternal bliss.

And the eternal consciousness is same as the eternal existence (otherwise, consciousness will be non existent & also that, existence will only be non conscious or inanimate.)

That alone is Brahman - thou art.

Hari Om.

D] LIGHT OF PERCEPTION

That by what one sees in the day -is the light of Sun.

When the Sun is down, it is Moonlight & electric light; that by which one perceives.

When the moon has waned & electricity is off, one perceives by the light of Fire.

When the embers of Fire has cooled off, one perceives by the light of sound (Q- Hey ! who is there? A- I am here.).

When yet the voice has fallen silent, there is yet the perception of I ness & Am ness, by the light of Self consciousness.

In dreams, one sees the days & nights of dream world, lit up in the light of, again- the self (consciousness).

That light of self, needs no other light to illumine it...... it is SELF EFFULGENT (Swayamprakasha).

That self is not, as a core in the body mind.

It is the self, in which the body mind is & it is also, again that very self which is in the body mind..... like space, the all pervasive.

The body mind, is idam (this/object).

The self is Aham (Am/subject).

And "Tat Twam Asi" (That thou art).

Hari Om. (Br. Up-4. 3.)

E] "When i searched for God; i found the Self.

When i delved into the Self; i found God."

SRAVANA

That which can not be objectified.

Thus beyond words;

from which the mind falls back.

It is attributeless & not limited by another.

It is infinite existence consciousness.

It is Brahman.

MANANA

That which objects to objectification; has to be the non objectifiable, pure Subject, The Self.

That which is not limited by another; is either Shunya or Poorna.

Shunya or Void is non existence, hence not that.

It has to be all encompassing & one alone, so as not to be limited by another, while being existence itself. The Poornamidam poornamidaha; Brahman.

Thus the Self is the all compassing non dual Brahman.

"Ayam Atman Brahman."

All complex ideas & matter can be explained by means of more simpler & more pervasive fundamental ideas & matter.

However it is more difficult to explain the more simpler & fundamental ideas & matter.

What to say of the most simple & most fundamental of all;

Pure non objective Consciousness !!

All know that it is.

Yet no way, how to explain it.

This is not knowing,

but INTUITION of being that.

"Aham Brahmasmi".

Hari Om.

F] MIND = THOUGHTS AND THE ABSOLUTE

Words convey meanings of genus, action, quality & relation. Brahman is beyond these, thus words & thoughts fall back from, before reaching it.

After "not this; not that", negation, there is the intuition of something higher than this. This is positive affirmation of the Absolute & not a complete negation. The absolute remains unnegated at the end of neti neti.

When the notion, that the self is this(body mind intellect); is negated. The ego notion dissolves.

The mind in thinking parlance, dwells in the realm of subject object dualism. The self transcends this duality. Thus the true nature of self is always a mystery to the mind.

Yet it is possible to pass into uncharted territory beyond borders of mind, into the realm beyond all cognitions & beyond the feeling of "aham brahmasmi".

After all, if it is Brahman (Absolute) alone, then who feels which & by what?

One is the knower of self which is aware of oneself as the unbroken infinite singular continuum, devoid of agency & who has lost the feeling of being the witness or the absolute.

Attainment of self is not an act of karma, as it is not gaining something, which one does not have. It is just the knowledge of self (Tat Twam Asi); which is already existing but forgotten due to ignorance.

The non-difference between the knower & that known, is the culmination.

It is only removal of ignorance by knowledge. This teaching is not possible by empirical means of knowledge, but can be communicated by agama, as that which is "Other than the known & higher than the unknown."

Hari Om.

G] THE GOD OF VEDANTA (BRAHMAN)

When the cogniser (asmat), has divested the act of cognition from & in itself.

When the cognised (yusmat), has been sheared of the attributes of nama roopa.

There remains the merged entity of absolute inexpressible nonduality... the essence of one & all..... The Brahman of upanishads.

Hari Om.

H] "TAT TWAM ASI"

The final nature of SELF, is not an Objective knowledge.

Neither is it a SUBJECTIVE experience.

It is just infinite SUBJECTIVENESS, sans Objectiveness.

Hari ॐ.

115

BONDAGE & LIBERATION

BONDAGE

Is ignorance, due to veiling of the self & its subsequent projection as the nonself. It is subjectification of the objects of experience; such as the body, prana, mind, intellect & the causal bliss. All of which are experienced, transient & jada, thus an object (ignorantly taken as subject/self). This is the result of beginningless ignorance, collected in past transmigrations, culminating in vasanas, doership & enjoyership.

The nonself body mind intellect are considered as the self, resulting in karmas of doership & enjoyership, with enjoined karmaphalas (for body mind intellect); thus causing transient joys & endless sorrows of birth to death experience. The cycle of bondage.

The jagat, body, mind, intellect are only an appearance, the essence of all of which is Brahman. Thus they are per say not a cause of bondage. It is the false notion of identification of the body, mind, intellect as the self; which is bondage. Wrong identification leads to duality, from it raga dvesha, from it desires, from it karmas & karmaphala, then rebirths.. thus bondage in transmigration.

LIBERATION

Is removal of the error of ignorant perception, by knowledge. The ignorant consideration of the subjective self, as the objective body- prana- mind- intellect is removed by knowledge; to establish in the real subjective self- the Atman. A process of unlayering (upadhis), the upadhi layers such as body, prana, mind, intellect; which overlaps the self & assumes self hood by projection. The undressing of upadhis & embracing of self; is liberation.

The self or Atman, is ever free in all time frames, only unrealised due to ignorance of beginningless transmigrations. Knowledge removes beginningless ignorance instantly, like sunlight, which removes darkness from a cave closed for ages, right here & now. Liberation is realization of oneself as the ever free Atman & remaining established in it after removal of doubts of abhavana, asambhavana & viparita bhavana, from a brahmanistha guru or by grace. The result of realization is the culmination of search for one's essential nature, which was ever there, yet hidden. This essential nature, which is Atman; is the same in all.

Liberation is the established nondual conscious state called Turiya, which pervades also the transactional conscious states of waking, dream & deep sleep. As the dream is illusory to the waking, so is the waking- dream- deep sleep; an illusion from the transcendental non dual state. The world with its horrors & bliss; births & deaths, remain as it is. Only the viewpoint of realized, changes irrefutably.

Hari ॐ.

116

JEEVANMUKTI & VIDHEYAMUKTI

A] A JEEVANMUKTA ALONE ATTAINS VIDEHAMUKTI=

VIDEHAMUKTI, is a state when=

1. The gross body of annamaya & pranamaya falls at the end of prarabdha, to dissolve in the panchabhutas.

2. The subtle body of manomaya & vignanamaya, dissolves in the nondual totality of consciousness, without further embodiment; since there is no desire or sankalpa, to create further karmas.

3. The seed of causal body of ignorance is already roasted in the fire of self knowledge, while living.

Of the three characteristic of Vidhemukta, explaining the dissolution of gross, subtle & causal body; into the totality of Brahma swaroopa. It is clearly seen that the dissolution of subtle & causal body happens already when the gyani is living; which is what is the state of JEEVANMUKTA. This is, as a result of-

1. removal of projecting ignorance of the body mind intellect as the self. Thus there is no doership or enjoyership, hence no karma for further embodiment.

2. There is absence of veiling ignorance of self, due to Atmagyan. The Atman as self is already realised, while living.

3. There is no projection in dualities, in jagat. Since all is seen as the self (in essence).

It is the only added dissolution of the gross body & prana, at the end of prarabdha, to the already existing state of Jeevanmukta; which makes a Videhamukta.

Thus it is only a Jivanmukta, who becomes a Videhamukta.

Hari Om.

B] SODASAKALA PURUSHA & VIDHEYAMUKTA

(last Q & A of PRASNA UPANISHAD)

The purusha is the Atman, free of attributes, substratum of all, undescribable & nontransactional. It is existence-consciousness-bliss; pure without upadhis. It is neither created, nor does it create anything, even the 16 components of a being, known as the 16 kalas.

The mind of a seeker adjusted to the transactional illusion, is unable to comprehend the transcendental reality. Thus mother shruti, in order to reach the transcendent total space; first describes the so called limited pot space by limiting it with a transactional upadhi of pot (body mind) & then breaks the upadhi of pot, to prove that the pot space is & was always, the total space.

The upadhi of a jeeva is explained as composed of 16 parts (kalas), which appear in & from the absolute self; though in reality, it only appears but not actually is.

The origin of kinetic jeeva- jagat, from the potential Atman, is effected first by the establishment of PRANA (will/dream of Hiranyagarbha); the first kala.

Then the jeeva bestowed with prana, needs a moitivation factor for any action (karma) or purpose (bhakti, gyan or meditation). A factor of confidence to undertake, something not done before. This is kriti hetu or SRADDHA, the next kala, needed for every purpose of doing & knowing in life.

The next five kalas are the 5 pancha bhutas, starting from the subtlest to gross; namely SPACE, AIR, FIRE, WATER, EARTH.

Everything & being is composed of admixtures of the five pancha mahabhutas.

The composed jeeva & jagat, needs for transaction; organs to perceive & organs to do. The Gyan & Karma INDRIYAS. The indriyas are compositely the 8 th kala. The senses are linked to the pancha bhutas. SOUND from space, TOUCH from air along with sound. SIGHT ftom fire along with sound & touch. Similarly TASTE is added in water & SMELL in earth.

The transactional jeeva jagat, needs the free will, doership & enjoyership, for this creation to go on in the cycle of karma. For doership enjoyership, there is MANAS (mind intellect).

The 9 th kala.

The jeeva with senses, needs food for each sense organ; to thrive in need & enjoyership. This is ANNAM, the 10 th kala. A composite experience of food for different sense organs, gives a transactional experience of totality for the concerned individual, which is in no way the total experience at any time, before Atmagyan.

The food provides VIRYAM (vitality), the 11 th kala, which helps action and propagation of jeeva.

The actions, then needs single pointed focus & concentration of thought, so as to achieve its goal in doing & knowing. This is TAPAS, the 12 th kala.

Even with concentrated single pointed focus, sometimes the waves of ignorance(Maya); are a cause for detraction for a seeker. At such times, a sacred chant/saying/japa; helps a wavering seeker, back into the right path. This is MANTRA, the 13 th kala.

Depending on the previous factors, there is accured KARMA, the 14 th kala. The karmas are enjoined with, karmaphala naturally.

Depending on the result of ones karmas, one attains to different states of existence as an effect of the causality of karma. These are the LOKAS of transmigration. The 15 th kala.

The last, 16 th kala is NAMA, which is the synopsis of false ego. For a jeevanmukta who is realised as, not the body mind. There is no NAMA ROOPA, only Brahman. The NAMA, of such a gyani is akin to a mantra, for future seekers to hold on to in the audrous path of atmagyan; when the master is embodied or disembodied.

The PURUSHA, is the purnattva or puri shayanat, the resident or the only truth, in the dream city of 16 kalas.

The dream story of 16 kalas was said to arrive at the only truth THE SELF, like a dream of charging lion, which awakens one from dream to awakening.

Hari Om.

C] MAHASAMADHI=

A jeevanmukta looses the adhyasa of body mind intellect ego, at the very moment of self realisation.

Yet the body continues its prarabdha, till it lasts. Doing actions of the will of supreme totality, for the benefaction of all.

Such actions are absolutely without doership or enjoyership, hence without karmas of egoism.

When such a jeevanmukta is freed from prarabdha, the body (Gross) merges into panchabhutas.

The senses merge into their respective deities.

The subtle mind intellect merges into the pure consciousness.

The darkness of causal ignorance was already absolved in the effulgence of Brahma Atma eikyam. Into a state of Vidheyamukti, as seen by an ignorant onlooker.

To the gyani, however; there is no realisation of Videhamukti or death. As the ignorant, I ness of body mind intellect, had already been absolved at the moment of jeevanmukti. Also the equipment of mind intellect, needed to realise is already, dissolved in the nondual consciousness; in a state of manonasa, at jeevanmukti.

This is what is Mahasamadhi, when of the 16 kalas of a being are merged in the nondual absoluteness of Brahman; while the name only remains as a guiding guru or mantra, for seekers in gyan or bhakti.

It is akin to the pot space(atman), becoming one with the total space (Brahman); when the limiting adjunct of pot(body mind) breaks(prarabdha). The pot space was always the total space, not different. Yet appeared different due to the superimposition of the gross pot.

Hari Om.

D] NAMA=

The last of the 16 kalas, that constitute a being.

For an ignorant being, the nama changes from birth to birth, according to the roopa, that one attains by transmigration; resulting from fructification of sanchita karmas & vasanas.

For a self realised master, the remaining kalas merge in the non dual substratum of Brahman; while the 16 th, kala as nama, remains as a guiding & motivating force for future seekers on the quest of Atmagyan.

The embodied master, can not remain for ever. Nor can it be with all seekers, at the same time.

The name of realised master, is like a pass word; in the internet of transcendence. Which connects the seeker at any place, at any time.

It is an all pervasive map of guidance on the path of Brahma Atma eikyam, which is there for all seekers. Since the master is now the all pervasive Brahman, itself.

The nama of the Lord or the guru, is like a mantra; which enables one to overcome adversities on the path of self realisation, when it happens inspite of single pointed concentration.

The nama, of a realised master is the potential power of atmagyan; which is unleashed as grace unto a seeker, who chants it as a japa.

The power of Nama, is there for both, who chants it knowingly or unknowingly.

Hari Om.

E] SRADDHA

Means, conviction or motivation for any action or knowledge (kriti- hetu).

To do or to know.

It is a faith to endeavour into something, not done previously, in this body mind.

It is both an initiating & sustaining factor for any effort.

A form of self confidance or belief in oneself, to do; in terms of action or knowledge.

Sraddha to shruti, Smriti & Guru, leads one to the blessed realms of eternal bliss, by sravana, manana & niddhydhyasana.

For any success in vyavarika, one needs sraddha in the means to do the work or in the books, to learn the desired knowledge.

Similarly in paramarthika, one has to have sraddha in the teachings of Shruti, smriti; imparted by a brahmanistha guru. Otherwise the blissful infinitude of transcendent remains unknown & unlived.

Hari Om.

F] SATYASANKALPA OF JEEVAN MUKTA

Satyasankalpa of Jeevanmukta, literally appears to be a misnomer. It is actually a language of paradox. A jeevanmukta, who has realised the self as not the body, mind or intellect; how can there be a sankalpa. To such a being, there is no doership or enjoyership, nor is there any desire.

Yet in the transactional prarabdha, there remains the body with karmas & mind intellect with thoughts and sankalpas. But such body minds are not at all identified in individuality, the total cosmic body Virat or the cosmic total mind hiranyagarbha; uses the body mind of a jeevanmukta as an instrument to fulfill sankalpa for total cause. When a jeevanmukta is singularly focussed in the non dual consciousness without distractions of individual desires or thoughts of body mind, the potential power of Iswara manifests through them, to fulfill sankalpas for total bliss. To a bhakta it is grace, to a yogi it is power of kundalini & to a gyani, it is satyasankalpa. The common factor being absence of doership & enjoyership of the jeevanmukta. The sankalpas arise from the total mind, in the instrument of body mind of jeevanmukta & it is, the Hiranyagarbha with power of Iswara, that fructifies it.

As is the mind, so is the being.

For a jeevanmukta, the mind is cosmic totality, so is its outcome by the totality without individuality.

A seeker of liberation, when offers the oblation of pure mind, total detachment & single pointed determination; to a jeevanmukta is graced in the path of liberation. Though a jeevanmukta can not bless an individual, for all individual notions have obliterated & replaced by totality. Yet grace is there, since individual seekers liberation, is a boon for the totality of jeeva.

Hari Om.

G] DESIRELESSNESS OF JIVANMUKTA

A jeevanmukta is one established in the truth of, self in all & all in the self. A state of nonduality, where there is not a second being or thing, all is the self/ Atman.

The ignorant identification of the body, prana, mind, intellect as the self is burnt in the fire of gyan of self as Atman, in one & all.

Since all is the self, there remains nothing to aquire.

Since all is the self, there is nothing to renounce.

It is not a state of, all desires fulfilled. But a state of all desires, anhilated.

Since a jeevanmukta is not the body. There arises no gross desire for the body. Since one is not the prana, there is no desire of pranayama. As one is not the mind, there is no desire of emotion or thought. Since one is not the intellect, there is no desire of knowledge even. That by which, all is known; is already known, as the self, which is the same in all.

Such a being, revelles in, all in the self as action in inaction (all in Atman), as atmarama.

Such a being also plays as the self in all, as inaction in action (Atman in all).. Atmakrida.

Since all notions of individuality has merged in the unitary totality, there remains none or nothing to desire.

Hari ॐ.

117

SELECTED VEDANTIC SHLOKAS

(FOR MANANA).

A complete elaboration of a subject is a Sastra. Adhyatma is knowledge of the self. This is discussed under Anubandha chatushtaya, comprised of adhikarin, visaya, sambandha & prayojana.

The qualities of a qualified seeker (adhikarin) is clarified by slokas of relevant upanishads like Katha up. in lesson 2 & 3: with an exposition into sadhana chatushtaya.

The hallmark of a Guru is revealed as shotriya, brahmanistha & compassionate. In lesson 2, by shlokas of Mundaka Up.

The methodology to approach a Guru in humbleness, dedicated service of body mind as a totality, is mentioned as samitpani, in Mundaka Up. in lesson 2.

The Guru then expounds the knowledge of Brahma Atma aikyam, by Mahavakya Vichara.

The implied meaning of That Brahman, is the same as, This Atman, in its fundamental nature as consciousness. To ultimately realise; the self is the one and only Brahman.

As given in lessons from 4-11.

The methodology of Sadhana, to remain established in this gyan; not only as a knowledge of philosophy, but a living realization, is also explained. In lesson 22-23.

The abhavana of the supreme gyan is removed by shravana from Guru & Shruti.

The doubts & dilemas are removed by manana. Finally viparita bhavana is removed by nididhyasana, to a state of uninterrupted state of bliss or meditation. As elucidated in lesson 12-16.

The outcome of such a gyan, leads to Jeevanmukti which culminates in Videha Mukti at the end of Prarabdha. The hallmarks of jivanmukta & Vidheyamukta is give in lesson 17-21.

The entire gamut of Atmagyan is slowly nourished from the quality seed of an adhikarin, by the nourishing gyan of a guru rooted in brahma atman aikyam, into stems & leaves of sadhana, into the fragrant flowers of jeevanmukta, ultimately to drop as the sweet nourishing fruit of Vidhemukta..." Urvarukamiva bandhana mrityur mokshi mamammritam."

Salutations to Gurudev & the Guru parampara, for such a beyond mind realization.

Hari Om.

A] The first sloka of Isavasya upanishad, is condensate of entire Vedanta.

ईशा वास्यमिदं सर्वं यत्किञ्च जगत्यां जगत्।

तेन त्यक्तेन भुञ्जीथा मा गृधः कस्यस्विद्धनम् ॥

All that there is, in the three periods of time; moving or unmoving. Is pervaded or covered by the supreme existence consciousness (Brahman).

Such a teaching is an upasana when one sees the objects of the creation as Iswara. When it is an intuitive realization, of the existence consciousness as the pervading truth in all trasient objects, it becomes self realisation.

Established in the above truth, when a mind intellect is endowed with discrimination(viveka) of what one is(sat chit ananda), from what one appears(nama roopa). The established viewpoint of immanent nama- roopa-vyavara; shifts to the transcendent existence consciousness. Thus one is established in Brahman.

The culmination of viveka is vairagya or renunciation of the ephemeral (nama roopa) & unitary nondual identification as the eternal pervading truth of existence consciousness, which is the self in one & all. Thus the self is enjoyed & protected in the realm of infinitude, away from the superimposed ignorance of a finite being.

The quest for infinite bliss is a choiceless purpose of every life.

The thought to covet anything, gives rise to desire. From desire originates love, hate, anger, jealousy. These then manifests into karmas & subsequent karmaphalas. Thus is one ensnared in transmigration & led away from the state of unending bliss into unending sorrow. The very antithesis of lifes purpose. Non covetousness is the way to overcome sorrow.

With established knowledge of this sloka of Isavasya upanishad, when all is realized as the self. There remains none else; that is there to gain & acquire.

Similarly when all is the self; what else remains to be renounced?

Sarvam Brahma mayam.

Hari Om.

B] Significance of the Guru as seen in the Praśna-upaniṣad mantra (6. 8) "te tamarcayantastvaṁ hi naḥ pitā yo'smākamavidyāyāḥ pāraṁ tārayasīti"?

The significance of Guru, as in Prasna Upanishad=

The biological father & mother who has given birth, to one, as this embodied being of human life; are one of the most revered & worshipable, in this world. Since in human body mind intellect only, one can persue Atmagyan for self realization, which is the one and only auspicious goal of life, that conferred the gyan, knowing which all is known & one is in absolute bliss & fearlessness. Such is the high pedestal for parents who has given one, the instrument called body mind intellect; for a purpose.

The brahmanistha Guru who has guided the seeker in the motif of "Asato ma sat gamaya, Tamaso ma jyotir gamaya, Mrityur ma amritam gamaya."

Is the progenitor of a new birth in knowledge from ignorance, from finiteness to immortality & from sorrow unto eternal bliss. The revelation of Sat Chit Ananda.

This enables one to sail the ocean of innumerable transmigration, infested with pitfalls of birth, disease, sorrow, old age, disease & death. Such a realisation is greater than any conceivable worldly birth.

So the giver of such realisation is the supreme parent, to whom shall be the supreme salutation.

Guru Om. Hari Om.

C] indiiyebyah para hayartha,

arthebhyasca param manah,

manasastu para buddhi,

buddheratma mahan parah,

mahatah paramavyaktam avyaktat purusah parah,

purusanna param kincit sa kastha para gatih..... katha upanishad.

EXPOUNDING THE SUBTLETY OF SELF/BRAHMAN (In katha upanishad)=

The sense organs are considered to be the instrument of perception & the first step in the spectrum of gross to subtle. The sensory objects in form of smell, taste, sight, touch & hearing are more pervasive than the sense organs. The mind is the next subtle as it is more pervasive, since it can perceive in subtle, inspite of absence of gross objects. The intellect is more subtle as it capable of discriminating the thoughts of mind. The vayasti intellect is a part of the samasti intellect, which is more subtle & pervasive. The total intellect which is the samasti subtle, is created out of the unmanifested causal Maya/Iswara; which is more pervasive. The substratum essence, of the unmanifested is the supreme Purusa. Which is infinite fullness & the resident consciousness of all.

The pinnacle of subtlety, beyond which there is nothing. It is unexplainable neti neti. But is not(neti), nothingness or shunya.

SENSE OBJECTS ARE SUBTLER THAN SENSE ORGANS

The sense objects are considered in terms of their sensory essence as smell, taste, sight, touch & sound.

Under such a consideration, the sensory objects or stimulus are more pervasive, than the perceiving sense organs (which are less subtle).

The visual stimulus is a vast spectrum of cosmic, ultraviolet, visual, infrared & microwaves. The sense organ, eye; can perceive a limited range of VIBGYOR, amongst the entire available range.

Similar is sound, comprised of ultrasonic, sonic & subsonic. Of which the ears perceive only the sonic range.

In taste also, there is perception of sweet, sour, salt & bitter. There are many more tastes not perceptible to human tongue.

Similar are the states of smell & touch.

If there was no stimulus of sensory objects, there would be no sense organ for such as there is no sense organ of chemical perception in humans, as found in snakes.

The sense organs are only an instrument for the objects, which are thus more pervasive & subtle.

Hari Om.

D] "bhidyate hrdayagranthi, chidyante sarvasamasayah, ksiyante casya karmani, tasmin driste paravare.".. Mundaka uo. 2. 2. 8.

explains the prayojana of (anubandha chatusthaya), Brahmavidya/ Upanishad.

1. Cuts the knot of Hrdayagranthi.

2. Removes all doubts.

3.   Removes bondage of karma into Naiskamyasiddhi.

For one with aparoksha anubhuti of Atman.

THE KNOT OF HRDAYA-GRANTHI

Is the three knots of AVIDYA-KAMA-KARMA.

THE KNOT OF IGNORANCE=

Hrdayam is Hrt(supreme atman/consciiousness)+ ayam (this body). The Atman is real & eternal, whereas the body is mithya & ephemeral. The avidya(ignorance) of the immortal self(as Atman) & the adhyasa of the mortal body as the self is the greatest ignorance. The ignorance of self or ones real nature.

As to, since when is one ignorant of self? Since times eternal...beginningless.

But ignorance ends with knowledge.

Self ignorance ends with Atmagyan.

When the body mind intellect, is considered as the self due to ignorance of the immortal Atman as ones real self; there is the initiation of enjoyership of desires, with subsequent karmas to fulfill it.

Thus in the triad of avidya- kama- karma. a jeeva is led into the mirage of karta- bhokta bodha of jagat as a samsari.

In the tree of jagat, the root is the ignorance. The trunk & branches of desire arise from it. From the branches of desires, there arise the karmas & karmaphalas as flowers & fruits with seeds, to give renewed embodiment.

Ignorance is thus the root (main cause), of binding of the hrt(eternal atman) with the ephemeral(ayam/body).

THE KNOT OF DESIRE (KAMA)

When there is superimposition of the body mind intellect, as the self; instead of the blissful & infinite Atman (as self), due to ignorance. There arises the second knot of bondage. Atman which is full & infinite bliss, needs no desire, to be full or to be happy. Whereas the avidya adhyasa of body mind is finite & thus desires for fullness & joy, for body in gross & the mind in subtle arises. The thoughts of desire arise in mind like series of waves which induces body into action. The sea of mind made turbulent by waves of desire, makes the jeeva restless & loose its tranquility, till the desire is apparently fulfilled. Only to give rise to another desire in a geometric progression. The the objects of desires in vyvarika are themself finite & its fulfillment is incapable of giving infinite lasting joy. The thoughts of desire reap transient joys on fulfillment, yet there is creation of imprints of vasanas in the causal body which are long lasting & emanates new desires later, to aggravate desire with dissatisfaction... in repeated bonds (knots), of transmigrations.

THE KNOT OF KARMA

Any action is for aquisition, modification, purification or destruction of any object in gross or subtle. Desire is the initiator of all actions. Ignorance is the initiator of desire.

Every outcome of karma (karmaphala) is to be exhausted, be it sanchita, prarabdha or agama; in this or later embodiments. Thus karma is the knot of transmigration experienced as doership(karta bodha) & enjoyership(bhokta bodha). The enjoyership may be in joy/sorrow or a mixture, but it creates vasanas in the subtle, which is a projenitor of further desires & further karmas.

The avidya of oneself as the body mind is the root cause of karma.

The atman which is ones real self (nature), is all pervasive- hence non aquisible; is without upadhis- hence non modifiable; is ever pure- hence non purifiable; is unborn eternal- hence indestructible. Thus there is no karma in the paramarthika self(Atman).

Hari ॐ.

118

REFLECTIONS IN & OF BRAHMAN

Upanishad says that Brahman pervades the entire visible and invisible Cosmic manifestation. It's said that Brahman is without time and space.

If so, why the same is not reflectd in the inanimate/lifeless things and space?

Brahman pervades the universe as existence consciousness.

It appears, depending on what reflects it. A red rose will only reflect red color, not green.

The gross (inanimates) reflects the existence mainly.

The gross and subtle (Viswa & Virat, those with body and mind), reflects both existence and consciousness, in individual & cosmic level.

The subtle only; as Taijasa & Hiranyagarbha reflects only individual & cosmic consciousness.

The causal reflects the bliss of non objectification in individual(pragyana) & cosmic (Iswara).

All however is a reflection only of the effulgent Brahman, which is inapparent. Like the light in space, which is fully there but appears dark, till a planet, satellite or meteor reflects it, to make its presence observable.

Hari ॐ.

119

ALATASHANTI IN VEDANTA

"A flaming torch in motion, appears as straight & circular lines, that disappear when the motion of torch Ceases."

* THE curved & straight lines appear only with motion of torch.

* When the torch is motionless, the lines do not remain or go elsewhere like real.

   They just disappear; since they are not real but appearance only.

* The lines do not come from any external factor or from the torch, hence no causality.

* The lines are unreal, only the torch is real.

Similar is the pure consciousness, which is motionless, since it is omnipresent. Yet is set in motion by ignorance (the desires).

* In such an ignorance of motion of consciousness (torch), there appears the jagat (lines).

* When the apparent motion of consciousness is stalled as in deep sleep, desirelessness or self realization, all the reality of appearing jagat vanishes. Thus no real origin.

* The elements of jagat is not produced from consciousness or from anything outside, (no real causality), ignorance alone is the cause of appearance.

* The appeared elements, like real; do not go elsewhere or back into consciousness; their apparent reality just vanishes.

* The elements of jagat, like the lines are apparent only. The torch/consciousness alone remains as real, when motionless.

* In the beginning and end, there was the torch/consciousness alone; no lines or jagat.

That which is absent before the beginning & after the end, is also absent in the middle, like a mirage.

Hari ॐ.

120

IS VEDANTA NEEDED?

IS THERE NEED OF DISPASSION TO WORLDLY LIFE?

STORY TIME (1)

Welcome to,

W(orld). DIS(ere) Theme park,

At 8. 30 am entry time(birth); enters many a person who has the necessary entry fee (prarabdha). The park (jagat) is abuzz with life, activity & experiences. There are rides, movies, games, jackpots, shows, food stalls... and many more. The desire differs for different entrants. Some have the desire to finish all the rides, some have come to enjoy a particular ride again & again, some are attracted to adventurous dangerous rides for the thrill of adrenalin. Some enjoy the bliss of Soaring. There are one's in joy of winning, while some are glum at loosing a game, some just contented to play. Yet the park, has to end at 7 pm (end of life in jagat). Most will love to come back again to repeat it all over in a different park or realm or to try out the unfinished experiences in same realm or park, oblivious of closing time viveka. Transmigration Goes on. No harm in enjoying the artha, kama, power, fame, adventures of jagat. Yet it has to be within the framework of law (dharma). One is not supposed to steal, usurp others rights or harm others mentally, physically or in thoughts; for one's entertainment. Dharma should enjoin the karmas of desires of Artha & Kama The guidelines of karmakanda.

There are few entrants sitting in the lounge near the entrance, keeping a watch on the closing time. They have come with their grandchildren or children to enjoy; while themselves are unaffected by the activities, eager to go home at close (mumukshu).

One may say that they have already enjoyed in childhood & youth, following which this dispassion arises, out of fulfilled desires. True.

But mokshya & vedanta is on a much larger time frame. A single life is too less a time to fulfill worldly desires & then contemplate & gain self realization or mokshya.

Many a lifetimes have been spent in experience of Tamasic, then Rajasic & Sattwik persuits..... at the evolutionary end of which, does the viveka of transient (finite), from the eternal (infinite), does arise.

Then starts the path as a seeker, in search of a guru & vedanta. To get the unanswered; answered.

This atmagyan or vedanta is a kingly secret, protected from those not eligible (adhikarin). It is not protected by soldiers, pandits, gurus or esoteric language. But protected by the lure of Maya (jagat), and a spontaneous disinterest in those in whom desires of world, yet remains. A self protective mechanism.

STORYTIME 2

Nachiketa is a young boy, who reached before Lord Yama, out of his sheer single point determination to uphold dharma. There is immense viveka & vairagya even at such early childhood, which had not the time for all jagatic experience in such a short time of this lifetime. The only explanation of such dispassion is only by experiences of past life in quest of such truth, which was not attainable in that life time. As Krishna has said "one shall start from where one has left on this path." Similar is the childhood of Sankara bhagwatpada.

Nachiketa was given many a boon by lord Yama, in form of power, long life, progeny, riches, joys of heaven on Earth.

But he did not waver from the discriminating choice of Shreyas (the eternal/good); over the Preyas (efemeral/preferable).

Anything with a name & form, has a beginning, thus an end.

That which is without attribute and is not this- not this; yet all pervading. Is without a beginning, thus without an end. That is pure existence - consciousness, without a upadhi. This is common to all. To delve into such queries, as to when it arises, is the path of Vedanta, then one is a seeker. Then when all desires are dissolved in the only burning desire of Atmagyan, does the self effulgent Self reveal it self.

Hari ॐ.

ON THE JOURNEY TO SINGULARITY

Thoughts Of This Mind

1. Puja vritti- To do all actions mentally as a puja/service to the supreme Brahman (formless)/Iswara (in form).

2. To accept all outcomes of thoughts & actions, known & forgotten, as Prasadam, thankfully, & in joy.

3. To see the divine (Brahman/Atman) in every temple (body/mind); mentally. The temple may be attractive/repulsive; body mind jeeva or object.

4. To establish in the fact, that the divinity residing in all the appearing temples of body mind or objects, is the same divinity that resides in the body mind temple of yourself.

5. The temples of body mind & objects has a beginning & end, thus transient appearance only, while the essence of residing divinity of all that was, is & will be, is the eternal Brahman/Atman. To constantly detatch mentally from the transient qualities of every action & object, unto the eternal principle of each.

For every object & action, there is-

Transient quality-name, form & transaction.

Eternal principle-Existence, Consciousness, in varied proportions.

6. The final outcome is not to gain something, but to wash away all the transient five layered dirt gained over umpteen lifetimes, so as to be that which one already is, just forgotten.

Hari ॐ.

122

MEMOIRS OF A DREAM OR NIGHTMARE

I dream a dream, where over ages of mutation & natural selection, there was a blessing of so called mind, unto me.

The all giving nature, which was also a teacher; gave me all that was needed for blissful coexistence. Yet I was not satisfied with it & yearned for needs to hoard for lustful sensory gratification. I used my mind & intellect to harness the powers of nature, to become all powerful, lording over nature & other life & non life forms. My ego boosted my sense of invincibility.

In the name of civilization, i have taken down many a natures creation to its extinction. Even amongst our fellow brethren of homo sapiens, i have subjugated the less blessed & fortunate. In the name of my self, family, society, nation, race, ideology & religion; i have waged wars of annihilation & destruction. I have successfully usurped the living environ of other life forms for my surplus greed of sense gratification, which is not my need for survival. The Words; sharing, compassion & love, has lost its universal value, now replaced by selfish agendas. I am so called a civilized race, which kills other life forms & also fellow beings, masquerading under masks of species, race, nation, religion, gender & what not.

I have enjoyed the glory as if, the master of creation, lording over mother nature for long.

Nature had given the power of mind to be a monitor of peaceful coexistence, but my ego & greed, transformed it into a Frankestine's monster with dictatorial attitude. The priorities were set from me, my family, my society, my community, my state, nation, and finally mother Earth (if at all). Which should have been just the reverse.

Then the teacher (Nature), decided to correct the errant pupil (me); by punishment. It gave gentle reminders of famines, earthquakes, volcanoes, sunamis, global warming etc. But intoxicated in the lust of power & lordship, I failed to be taught. The anguished cry of mother Earth & nature, fell on deaf ears enamored in the music of sense gratification.

One fine morning, i wake up to an invisible nemesis. A virus, to which all my hoardings of power & possession is a useless futility. The very health system that was considered a white elephant, is now my only search. My lungs cry out for lifesaving oxygen, and the very forests and nature that gave me that & immunity, i had destroyed in creating my path of civilized (so called) progress.

To day I am encaged, in bondage of four walls, fearing every human contact; while the sky is bluer, the birds are flying happily, the sunset is pristine & beautiful, more than ever.

The so called death will take many a body minds, in this cauldron of misery. Yet will leave behind many a fortunate few for redemption & contemplation of what nature wants to teach the residual humanity.

But shall we?

The forgetful humanity will probably start all over from where it left, taking it to be a nightmare only.

Those of us who shall pass on, will only rue; if this was only a dream. But alas, it is a living nightmare, not a dream.

Hari ॐ.

SHANTI MANTRAS & ITS SIGNIFICANCE

The mantras, which may be in first person singular, second person dual or third person plural, form.

The shanti mantras are an invocation before onset of study of Upanishads, when the seeker is not yet realized. Later on at the end of upanishadic teachings, when being realized, there is ample resolve, courage & knowledge to progress in the spiritual path.

It is an invocation to connect to the grace & blessings of the supreme through the channel of the Guru. Thus an expression of shraddha, bhakti & service to the Guru.

It is also an expression of resolve & commitment towards a purpose, here Brahma gyan.

The shanti mantras are also an exposition to the means & purpose of objective, here being Brahma Atma eikyam.

Initially it begins with invocation in first person, when the seeker is in body mind ego due to ignorance of self.

Then there is invocation in duality, when the seeker feels the connection with guru.

Finally with further progress, when there is gradual realization of all, as the various name form of one & only Brahman, then there is invocation for the plural, realized as the one self.

The shanti mantras are infact the first step of Vedanta, which connects the finite & known to the infinite & unknown.

Every mantra starts with Om, as an invocation to the supreme Brahman, though there may be salutations to individual Devas, in the mantra.

The end of each mantra repeats, Shanti three times, to invoke control over Adhidaivik, Adhibhautik & Adhyatmic obstacles, in the spiritual path.

Hari ॐ.

RG VEDA SHANTI MANTRA

"Om van me manasi pratisthita, mano me vaci pratisthitam avir avirma e dhi, vedasya ma anisthah srutam me ma prahasir anenadhi tena horatran sandadham yrtam vadisyami, satyam vadisyami, tan mam avatu, tad vakta rama vatvavatu mama vatu vaktaram avatu vaktaram. Om santih santih santih."

It is invocation of the supreme as Om, with resolve in the means & purpose of brahma gyan.

May the sayings be in accordance to thoughts of mind. May the thoughts be expressed as speech, without duplicity. When there is harmony of thought & speech, then the following action will be synchronous, without confusion. The mind & speech may enable one to realize the truth of Vedas.

Since the self effulgent Brahman, is the only one chosen; may there be grace of Brahman, to reveal itself to me.

May this mind not forget the Vedic teachings that are heard, nor should it loose the realization of self obtained in grace of the Atman.

As a means to this purpose, i resolve to single pointedly, devote all day & night reveling in the upanishadic studies.

I also pledge to speak only the truth expounded in the shruti & also to live the truth, for which i pray to seek grace of the supreme Iswara.

May the truth & essence of Vedas protect me & my Guru, both physically & mentally; so that the purpose of guru sishya connection be manifested in full measure of brahma atma eikyam.

O supreme lord, bless me, so that there is no adhidaivic, adhibhautik or adhyatmic obstacle to the chosen path.

Hari ॐ.

125

SHANTI MANTRA OF SAMA VEDA

"OM apyayantu mamangani vak prana s caksuh srotramatho balamindriyani ca sarvani.

Sarvam Brahma upanisadam ma ham Brahma nirakuryam, ma ma Brahma nirakarot,

anirakarana mastva nira karanam me stu.

Tad atmani nirate ya Upanisatsu dharmah te mayi santu te mayi santu.

Om Santih Santih Shanthi."

The prayer=

The seeker prays to the supreme as Iswara, for being blessed with healthy -body, organs of knowledge, organs of action, & physiologic functions full of vigour along with conductive mental health.

The Prayojana=

This is not for use of fulfillment of finite worldly desires, but for self realization at the end of the arduous spiritual path.

The Resolve=

I dedicate to realize this Brahman, which is the essence of all perceived & experienced.

May not, i or anybody ignore this truth as the unconditioned Brahman or as the conditioned Iswara. May not the conditioned truth, Iswara; ignore me or anybody from grace. Let there be Sraddha, without which there is neither culmination of devotion in bhakti or knowledge in gyan.

The Means=

The virtues of sadhana catustaya as enjoined in Vedas, may be my strength on this path of Atmagyan. The repetition of such yearning, indicates this to ba a firm resolve, & one & only choice of Atmagyan.

Let there be blessings of protection from adhidaivik, adhibhautik & adhatyamik obstacles on this path.

Hari ॐ.

126

ATHARVA VEDA SHANTI MANTRA

"Om bhadram karnebhih srunuyama deva, bhadram pasyemaksabhiryajatrah, sthirai rangaistu stuvamsastanubhirvyasema devahitam yadauhuh, svasti na indro vrddhasravah, svasti na pusa visvavedah, svasti nastarksyo aristanemeih, svasti na brhaspatir da dhatu. Om santih santih santih."

A prayer for the singular seeker on behalf of the plural, to the deities, for specific seekings.

May we always see & hear, that which is auspicious. That which we hear, is our speech & silent thoughts. These ought to be auspicious. There is the need to avoid hearing & seeing that which evokes passion, lust, greed, anger & other vices.

Auspicious is that which unites with the self or Supreme. Such auspiciousness is the hallmark of shruti, Iswara/Brahman, & Atmagyan. While worldly desires are its detractors. In order to practically live such auspiciousness, there thus has to be sraddha (to shruti); bhakti(to Iswara); manana & niddhidhyasana (in jnana), with dispassion for the worldly(vairagya).

A prayer for good physical & mental health for the destined lifespan (not praying for longevity); so as to be able to devote in chanting lords name(Bhakti yoga); to dedicate all works in dedication to lord (Karma yoga); to live in constant contemplation of atmagyan(jnana yoga). The prayer of complete yoga. The prayer for a meaningful life with a noble purpose.

Prayer to deities for Knowledge(Brihaspati), with unsurpassed energy(Sun), resulting in enjoined karmas(Indra); with swift removal of distractions(Garuda)...... then all is auspicious(Bhadram).

Hari ॐ.

THE SUKLA YAJUR VEDA SHANTI MANTRA

ॐ पूर्णमदः पूर्णमिदम् पूर्णात् पूर्णमुदच्यते |"

पूर्णस्य पूर्णमादाय पूर्णमेवावशिष्यते ||

Om,

That essence of all which is SAT (existence); is complete/absolutely full/ infinite.

This creation of perception is also full in sthiti.

From the absolute fulness, this perceptible full universe of nama roopa, appears to arise in sristi.

When from this full or infinite world of nama roopa, the infinite names & forms are removed in laya. There remains yet, the absolute infinitude of SAT (existence).

May there be protection from Adhidaivik, Adhibhautik & Adhyatmic obstacles.

Since reality & appearing world are both stated to be infinite, which is a mathematical improbability (as infinite can never be two, since one will limit the infinitude of the other. Infinite is only nondual.) Thus creation is an appearance in the absolute, without any change in the absolute.

That reality(Brahman), is existence(satyam), consciousness(gyanam), which is infinite(anantam).

This creation consisting of nama roopa vyavarika is also beginningless. However its essence of existence (Sat), is borrowed from that absolute Brahman. Without this borrowed existence, the creation does not exist. It is similar to different ornaments of gold. When gold is taken out, the bangles, rings, necklaces etc. simply dont exist.

That (Brahman), is attributeless, hence infinite. Attributes are the cause of finiteness.

This creation of appearances, which appears (thus not asat); but thrives on borrowed existence(thus not sat); is mithya. It appears but is not is. This is the beginningless Maya, the causal ignorance. Ignorance is always beginningless, but ends in gyan (here Brahmagyan).

When this beginningless Maya(name & forms) is removed in cosmic dissolution or by Brahmagyan. There yet remains the eternal existence consciousness infinite Brahman. Infinite minus infinite is infinite.

When an ignorant thirsty desert traveller sees water in the distance. One is lured in action towards the water, to quench the desire of thirst. Alas the water with all its ripples & real reflections, keeps moving away & away. The name, form & function (reflections & ripples) of water is complete in ignorance, while the substratum of sand & air; though always existing, is not evident. When with knowledge, the sand & air are known to be the cause of this appearance called Mirage, there is no desire to quench thirst from that water, nor the karma to run after it. The appearance (mirage water); is incapable of any change in the substratum(not a grain of desert sand is made wet by it).

The mirage (creation), may remain appearing, but the viewpoint of the jnani changes into the realization of its mithyatva.

So long as there is ignorance (of Brahmagyan), the creation appears infinite in name & forms; since it is beginningless.

While the substratum of existence consciousness, from which this creation borrows its existence, though ever present, is completely veiled.

When this veil of beginningless, apparent, infinite, ignorance is taken out by knowledge of Brahmagyan; The pure attributeless existence remains as the complete infinite essence of all appearances.

This mantra is the summary of entire Vedanta. It is an elaboration of Brahma (Poornamidaha/Tat) - Atma(poornamidam/Twam); eikyam (asi).

Hari ॐ..

HARI ॐ.

TAT SAT.